BUILD YOUR
BEVERAGE
EMPIRE

Jorge S. Olson

*To all of you with an entrepreneurial spirit
and a desire to succeed.*

Masterminds and Online Courses

Build Your

Beverage

Empire

Course

Your next step in the quest for beverage domination is the Marketing Mastery Beverage Course.

If you're ready to get your product into mass retail accounts all over the USA, contact us today. We'll help you with your project or idea. You can also join our masterminds and mentoring programs. Contact us today:

www.LiquidBrandsManagement.com/beveragebook

TABLE OF CONTENTS

INTRODUCTION

"DEVELOP YOUR BEVERAGE FOR ONLINE SALES AS WELL AS WHOLESALE DISTRIBUTION.

COVID CHANGED THE RULES ON HOW YOU CAN MARKET TO YOUR PERFECT CONSUMER."

INTRO

Post-COVID Beverage Strategy

When COVID started changing society and businesses, a beverage entrepreneur persisted in getting me on the phone. I wasn't working or taking clients at the time, but I decided to call her back after a barrage of voicemails. She told me about her beverage project; her passion and vision were so compelling that she changed my mind at the end of the call, and I decided I had to work with her.

Before the stay-at-home orders, we managed to schedule our first strategy session. Before COVID, the strategy session would have been, "We'll cover your funding, target market, and wholesale distribution strategy first, and tackle product development after we've figured out the first three."

During the pandemic, I found myself changing the way I approached launching a new brand. I had to do the same soon after, as one of my friends invited me to launch our hemp products brands. Despite COVID, or maybe because of it, I participated in fifteen new projects, including the new strategy or traditional wholesale distribution combined with a parallel eCommerce strategy.

During COVID, I told my new client that we needed to focus on three things:

- ✔ Wholesale Distribution
- ✔ Amazon
- ✔ eCommerce

If you read the previous version of this book, you may remember that Amazon and eCommerce sales were mentioned briefly in the book, as sales were driven by wholesale distribution. After COVID, Amazon and eCommerce can be the difference between your brand surviving or crashing and burning.

What changed? Well, COVID changed everything. The beverage industry has been changing for a while; in convenience stores, there's significant consolidation. It feels like an oligopoly in the hands of Coca-Cola, Pepsi-Cola, Dr. Pepper Snapple, and Nestle controlling the refrigerators. On the other hand, natural stores are more open to allowing new products on the shelves and fridges.

The Ready to Drink alcoholic channel is the opposite, with stores and restaurants receiving open arms. Hundreds of microbreweries are emerging, and some of them have been acquired. Here in San Diego, we have one of the most active microbrewery towns in the nation, giving beer lovers great options with on-premises and even retail sales. In my last count, I saw one hundred and fifty-two breweries in San Diego; these are not home operations; they're businesses open to the public. You can check out the list on www.liquidbrandsmanagement.com/beveragebook. Placing these new beers in retail and on-premise accounts is not as tricky as their non-alcoholic cousins. Bars and restaurants accept them, retailers love them, and consumers like me are willing to give them all a chance.

Artisan beer is not the only rediscovered beverage to hit the market. We can learn plenty from White Claw, leading the hard seltzer category that exploded into the scene. Budweiser already responded with their Bud Light hard seltzer, which gives you an eye as to why large companies struggle to innovate. It isn't easy to strive away from the name brands they already own.

The newest addition to the microbrewing movement in San Diego is hard kombucha.

You would think that the beer giants like Miller, AB InBev, or Heineken would completely dominate the beer refrigerator. It was factual for a while until discerning and knowledgeable consumers welcomed the new Artisan beer brands. Will this trend one day extend to the RTD non-alcoholic sector? Soda has seen a steady decline over the years. The opposite is true for the new functional brands that are showing positive growth. However, most brands' wholesale distribution channel was still off-limits until COVID hit and changed it forever.

Rapid Knowledge Section

There is much information in this book, and it can be overwhelming at times, especially if you want to start with beverage development and quickly get some sales. I thought of this for a long time and decided that the best way to get you the information you need, when you need it, is to add a Rapid Knowledge Section to each critical section of the book. For example, suppose you want to attract influencers with an affiliate program that they can use to make money online while promoting your product. In that case, you'll get the hack fast. Later on, I'll explain in detail everything you need to know about direct marketing, affiliate market influencers, and selling beverages using social media.

Rapid Knowledge Sections is the way to hack this book. Get the information you need fast, use it instantly and get results. When you're in the beverage development phase, get the info you need; if you're pitching distributors and need the information to prepare for them, get it fast. Read the Rapid Knowledge Section for the quick guide if you decide to sell online through Amazon or your store, and you're keen on understanding keyword marketing and SEO.

"I'm the Deep Dive King, but sometimes you need the hacks."

This entire book is a deep dive; every chapter explores beverage development details, targeting your perfect consumer, wholesale distribution, online sales, and more. I'm the Deep Dive King, but sometimes you need the hacks. Don't worry about the details; this book is very meticulous, and I go into the nuts and bolts of the entire process of being a successful beverage CEO. You'll still get all of that.

The Era of Free Shipping

"Welcome to the Amazon Prime Phenomenon!"

I decided to upgrade my home office equipment with a DELL monitor and the XPS 13 laptop. I waited the next day for my shipment, nothing. I waited by the door the second day, and I was surprised when it didn't arrive. I started doubting my sanity, "Did I buy the equipment? Did I push the place order button?" After checking, I saw the order confirmation email, which confirmed the scheduled delivery date was one whole week from the purchase date. "How weird," I thought, but then I remembered that I didn't buy it from Amazon; I purchased it directly from DELL. I call this the Amazon Prime phenomenon; this is shopping in the era of free shipping.

COVID didn't change the industry; Amazon Prime started changing the industry a few years ago. Consumers didn't order their beverages through Amazon or other retailers, and beverage brands couldn't drop-ship their products directly to consumers; shipping was too expensive.

When I owned my wholesale distribution company, I tried to sell beverages and ship them by mail; I needed to send an entire pallet to profit. Shipping a case of 24 sixteen-ounce energy drinks was twenty-five dollars. Back then, I was experimenting with every selling method; I tried eBay, drop shipping to consumers, sending half pallets to Walgreens stores around the nation using the then-new UPS freight. It was hard to make any money. You can now buy a single can or bottle on Amazon, and it ships for free, whether you buy a twelve-pack or a bulky thirty-pound case of glass bottles. It's not free for us, the brand owners. Still, we can use Amazon without losing money on shipping, and we can use them to get next-day or two-day delivery and guarantee a great customer experience. If your beverage didn't get there in two days, the consumer doesn't think it's your fault; they know it's Amazon. Free shipping is freaking amazing! How big is it? Free shipping is the number one consideration for customers to buy your product online; a reliable store is second, and Amazon has both.

You should also invest in your store, not every buyer has Amazon Prime, and with the right incentives, you could captivate and convert your perfect consumer into lifelong clients. Remember, Amazon doesn't give you a whole lot of information on their customers. With your online store, you can market, remarket, upsell the way you want to do it, and ensure a fantastic customer experience.

Brand new consumer goods business models allow you to sell directly to the consumer. For example, you can create subscription boxes that you ship monthly to your customers or provide them with points to exchange for free shipping or send them a gift with a purchase. I'm currently exploring these two models for my products and clients. If your customer buys more than forty dollars that day, they could get free shipping for the order, but how about customers that spent three hundred dollars in a year? How about five hundred? Should they get free shipping? I also like the gift with purchase idea, where you reward your consumers with giveaways like hats or t-shirts as they buy more from you. Remember, the cost of acquiring a new client is high. Selling to your existing customer over and over again is free, so you should invest in keeping your direct-to-consumer customers very happy.

Selling directly to consumers gives you an opportunity over the giant beverage companies because you can position your beverage by injecting your personality. New social media age consumers don't like to promote your brand; they want you to be an extension of their brand. Facebook started this trend, then Instagram, and now Tik-Tok is extending it. The bottom line is, don't compete with the beverage giants on their turf with their own rules. Compete with them on your turf and convince consumers that you want to extend their brand. Collaborating with consumers gives your company a competitive advantage, and in turn, your consumers will share your brand on their social media accounts, making it go viral.

Artisan Beverages

"You can buy a pallet of your beverage instead of two truckloads."

Artisan beverages are no longer the homemade jars of lemonade sold at the farmer's market. They can be a beverage selling in natural channels all over the country.

The Artisan beverage market has changed, and that's great news for new beverage entrepreneurs. Finding the right bottler (also known as a co-packer) is vital for beverage companies. A few years ago, you had only a few bottlers on the west coast and a few on the east coast, and both required at least a truckload or two to bottle your drinks. Having two truckloads of product is no longer an artisan operation; bottlers forced new entrepreneurs to behave as large beverage companies with considerable inventories. At one time, the minimum order of cans was ten thousand cases of twenty-four cans. The minimum bottling volume was five thousand cases, more than two truckloads, and far too expensive for a start-up. This old model's result was that brands spent all their money in production instead of marketing, and beverages expired in the warehouse, bankrupting the company in the process.

I needed to find bottlers with a new business model. Yes, keep producing your large production clients, but buy another bottling line to make smaller quantities of beverages, say a pallet. Don't buy ten thousand cases of cans with printing; buy them without any printing and label them as you go or sleeve them with a label. I started looking for small-scale co-packers a long time ago, and they were tough to find and far too expensive to sell to distributors and retailers. Now, with more bottlers all over the nation, you can start with a pallet or two instead of the old minimums of two truckloads. What does this mean to you? It means you can spend your money on marketing instead of inventory. Yes, you pay a bit more to have a small production run, but who cares? When you're starting, it's all about cash flow, and short production runs get you to positive cash flow faster. With modest production runs, you can also test products. What if you start with four different flavors, and two sells, but two don't? Not to worry, you only made a pallet of each so that you won't lose truckloads of products, and you can develop new flavors quickly, knowing that your inventory investment is minimal.

You can run small production with bottles and cans as well, even with slim cans. You can do it with vitamins, carbonation, and natural ingredients. The bottling world changed. You, the entrepreneur, are now better off than even two years ago when you needed at least fifty-thousand dollars to test one flavor of one product.

Online Direct Marketing

"Connect with your perfect consumer, turn them into brand ambassadors, and leverage that into wholesale distribution."

Online marketing is no longer an online strategy, and direct marketing is no longer a mail order or catalog business. Direct response marketing is nothing new. It began in newspaper advertising and sales letters, but now we use it to construct online audiences that best suit our products. Yes, many entrepreneurs use direct response marketing online. I use it on every platform you can imagine, especially the big three search engines, Google, YouTube, and Amazon, plus social media. The strategy is simple. It would help if you could know how every advertising dollar you spend is performing. Online marketing gives you that transparency, but that's not new; I've been using these strategies for twenty years. New is using online direct response to leverage wholesale distribution or sales to distributors, retailers, and consumers.

Internet marketing can now make an incredible difference in your sales to distributors, retailers, and consumers. One of my favorite strategies is opening a few retail stores and running a Facebook or Instagram campaign. I target consumers in the same zip code and send them to buy at those stores. The retailer will love you for sending them business. Consumers might buy at those stores or go to Amazon or your website to purchase there. The internet can help you produce ultra-targeted marketing campaigns aimed at your perfect audience and can send them to your store as well as your retail customer. The price of all this marketing can be ninety percent cheaper than one billboard or radio ad.

Amazon is jumping on the online advertising bandwagon, allowing you to advertise in their store and outside of their store with brand new tools and platforms, including Amazon DSP, Amazon Posts, Amazon Live, Alexa Audio Ads, Posts, and custom advertising solutions. Amazon is even giving you the tools to measure how your social media advertising performs in your Amazon store; this is called Amazon attribution.

The Basics are The Same

"Online and offline, using distributors or Amazon, it's still wholesale distribution, and the basics are the same, get a solid supply chain and master consumer interaction."

Don't worry. We'll still cover all the basics of beverage formulation and development, supply chain, selling to distributors, placing your product in and out of the refrigerators in convenience stores, supermarkets, and the natural channel.

Your goal after reading this book should be to finish your entire business model. What do I mean by business model? Your business model is all the information you need to execute each section of your business plan.

Your business model could include:

- ☑ Discover Your Unique Value Proposition

- ☑ Communicate your Unique Selling Proposition

- ☑ Create a business plan

- ☑ Write your investment deck

- ☑ Secure investment

- ☑ Develop your Beverage

- ☑ Sell and Distribute

- ☑ Market to your Consumer

We'll be talking a lot about business models as it's a significant goal for your beverage or any other business that you start.

Build Your Beverage Empire!

Rapid Knowledge Section

To Build Your Beverage Empire, you need to stop and think for a minute. Take out a notebook and visualize what you want for your consumer; what value will you provide? Will you make them happy? How will you do that? How will you make a positive impact in the life of your perfect customer? After you figure that out, write down how you'll communicate that to everyone, and by everyone, I mean the consumer, retailer, distributor, investor, and your employees. That's the hack to your business model. Close your eyes and imagine how that would look, how that would feel, imagine how your company would work to achieve that goal.

Write down how you'll get that product to that happy, perfect consumer, maybe using a subscription gift box, or by selling it in Whole Foods, or Costco, or 7-Eleven, or how about Amazon or in-house parties? Write down all the ways you can deliver the product to your perfect consumer and put a budget together. How much will it cost in advertising, employees' salaries, shipping, retailing, distributing, commissions? Using this new budget, calculate how much you want to grow and how much money you need to achieve your goals. For example, if you're going to open one hundred thousand stores in the entire country, and the price per store is three hundred dollars, you'll need thirty million dollars. That's a lot of money, but then again, you don't need it all at once, and if you want to grow to one hundred million dollars, that's what you need. Congratulations, you just hacked your beverage financial model; you can apply it to a wholesale distribution model, direct response, online sales, or anything you want.

The Beverage Success Formula

"Here is my step-by-step beverage success formula. It's the same formula I use with my products; take it, apply it, and tell me how you fare with it."

What to do next?

This book is about what to do next! "What to do next" means what you need to do daily, weekly, or monthly. It means knowing precisely how much to spend in the formulation, production, cost of goods sold, marketing, and retail stores acquisition; in other words, the entire planning and execution of your Beverage Empire.

What are your expectations for creating and launching a beverage company? What information and experience do you need to achieve your goals? How can you shorten your learning curve? These all should be your personal goals not only for your new beverage venture but for how this book can help you achieve your short-term and long-term goals in Building Your Beverage Empire.

Yes, you need to know the highly detailed information such as beverage development costs or how to land your perfect distributor, but the problem is not what you know; the problem is in what you don't see that you don't know. In the annoying issues you'll face, those you learn by making mistakes are the unknowns in the industry. I'll let you in on a bit of a secret; nobody is as good at making mistakes as I am. I can make a large number of errors in a short time.

The perfect mentor – I've mentored hundreds of beverage entrepreneurs in the last twenty years. This book is now a collection of terms, mistakes, failures, successes, best practices, and information from not only my experiences but those experiences from hundreds of new beverage entrepreneurs as well as seasoned beverage executives, distributors, and retailers. Allow me to be your mentor; I won't hold any punches, delivering the good, the bad, and the ugly.

I'll try to make the information relevant with different takeaways at different moments in your beverage venture. In the beginning, I'll show you how to get started and save time and money in development, procurement, and production. Once you have your product in the warehouse, I'll indicate how to find your best distributor and retailer, and in growth mode, you'll hear how to manage growth and cash flow and establish better loyalty programs across the supply chain.

Is there a secret formula for starting a beverage company?

What if someone could tell you the secret formula for creating a beverage that will sell, how to sell it, and what it takes to take it nationally from San Diego to New York and even internationally?

"You should begin your business modeling with the end of the story, with your client happily enjoying your product at his house, in a bar, or at the beach, and never with beverage development."

What if you also knew the mistakes new beverage entrepreneurs make and how much each of them spent in time and money, and their success rate? This way, you could make your budget, avoid all costly mistakes and all that wasted time.

Yes, you'll receive this information in this book and much more. Yes, there's a formula for creating a beverage that will sell instead of one that tastes good. How about we start with that information right here at the beginning of the book, so you don't have to wait too long to get to the good part?

So what is the correct way to develop your beverage? How can you create a disruptive product and create an instant best-seller nationwide? The strategy is straightforward but counterintuitive. Please stop researching the internet, stop visiting stores, and start visualizing exercises.

No, imagining and visualizing your way to beverage success is not the theme of this book; that's not the type of visualization I mean. You see, most people think of a product and then start researching the ingredients, then formula, and production; this is the worst thing you can do. It would be best if you began the opposite way entirely. It would help if you started your business modeling with the end of the story, with your client happily enjoying your product at his house, in a bar, or at the beach. This consumer is your ticket to beverage empire heaven. It would be best to understand everything about this person, how they think, how much money they make, where they shop, their age, gender, and everything about them. You will find how to motivate your perfect consumer or Avatar, make the consumer try your product, and buy it time and time again. The goal is to have them as loyal customers, even alpha consumers. Your alpha consumer, also called your Avatar, or perfect customer is a super-loyal customer who recommends your product to their friends and family and through social media.

This super consumer is the basis for your beverage empire. Yes, you will need the right retailer and the proper distribution. Even with the best beverage distributors and stores such as 7-Eleven, Walmart, and Kroger taking your product, you won't survive without your consumer. On the other hand, if you find a perfect consumer with the product they need, you don't need to worry much about your supply chain as it will come to you.

So how do you find and sell to your perfect consumer over and over again? You do it by developing an emotional connection with them! Yes, you'll probably need innovation and a value proposition to get noticed, but it's not as important as establishing an emotional connection. Remember, most buying decisions are based on emotions, so naturally, you need to make emotional connections with your audience or customer base to turn your excellent tasting beverage into an ideal selling beverage.

After you develop a great marketing plan for an emotional connection with your consumer, you'll work on your value and selling proposition, showing consumers, distributors, and retailers that you're distinct, better, unique. In other words, "don't be a copycat." Don't just think of the same old product with a different label, size, flavor, or an extra ingredient. For example, if you're creating an energy drink, don't do an eight or sixteen-ounce can with a better taste and aim to compete in bars and convenience stores as that's precisely the definition of a copycat, and the market will notice. Suppose you flip the energy drink example and create a truly unique value and selling proposition. Then you make a brand new delivery system for your beverage, much like 5-hour ENERGY did with their packaging in a two-ounce shot selling for $2.99 and shocking the marketplace with a brand new category. In that case, you forget about distributors, convenience stores, and bars altogether. Maybe you sell with MLM or with Direct Response selling directly to consumers by the case. Any combination of these examples will qualify your product as a disruptive consumer good.

So What's New in Beverages?

The more things change, the more they stay the same! Much has changed since I first wrote this book with my friend and former business partner Carlos Lopez, especially after the COVID pandemic and the small entrepreneurs' social media empowerment.

I rewrote the second edition of this book in 2016, a complete rewrite filled with years of new experiences from my projects and mentoring new beverage entrepreneurs. I had two main motivating drivers for rewriting the second edition of this book. One was all the industry changes; the other was realizing that graduate and undergraduate university programs used this book.

The functional category is sweeping the non-alcoholic marketplace. The ready-to-drink alcoholic scene is bubbling with new and exciting microbreweries producing hard seltzers, hard kombucha, and, yes, beer.

I always called the combined world of functional beverages "New Age Beverages"; leading the way was Red Bull, followed by

Monster and Rockstar, Vitaminwater, 5-hour ENERGY, coconut waters, and a plethora of RTD teas. The new growing category is called "Functional-RTD Tea-Bottled Water," but to make it easier, we'll refer to it as "New Age Beverages" or "NAB." In it, we'll also include all the new alcoholic beverages such as microbrews, hard kombucha, energy malt beverages, flavored spirits, hard seltzers, and newcomers such as new exotic wines and other spirits from regions across the world, such as the growing portfolio of Mezcales and Tequilas, now with new exotic fruit infusions.

The COVID Shake-Up

The COVID pandemic changed the industry so much it forced my hand to revise the book again. Even my mentoring services changed, and COVID compelled me to create an online course to help more people at a lower price than my high-ticket mentoring prices.

COVID changed the way consumers purchase beverages, especially with online shopping and the advent of delivery services like Doordash. Your online strategy for sales, delivery, and consumer outreach is entirely different from what it was before COVID, and it's all good news for you.

Even more changes happened in business modeling and the approach to selling products in stores. You'll see a lot of consolidation of products in the refrigerator doors and far less independent products in convenience stores, but don't despair; we've seen new doors open up in supermarkets, the natural category such as Whole Foods, and other targeted sales channels. The entire natural category has taken consumers and retailers by storm – from natural sodas to organic Amazonian fruit juices and extracts; the door is wide open for you to discover the newest, coolest superfood and squeeze it into a shelf-ready bottle.

The emergence of merger and acquisition teams at Coca-Cola and the other large beverage companies and investment firms is the best news for new beverage entrepreneurs. You now have more companies looking for successful small beverages with some traction to invest in them, buy or even take public. These investors don't usually look for ideas; they look for traction; this means your product is made and tested with a few distributors and accounts.

Another notable change and the one I like the most is Social Entrepreneurship; this is new to the beverage industry and business. I'm personally a social entrepreneur. I invite and challenge you to become one yourself, be part of something even more significant than dollars, than self-accomplishment, but success at a grander scale, success for yourself and your family, and expand it from there. Use your business to make a community thrive, fund a school, or donate a portion of your winnings to a noble cause. Social Entrepreneurs tend to be dreamers, and they don't accept reality. They want to change it, and they use business and the economy as their primary tool.

Your Core Values

One thing has remained the same. The approach to product development and innovation are the same best practices that you found years ago are still in place today:

- ✓ Start with your target market and work backward

- ✓ Be innovative; don't just copy a product with a different formula

- ✓ Contact distributors and retailers before production

- ✓ Create a best-value proposition

- ✓ Create a best-selling proposition

- ✓ Tie it all up with the packaging that targets your perfect consumer

- ✓ Ensure it is distributor and retailer friendly

These seven steps can be your roadmap for a successful beverage empire. It seems simple; however, it's not. Starting at the end and moving backward is not what comes naturally. It's the opposite of what comes naturally. What most entrepreneurs want to do is get a formula and produce. I'm looking to change the narrative and gain intelligence from the market before you go into business.

I recently got a call from an entrepreneur who developed an energy drink targeted towards the Hispanic market. He wants to export it to Mexico and sell it to OXXO, a sizeable Mexican chain of convenience stores nationwide with over sixteen thousand stores.

After chatting, he realized he didn't have the proper paperwork to import his product into Mexico. He's also not familiar with OXXO's purchasing policies requiring him to "pay to play" and dish out hundreds of thousands of dollars in slotting fees. Furthermore, this beverage entrepreneur didn't know that FEMSA owns OXXO and Coca-Cola in Mexico, and they only sell Coke's products.

I realized this beverage entrepreneur was not ready in a single phone call, and I didn't take him seriously because I've worked with the OXXO chain. I know the buyers and how they purchase; I know they don't buy energy drinks. In this case, I knew the entrepreneur was clueless about exporting and doing business in Mexico. I've worked with a few Hispanic energy drinks already, and I know the market and where we can and cannot sell. I also owned a large distribution company in Mexico, including a Miller Beer distributorship. I've exported Monster Energy, Rockstar Energy Drink, and 5-hour ENERGY. What I want to say is that I've worked with Energy Drinks in Mexico!

?

New to Beverages?

Would you be surprised to know that most people who start a beverage company are not from the beverage industry? This fact poses an interesting problem. Before diving into beverage entrepreneurship, most of you have to start working in the industry without having two, five, or ten years of experience.

If you're a salesperson, merchandiser, or marketing manager in the beverage industry, you'll recognize a few things in the book. If you're a salesperson for Pepsi, Coke, or Miller Beer, you know how many accounts you can visit per day for convenience stores, supermarkets, or on-premise accounts such as bars or restaurants. You also learn how to list new products into existing accounts and understand the time and energy it takes to do this. This experience would serve you well when going after new accounts or calculating sales per store per month. If you're a merchandiser, you know how to fight for shelf and refrigerator space, keep the store manager happy and place the product in front of the consumer. You might place poll signs outside the store, stickers on the refrigerator door, and posters on the windows.

Being a veteran employee from the beverage industry doesn't guarantee success as a beverage entrepreneur. As an entrepreneur, you're entering the big picture side of the industry. You have to think like a general, not a frontline soldier, not even a sergeant! You have to learn to be a CEO. If this is your first entrepreneurship venture, you should also learn how to be an entrepreneur, manage risk, expectations, and, like any great entrepreneur, prepare to make things happen. Yes, you must get as much experience in the beverage industry as you can, but don't underestimate the power of learning marketing, management, and entrepreneurship. Look for valuable mentors, enroll in courses, and read as many books as you can on business-related subjects. It will pay off.

Who Should Read This Book?

- ☑ New Beverage Entrepreneurs
- ☑ Existing Business Owners
- ☑ Wholesalers and Distributors
- ☑ Salespeople at Beverage Companies
- ☑ Beverage and Consumer Goods Executives
- ☑ Formulators, Developers, Co-Packers
- ☑ Mergers & Acquisitions Managers
- ☑ Beverage Investors and Analysts

I initially wrote this book strictly for entrepreneurs launching their beverages. After publishing the book, I received calls from senior management at Coca-Cola, Red Bull, Pepsi, SAB Miller, Unilever, and other large and small companies, distributors, wholesalers, and university students. The most surprising conversations were with existing beverage professionals. They got as much from the book as new beverage entrepreneurs.

I'm writing and revising this book for the newcomer this time around, but I included much more high-level information that beverage veterans will appreciate. My editor advised I write an entirely new book for the beverage industry, a beverage-MBA type book. In the end, I decided to make the book much more extensive and include the two books in one. You will benefit from the 101 introductory courses and the MBA all in one. After all, when you're an entrepreneur, you need all the help you can get.

Who should read this book? Entrepreneurs will still get the most juice from the book, as they have the most to gain and the most to lose from the industry. An entrepreneur can spend two years and $200,000 learning what you'll learn in a couple of days (or weeks) reading this book. Managers and existing beverage executives will surely get something from the book, but they don't have their savings at stake like entrepreneurs usually have.

Unbounded Growth & Opportunity

The beverage industry has been growing tremendously in the New Age, Functional, and even Alcoholic Beverage Categories. That growth knows no bounds. Sales and projections continue to prove that beverages are a stable business to be in— one that only grows by the year, even as some of the most relied-upon, popular drinks start to dwindle and fade. Regular sugary sodas are slowly disappearing, and something bigger and better is replacing them, something consumers can't get enough of. There is a whole new category of beverages that includes:

- Energy Drinks
- Vitamin Waters
- High-End Waters
- Iced Coffees
- Natural Sodas

- ✓ Shots

- ✓ RTDT (Ready To Drink Teas)

- ✓ Kombucha

- ✓ Nutraceuticals

That's not all. You also have liquid vitamins, flavored vitamins, gummies, shots, all using different delivery methods. Vitamins and Nutraceuticals are also a new category for you to explore. Think of how you can infuse existing consumer goods with vitamins and minerals by delivering a nutritional beverage to kids or the elderly in need of protein. I'm currently working with extraordinary entrepreneurs developing superfood carbonated beverages and liquid vitamins.

There is also a new wave of alcoholic beverages, including seltzers and mixed ready-to-drink specialty mixes. New microbreweries are developing craft beers and, my favorite, unique flavors of hard kombucha. I've also seen new and exciting Tequila and Mezcal brands hit the market.

CBD, CBG, and Hemp made a splash after the Hemp Bill passed in 2019; these products are not new. My first client in the beverage hemp space came five years before the government signed the Hemp Bill into law. CBD is hot, and CBG is next, with CNN and other cannabinoids to follow. I'm currently working with ahead-of-the-curve entrepreneurs who are developing many drinks containing cannabinoids. The idea of using marijuana in drinks is also gaining traction, and when marijuana is legally able to cross state lines, the distribution will be much easier. I also helped develop and launch a drink containing marijuana in San Diego, now the number one drink in California dispensaries.

What was new and innovative when I first wrote this book only a few years back is old news today, and companies like Fuze, Red Bull, Monster, Rockstar, Izze, Fiji Water, Vitamin Water, and others are now household names. Some of them lead the category; in other cases, Coca-Cola and Pepsi purchased them for unbelievable valuations, at times in the billions as we saw with Rockstar and Vitaminwater some years back.

This book is your model—your vehicle, means, and comprehensive guide to success in the beverage industry. I wrote this book specifically for people like you. I wrote it to show the thousands of entrepreneurs and investors what it takes to produce successfully, launch, sell, and make money in the beverage business while building a sustainable business that has what it takes to succeed long-term.

Rapid Knowledge Section

To best organize your beverage MBA information, I arranged this book into three main parts. In part one, I'll introduce you to the beverage world and explain why this is the right business to invest your time and money in. You'll see how the beverage marketplace currently operates, and you'll have the tools to become an entrepreneur and CEO in the beverage industry.

In part two, we will dive into the behind-the-scenes world of Beverage Development and explain exactly how to create a beverage of your own. Here you'll learn the mechanics of producing a beverage brand from start to finish, as well as the costs associated with it. You'll master more about beverage development than 99% of the people in the beverage industry.

In the book's final part, you will see the big picture and obtain the most critical piece of the puzzle—the information you need to write and implement a solid business plan. This final part of the book explains the entire marketing process: how to obtain sales and distribution, approach beverage distributors and retail accounts, get reorders of the product, and then sell it off the shelves to those willing consumers. The sales and marketing part of the book will make or break your venture and your future, the part of the business that the vast majority of producers and investors never "get," and that is why most producers will fail.

Conquer The Beverage World

PART 1

Defining your Niche
Your Size & Profit
Market Opportunity
Types of Drinks

PART 2

Developing & Launching
Costs and Product Development
Target
Package, Taste & Ingredients
Production & Logistics

PART 3

Marketing
Sales
Distribution
Retailers and Consumers

Diagram 1 – Three Parts to the Beverage Book

Your Future Is Bright

That is an outcome that will be yours for one simple reason— you have this book, and you have me as your mentor! You now have in your hands a book that puts it all out there for you to test. You found the book that explains why some drinks fail and others go on to be outright successes. By the end of this book, you will be ready not only to develop an excellent beverage but also to sell it and turn it into a profit-producing machine! Your future and your business are waiting, so let's waste no more time. It's time to Build your Beverage Empire!

PART 01

OVERVIEW OF THE NEW
BEVERAGE MARKETPLACE

CHAPTER 1

$

How Much Profit Is There in The Beverage Business?

There is a lot of money to be made in the beverage industry. Still, many people with great drink concepts fail because they don't answer the most pressing questions first and ignore planning their beverage empire properly. Before deciding whether to invest time, money, and effort in this industry, you first must know where success in the beverage industry can take you. In the chapter "Build Your Beverage Empire," you got a seven-step system to build your beverage; this is your first formula for success.

The post COVID era released beverage delivery chains, allowing all of us to play in a level field against big beverage conglomerates; this means more money and faster money. You can be up and running with your Etsy store by tomorrow and sell your products instantly. If you need to bottle professionally, you can do so while building your WooCommerce store on WordPress for two thousand dollars and selling before you get your first production batch.

Rapid Knowledge Section

When you start your beverage, don't invest in production; invest in marketing. You'll run a small production run in only two flavors to test the marketplace. I work with producers that can bottle as little as one pallet of a beverage; this is important because the money is made in the long run, not in the first batch. After you produce a pallet or two, the real work starts. Test your business model and sell your product to consumers, distributors, retailers, or whoever your model calls for. Track your profit and margins and validate your business model by creating a spreadsheet with all of your prices and expenses related to sales, such as cost of goods, shipping, marketing, and distributor and retailers' margins. Are you still making money? If yes, now you can scale!

If you're selling the traditional way to distributors who sell to retailers, you should be making at least a 50% Gross Margin. If you don't make your fifty percent from day one, don't worry, but make sure you can make it with a decent production run. For example, if you produce your beverage for fifty cents, you should sell it to the distributor for one dollar. The distributor could take twenty to thirty percent and the retailer forty percent gross margin.

The Most Frequently Asked Question in the Biz

"How much will it cost to launch my new beverage?"

In my work with beverage entrepreneurs, I get asked one question more than any other: "How much will it cost to launch my new beverage?" And although it is undoubtedly important to know what you are looking at in terms of cost and investment, there are other important factors to consider as well. The questions should not be how much money it takes to start a beverage but how much it takes to sell to the consumer.

Cost and investment are irrelevant if you don't know the potential for return on that investment. Instead of approaching the question of cost first, we prefer to look at the other end of the equation; first, we pose the question, "How much profit can be made by starting and selling a beverage company?"

It's without question that you should set your goals first. As any venture capitalist or investment will ask you, "What is your exit strategy, and how strong are your financials?" In other words, what's your goal? How much money will your company sell in years one, two, and three? How much profit will you make? Once you reach a scalable model, will you sell your business, or is this a project you want to keep for many years to come?

As you read the book, have a notepad ready or your computer or tablet! Write down the quantities you want to sell the first three years of operation and what you think your profit margin on the sale of your products should be as well as your net profit. Do it as a proper mental exercise; for now, don't focus on the monthly profit and loss details.

Now that you have your big-picture goals, let's examine the current landscape of the market. For that, we must focus on two things:

☑ How much profit margin can you make as the brand owner?

☑ What is the size and extent of the beverage industry?

To simplify things, let's start by talking about profit margins and some general numbers you can use to see how much you might profit from a product or product line. Let's discuss the size of the beverage industry.

Profit & Margins in Beverage Production

First, a fact: when a beverage—any beverage—is selling between $0.79 and $0.99 to the consumer, that particular industry is considered "cold" as in, it's not growing and significantly profiting; sodas or carbonated beverages, for example.

A quick trip to your corner convenience store will show you that this is certainly not the case for energy drinks, tea, coconut water, vitamin waters, and other functional beverages. Many of these beverages sell from $1.00 to $1.99, and some sell even higher depending on where you shop.

While you're there, check out the new Kombucha or Hard Kombucha, selling for up to five dollars per bottle, or the new microbrewery beers snatching big bucks for one bottle or a six-pack.

"When your product commands a higher price,
that's when we say, "you're hot!"

Energy drinks and functional beverages have some of the highest profit margins and repeat sales in consumer product goods at every sales ladder level. High-profit margins are one of the biggest reasons the functional beverage category has become so popular today. Indeed, it is also enjoying rapid growth, but more importantly, the profits made in functional beverages are tremendous.

To give you an example of the potential and profitability, let's take the functional beverages as an example picking on energy drinks as they are priced relatively evenly across the board; we'll break down the average costs of production and sales prices for our energy drink.

Let's Start with Some Cost and Sales Numbers

Typically, it costs around $7.00 or $8.00 to produce a 24 can case of energy drink with 16 ounces of liquid in every can. That same case has the potential to sell for $24 to a distributor. It can also be sold directly to the retailer for $32 per case or directly to the consumer for $48.00 per case, using a website, mail order, or Amazon. These prices apply to large-scale production; minimum production runs can cost $12.00, $24 or more per case. It would help if you started thinking about fees and costs by the case, not the can or bottle, as this is how distributors and retailers will buy from you.

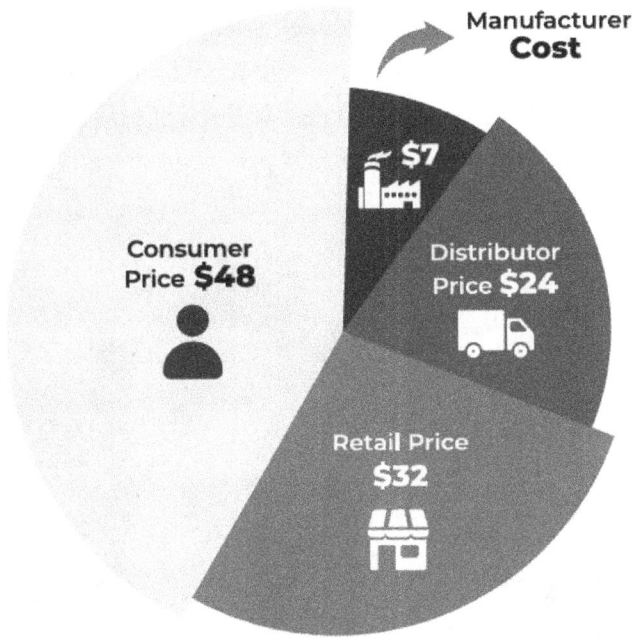

Diagram 1.1 – Costs from Manufacturing to the Consumer

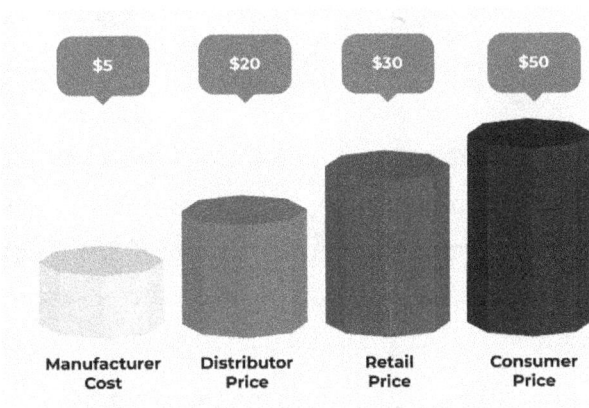

Diagram 1.2 – Supply Chain Cost of Functional Beverages

Taking the example of the $7.00 production cost per case, you can make $17, $25, or even $41 per case! These numbers could add up very quickly. Consider that the average truckload of 12-ounce beverages holds more than 2,000 cases. Even if you only sell at the distributor level, making sales of $24 per case, there is tremendous profit potential.

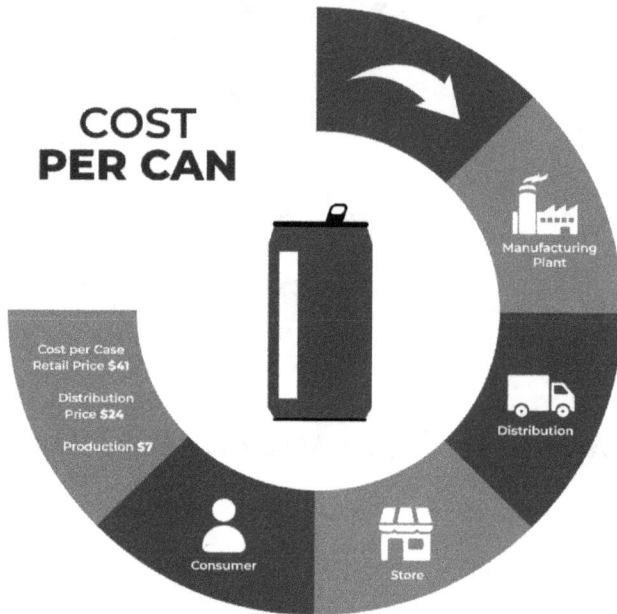

COST PER CAN

Cost per Case
Retail Price $41

Distribution
Price $24

Production $7

Manufacturing Plant

Distribution

Store

Consumer

Diagram 1.3 – Cost per Can

Translated into hard dollars and cents, this means you're making a 700% return on investment or a gross margin of 86%. That's a fantastic return seen in only a few industries; the beverage industry is one of those few.

You'll likely not make an 86% gross margin when you start with a small production run. To be sure, you should calculate a gross margin of at least 50%. Using our same energy drink example, if you're selling your beverage at $24 to beverage distributors, your cost can be as high as $12 for a 24 can case. If you're using a unique biodegradable bottle or one-of-a-kind all-natural ingredients and agave sweetener, you will not meet these numbers. Now you'll have to decide if the agave, bottle, and other ingredients are so unique and of so much value that you can sell at a higher price. This decision is what we call a UVP or Unique Value Proposition – something so unique and wonderful that it will convince consumers that the value is much more than the price. Now you can sell your product for $2.49 or $2.99 to the consumer.

A great example of a higher-priced product in the energy beverage category is 5-hour ENERGY. 5-hour ENERGY completely dominates the marketplace with no close second on the radar. According to Forbes magazine, they sell more than one billion dollars and have only been around for a few years. 5-hour ENERGY sells its product to the consumer for $2.99 for a two-ounce shot; wow! What a way to compete in the category – can you imagine the conversation? "Let's create an energy drink that's only two ounces but let's sell it for a dollar more than the 16-ounce drinks."

I was lucky to work on a project with 5-hour ENERGY a few years back. I connected with Rob McCormick, then Director of International. We met on LinkedIn through a large Beverage and FMCG business group I manage with close to fifty thousand members. I sent him a copy of the first edition of this book, and we became friends. My partner Sandro and I worked with Rob and 5-hour ENERGY to export the drink to Mexico. We met the owner, went to trade shows with the 5-hour ENERGY team, and saw behind the curtain their sales model. Their go-to-market strategy is one of the best and fastest-growing ones I've seen in my career. 5-hour ENERGY achieved this without beverage distributors, and they refused to compete with energy drinks inventing a new category in the process.

"What is your market advantage? Does the consumer think the same way? Or is it that you're just in love with your product?"

Keep in mind that what you think is valuable might not be vital to your consumer. If you want to charge an additional dollar because you have an all-natural drink with agave, it might not fly with your perfect consumer. Thus you need to test, call, and research. I've worked with at least three such cases, and it didn't work with that single unique value proposition. You could speak with consumers, distributors, and retailers during your Research and Development phase to ensure you possess a unique idea or one you can sell in the market. If you're planning on selling through distributors and retailers, you should speak with distributors and resellers. If you plan to sell on Amazon, you should pull all Amazon sales with similar start-up drinks. By the way, when you compare sales numbers, don't compare them to an established brand; they may be spending a hundred thousand dollars on advertising on Amazon; instead, pull numbers from smaller start-up brands and then research the brand to ensure they're a start-up. To get these Amazon sales numbers, go to Google and type "Amazon sales statistics" to see free tools you can use to get invaluable Amazon sales data. Imagine spending money developing and producing your drink only to have distributors or retailers tell you, "We already tried that ten times, and it didn't work; we don't want your product."

When you're researching your new beverage, run the numbers to find how many people look for your beverage category on Google and Amazon and how much profit you'll make for each drink you sell.

Ready-to-drink convenience store products or RTDs could carry the least amount of profit. Nutraceuticals, powdered beverages, shots, and canned alcoholic beverages have a low perceived value and sell for less at the store. You can choose to compete in the high-end tier of Vodka, Tequila, or other spirits; in the case of spirits, you could make much more than a 50% gross margin from the start.

If you have a superior high-end Vodka with a great unique value and selling proposition, such as a flavored or infused spirit, you can sell it for $39.99 with a cost of goods of $6 per case. Even after taking out the distributor price and selling it to restaurants and bars instead of retailers, you're making a $30 gross profit per bottle. A six-bottle case will put a hefty $180 in your pocket. You don't see these kinds of numbers in nonalcoholic ready-to-drink products; however, RTD beverages are fast movers, so you get your money through volume.

> *"Write down your goals as you ponder your business model. Do you want to secure funding and grow exponentially to exit? Or do you prefer to grow slowly and never sell your company?"*

An essential part of your investigation is pricing and profit. It goes hand in hand with your consumer research and your entire business model. Suppose your funding is limited, and by limited, I mean less than one million dollars. In that case, I recommend starting with the natural channel with stores like Whole Foods or selling to on-premise accounts such as bars if you have alcoholic products such as beer, wine, or spirits. Consider direct response, MLM, or other out-of-the-box channels if you have a non-traditional beverage such as a shot, vial, or powder. Without proper funding, don't go into the traditional market. You will not be able to support distributors or pay for advertising to keep consumers buying your product over and over again.

You should also have a reliable internet sales and marketing strategy; in a post-pandemic world, we know that you need to develop a relationship with your consumer, not just with your distributor. It would help if you were selling directly to your consumer using your eCommerce store and through Amazon or other large online retailers that you can leverage for marketing and free shipping. The good news with online marketing and sales is that you have many tools available to research sales on Amazon and marketing on Google.

Weaved into your cash flow strategy or your personal monetary goals for this business, you should have an exit strategy or at least a long-term strategy as your goal. Are you creating this business to run it for the next twenty years? Or will you sell it as soon as a big beverage company offers you a big check? Setting your goals is incredibly important because your growth strategy and running your business will change depending on these goals. If you would like to grow as fast as possible and sell your company quickly, you'll be more aggressive in growth and re-invest most of your money into that growth. If you're keeping your beverage empire forever, you'll probably want to grow slowly and get the absolute best distributors and retailers for your product, choosing them one at a time to make sure they fit your goals.

"IF YOU'RE LOOKING FOR FUNDING, YOU WILL NEED A ONE-PAGER."

CHAPTER 2

Size of the Beverage Industry

Rapid Knowledge Section

If you're looking for investment and need research for your business plan, don't spend hours on Google or tons of money to get this research; don't even include pages and pages of analysis in your business plan or slide deck. I've seen beverage business plans with five, ten, twenty, even thirty pages of industry research. Investors won't read this; they won't even read your entire business plan. Instead, prepare a slide deck using Google Slides, PowerPoint, or Keynote software and allocate one or two slides to the industry's state or size and no more. Try using diagrams or infographics to illustrate your point instead of paragraphs, and you can go to fiverr.com and purchase a couple of good graphics for a few bucks.

If you're looking for funding, you'll also need a one-pager; this is one page, and only one page, summarizing your entire business plan. Ensure you include the following:

- ☑ **Introduction** = Include your vision in one paragraph

- ☑ **Product** = Describe your product and how you plan on selling it

- ☑ **Market** = Explain the market size and how you plan on disrupting it

- ☑ **Opportunity** = Detail how much money you need, what percentage goes to the investor, and how and when the investor will get their money back

As a reminder, I have an entire course dedicated to this subject, including handouts and exercises, so you can benefit from all the documentation I use to raise capital. If you want to take this course, visit the following link:
www.LiquidBrandsManagement.com/beveragebook

Beverage Industry Research

The beverage industry's total size is estimated to reach a staggering $1.8 Trillion in 2024, and it's currently at $1.5 Trillion, according to the report "Global Beverage Markets" published by Research and Markets. This number is incredible, and you can use it in your business plan to show investors the potential of your project in this industry.

The new age and functional drinks market has become a serious competitor in the overall beverage industry. New Age and Functional categories are still enjoying double-digit growth in the beverage industry. In truth, the new age beverage and functional drinks market is sustaining big beverage companies like Coca-Cola and Pepsi as their carbonated drinks see declines and minuscule, even negative growth. Coca-Cola, Pepsi, and the other large beverage companies are in a frenzy to invest and acquire new and exciting companies because they need the boost that they're not getting from soda.

Size Perspective of the Beverage Industry

New age beverages and functional drinks comprise only a fraction of the industry, but this is the category, in fact, almost the *only* category that is growing and showing more and more potential. Several beverage categories make up the whole of the beverage industry, including:

- Carbonated soft drinks
- Bottled water
- Beer
- Wine and Spirits
- Functional Drinks (such as sports, focus, digestion, or energy drinks)
- Ready to Drink (RTD) Teas
- New Age Beverages (natural products, shots, etc.)

New age and functional beverages are just one category within the drinks market. Many in the industry include several categories in one giant category called Functional RTD Water and Tea because it encompasses the most significant growing categories in non-alcoholic beverages. And while it might seem that the old favorites of soda, beer, water, and wine are too ingrained in the marketplace to leave any opportunity, statistics show that just the opposite is true. It seems people have had enough sugary soft drinks and are turning to new forms of refreshment and beverages that can give them more.

If we look at the sales for just the top ten energy drinks alone—bearing in mind that this is just *Energy Drinks*, a sub-category of functional and new age beverages—we get a glimpse of the size and impact of the industry. In 2006/2007, the top ten energy drinks topped well over $743 million in sales, which was a change for the better of approximately 34.4% over the previous year. [1] In 2013, energy drink retail sales only incremented 6.7%, and the top three brands in the USA sold over $7.5 billion.

2014 ENERGY SALES

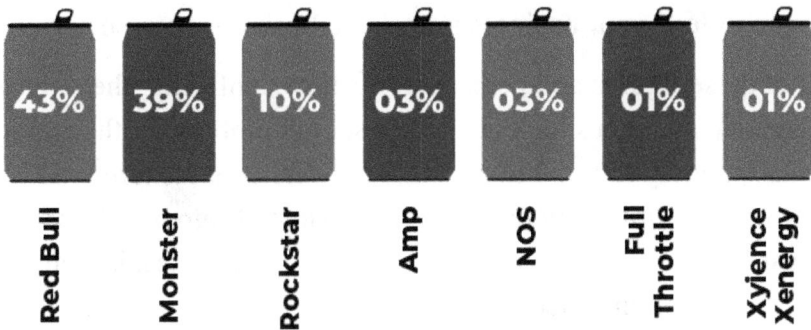

43%	39%	10%	03%	03%	01%	01%
Red Bull	Monster	Rockstar	Amp	NOS	Full Throttle	Xyience Xenergy

References
1. 2013 Data is from the top brands per, latest 52-week period, Total U.S Multi-Outlet w/ C- Store (Supermarkets, Drugstores, Mass Market Retailers, Gas / C- Stores, Military Commissaries and Select Club & Dollar Retail Chains) Provided by "IRI", a Chicago-based market research firm (@iriworldwide)".

2. 2014 Data is from IRI covering a 52-week period ending November 2, 2014 based on USA sales only and retailers not reporting.

3. Prior to 2013 the data was complied from data published by beverage industry insider. Bevnet.com

Diagram 1.4 – Energy Drink Sales

To put this into perspective, we have to point out that these are the numbers for just the top ten energy drinks—names like Red Bull, Monster, Rockstar, Full Throttle, AMP, NOS, and Xenergy. These numbers do not even account for the smaller players still seeing huge gains and making big profits. And these numbers do not account for the many other types of beverages in growing specialty segments like functional, specialized liquor, wines, vitamin waters, teas, coffees, and many others to consider. Growth figures for the overall energy drink category are now steady at around 7% in the current market, with domination from the big players that have run most small energy drink companies out of business. But don't let these numbers bother you as you don't want to compete with Red Bull, Coke, or Patron Tequila. You have to find a niche to exploit and create your market in that niche. Why would you try to compete with Red Bull developing another energy drink when they sell more than 5 billion cans annually worldwide with their 8,000 employees? These numbers are mentioned here as part of a big picture to feed your business model and business acumen.

All of these figures and percentages can be confusing, their actual impact elusive. Let's look at another set of numbers for the energy drinks category to put things in more understandable terms. Research performed by the Market Research Group has shown that in just five years, from 2002 to 2007, when energy drinks entered the US market, the energy drinks market grew 440%. In dollars and cents, that equates to a massive $6.6 billion in sales each year; but energy drinks continue to grow. By 2011, annual sales of energy drinks were projected to top $9 billion in annual sales. That means that for energy drinks alone, there was an additional $2.4 billion in sales up for grabs over the next couple of years that had not yet been accounted for at that time, and at least $6.6 billion in current sales that could be tapped by new drink products. Again, we're only talking about the energy drinks segment opportunity a few years back. According to Euromonitor, the top five energy drink brands sell almost $20 billion per year at this writing.

As a whole, the new age and functional category are posting an awe-inspiring growth each year. The functional beverage category showed sales of $63 Billion in 2015, with $17.9 billion from the USA. You can see a growing trend year after year in the USA without considering other beverages such as water, craft beer, liquor, and other new products. According to Statista, the functional trend shows in all food, with a global functional food market of $190 Billion.

What Do All These Numbers Mean?

Admittedly, the statistics, numbers, and data presented here and other beverage industry analyses can be complex and confusing. What's more, these numbers represent just the tip of the iceberg in reports and statistics. There is much more that can be learned and analyzed. We include this taste of statistical data here as an example of what the industry promises and what the future of the beverage market is capable of performing.

However, besides the straight facts, which we've done our best to present in understandable and meaningful terms, it helps us understand the data.

What you should know is that this $100 billion-plus figure is the amount of money consumers are paying for beverages in a given year at convenience stores, supermarkets, and so on. It is a retail figure, not a wholesale sales number. This figure represents the amount of money that changes hands over counters during a retail point of sale transaction. Unfortunately, I can't provide you with the wholesale totals or the manufacturers' sales totals to the distributors because I don't have them. Or, more accurately, because I can't get them. Most beverage companies are privately owned companies and don't share their annual sales with the regular public.

More importantly, though, to gain a perspective on the beverage industry's market and opportunities, you need to know these figures are based on something known as "scan data." Scan data are the sales figures compiled when you go to the market to buy a product, and they scan that bar code with a UPC scanner. Market retailers send their scan data to research companies like Nielsen's, and these figures are used to compile this information.

To take this further, you need to realize that not all sellers participate in scan data; only a portion of the retail beverage markets participate. Often liquor stores, bars, and even some big retail giants like Walmart do not join in scan data, so their retail beverage sales are not included in this reporting type. Thus, a market report may indicate exclusions such as "based on scan data not including Walmart."

So what does this mean for the size and opportunity in the beverage market?

The use of scan data can give us an idea about the beverage market's size, but it is not entirely accurate. The beverage market's size is probably much more significant than what is reflected in reports based on scan data. The feedback that we get directly from manufacturers is that the numbers out there simply do not add up; sales are genuinely more extensive than these numbers. Very frankly, beverages in all categories are selling in even higher numbers.

Scan data has an especially deceptive impact in the Functional, RTD Tea, and Bottled Water category because these drinks sell more at the convenience levels and small gas stations and family-owned stores. These places often do not scan data, so many sales are missed in many statistics reports.

There is a way to get a complete accounting of the sales in this beverage category, but you have to go directly to the producers or retailers themselves. Call a company now, and they may tell you what their actual sales volume is. These statistics still serve a beneficial purpose—they show us that sales of energy drinks and new-age beverages are brisk and still brisker in truth. In my research for this book, I called more than twenty privately held companies to discuss their experiences, strategies, opinions, and sales. Some shared private sales numbers and other financials but requested that I not publish them using their names.

A Growing Business

A few years ago, this New Age Beverage category was posting growths as high as 75%. Now it's back to average growth in the entire category. Still, this normal market correction means that the market stabilizes and readies itself for long-haul, steady, sustainable growth and profitability. Once a unique product hits the market, the category will blow up again!

Nevertheless, when it is all taken into account, it is clear that the only portion of the beverages industry with room for more products and opportunities is the New Age Beverage industry. With billions of dollars in additional sales projected through the next several years, the place with promise is this still burgeoning yet continually underserved segment of the refreshment beverage market.

"*MEXICO IS THE NUMBER TWO IMPORTER OF U.S. PRODUCTS GLOBALLY.*"

CHAPTER 3

Truckload Sales Opportunities

Rapid Knowledge Section

No matter where you sell your beverage, finding truckload sales opportunities gives you immediate cash flow and helps your valuation all at the same time. It also gets you partners who pick up the marketing slack so that you don't have to do all the marketing and sales heavy lifting. It's all about selling truckloads of a product without doing truckloads of work. If you trade in your market, like the USA, you need to support your distributors and retailers, but if you sell to partners, say, in Mexico, they can do that work and pay you in advance.

Find partners in other countries that are looking for great brands like yours and make them partners. Don't expect them to invest their money to grow your brand instead of their brand. Rather, give them an attractive incentive to invest, like offering stock in your company.

Currently, I'm partnering with international distributors for some of my and my customers' brands. These distributors are getting stock in my customers' private companies and stock in my pre-IPO company.

Don't know where to start? I have you covered! Go to LinkedIn and make sure you have videos and photos of your products on your profile banner and all over your LinkedIn profile. Ensure you post regularly, and join my Mexico Business and Sales Group to meet businesspeople from Mexico: https://www.linkedin.com/groups/56913.

Another hack is visiting ANTAD, the largest retail trade show in Latin America, held in Guadalajara, Mexico. I have attended many times in the past representing different brands, including Miller Beer and 5-hour ENERGY. When you go for the first time, make sure your brand has a trademark in Mexico, and look for partners that believe in your brand and can run with it.

International Sales Opportunities

We have mainly discussed the potential for profiting as a producer and seller of a drink in the United States or your home country. Yet, just next door could be an even wider-open market that is desperate to see their demands for beverages met. Yes, most of the book's strategies apply to all markets and not only the USA; however, most of the book's readers come from the USA.

This book sells worldwide, and I've mentored clients from Australia, Japan, Spain, Germany, Mexico, Peru, South Africa, the

UK, and Canada. But most of my readers and clients have been from the USA. My wish for US entrepreneurs is to sell internationally and international readers to sell in the USA.

Many North Americans and US companies do not realize this, but Mexico is the number two importer of US products globally, just behind Canada. Of even more interest to us as drinks producers, Mexico has a great demand for all types of US beverages, including energy drinks, flavored waters, sodas, shots, and all kinds of alcoholic beverages. It's a whole new market possibility waiting to the south. Also, Mexico is a vast beverage consumer; the country is one of the largest beverage consumers in the world per capita, consuming large quantities of soda, beer, energy drinks, flavored waters, and other new-age beverages.

The American beverage market is not meeting this massive demand in Mexico. Beverage exports to Mexico are underrepresented. According to the U.S. Census Bureau and the U.S. Bureau of Economic Analysis, only about $147 million worth of beverage exports goes from the US into Mexico each year, translating into a trade deficit of around $2 billion in beverages each year.

The demand for these beverages is so great that good beverage producers don't have to work too hard to tap into the Mexican drinks marketplace. Mexicans come to the US to export these products themselves because they simply have no products or production facilities in Mexico. Mostly big wholesale distributors and big retail outlets are buying American beverages by the truckload. This opportunity allows you to develop and export your beverages to Mexico and take advantage of a wide-open market many drink producers are missing.

If you have an enticing product, Mexican exporters will eventually find you. You could take the passive route to export to Mexico just by doing the following:

- ☑ Get your beverage into US trade shows. You can go yourself or place a retailer or distributor there to sell on your behalf. You can also hire a broker to attend trade shows for you.

- ☑ Make yourself easily accessible. Include an international telephone number, not just a US toll-free number, on all your sales materials. Remember to include your email and website address as well, and make sure all of this information is on everything—product labels, business cards, and brochures, too.

- ☑ Have the required information ready. Pre-determine your international price, which is usually lower than your US price, especially if the exporter pays transportation and export fees. You can make up the difference in volume. Know your product specifications—weight, dimensions, case count, pallet count.

With a passive approach, your drink could move into the Mexican market in months or years, but with a more active approach, you could be selling in Mexico in short order (NOW!). If you don't want to leave anything to chance, and you want to ensure your drink's entrance into the Mexican marketplace, take a more active approach and

- ☑ Learn about your target market

- ☑ Research what consumers are paying for similar drinks

- ☑ Calculate the import and transportation costs

- ☑ Negotiate the distributors' and retailers' profit margins

- ☑ Decide where your product can sell and how many of these outlets or stores exist

- ☑ Find new customers by attending Mexican trade shows

- ☑ Locate US distributors currently selling in Mexico

- ☑ Partner with beverage brokers doing business in Mexico

- ☑ Determine what support your new customer base needs

- ☑ Try promotional campaigns to retain or increase sales

- ☑ Provide retailers with Point of Sale (POS) materials when necessary

- ☑ Offer sales commissions

You can extend your sales or target them primarily towards beverage sales in Mexico by taking either an active or passive approach. Mexico is yet another market that further expands the opportunity of profiting in the beverage industry.

Leverage Your Current Opportunities

Some of you reading this book already have a clear advantage over the rest. Some of you out there have a built-in advantage; maybe you're a distributor or retailer, a small independent store, or a seller or developer with a robust online presence selling either beverages or complementary products. If you are one of these people or businesses, then that's all the more reason you have to go into the business of producing a new age drink.

For those reading this book who already engage in one of these businesses or who have that extra advantage, building a new age drink product line should be all the more attractive. You can eliminate many of the steps and place your beverage products forefront of your sales.

If you are a distributor (and not necessarily just a beverage distributor, although this would be best), you have already established a relationship with retailers. Because of that, they might help you out. If you've had a good working relationship, retailers might get behind your product and give it that extra push to move it off the shelves.

Many distributors haven't yet woken up to this opportunity, creating their beverage and distributing it through already established sales channels. These businesses continue to be approached and build up new brands for others to find that they are traded up or down for another distributor in five or six years. Their competition ends up reaping the real rewards of their hard work and sacrifice. For us, as beverage incubators, it's easy to empathize with people in these situations and help them develop their brands to keep this from happening again. It's easy for the distributors to see the benefit of owning the brand, letting go of those without loyalty, and replacing them with the most loyal product developers of all—themselves!

This effect is not limited to distributors, though. The same effect trickles down to the retailers. Retailers, like distributors, also have a lot to do with building brands. Retailers lose space on their shelves to promote new brands. They'll make good money on new products at first because hungry producers will offer them significant profit margins of 30 or 40%. Once these retailers get the drinks selling in high numbers, that profit margin is cut, and the producer charges the retailer a 5% higher wholesale price. The retailer begins to wonder why they should keep giving up prime selling real estate and shelving to a producer that keeps squeezing him into a smaller and smaller profit margin. He begins to think about moving on to the next new producer to enjoy those more significant profit margins once again. The smart ones start to understand that if that next new product were his, the entire profit margin would be his, and it would never be reduced.

People in these positions have a clear advantage; truthfully, the benefit is in their already established sales lines and the business-to-business networking based through the primary business. Readers in these types of positions already know where and how they'll sell their drinks. The benefits are so clear that often we wonder why we don't see more retailers and distributors developing their drink product line. For those who have heard the call, we invite you to get serious about creating your beverage and tell us all about it.

Private Label Opportunities

Each distributor, retailer, restaurant, store, or bar owner should have their own drink. If you do not, you are losing money marketing other people's drinks when you could be reaping all the profits yourself since you already have established sales outlets.

As discussed for distributors, retailers, and the hospitality industry, if you are already in the business in one or more ways, you are already paying for the high costs and infrastructure components like sales, transportation, and warehousing. You can produce several drinks (like non-carbonated products) for less than you can buy from the local distributor. These include drinks like:

- ☑ Sports drinks

- ☑ Enhanced waters

- ☑ Teas

- ☑ Wine

- ☑ Spirits

You can double or triple your profits on similar drinks you sell for others by selling your private label drinks and producing them at less cost. You can even sell at a lower retail price over others' products on your shelves and in your coolers. What's more, you can build a brand for your business through your label and further promote yourself with every private label drink that walks out your door.

Getting on Board with New Opportunities

The sales statistics, the unaccounted sales data, and the thirsty markets inside and outside the U.S. prove that the time of the new beverages has arrived. All alcoholic and non-alcoholic NAB's are the *hot* drink product, the only ones with promise today. If you position yourself with an even more significant advantage through marketing, sales, or distribution, the opportunity for quickly profiting from the NAB craze is still more considerable.

Everyone is looking for new functional beverages. Consumers know what they are, and they are looking to buy them. Bottlers are looking for more bottling businesses, distributors and retailers are looking to enhance their product offerings and sales, and bars and restaurants look for new wines and spirits to serve younger clients. The functional drinks market is big business, and it's only getting bigger.

"YOU'LL LEARN FROM YOUR MISTAKES, BUT MORE IMPORTANTLY, YOU'LL LEARN FROM MINE."

CHAPTER 4

Do's and Don'ts in the Beverage Industry

Rapid Knowledge Section

- **Do**: Bottle a small batch of your product, investing heavily in marketing.

- **Don't**: Invest in a large production run to save money.

- **Do**: Be a beverage CEO and hire the best talent.

- **Don't**: Try to be a designer or beverage formulator.

- **Do**: Develop a sales-based business model.

- **Don't**: Fill it with industry research.

- **Do**: Raise as much capital as you can as fast as you can.

- **Don't**: Worry about dilution or control; get an intelligent advisor.

Falling Forward

"You'll learn from your mistakes, but more importantly, you'll learn from mine."

I've heard the analogy that being an entrepreneur is like jumping off a plane and figuring out how to build a parachute before landing. I don't like that analogy!

Yes, I'm a risk-taker, and I take significant risks with my time and projects; however, I don't risk my customers' companies. I only mentor in sectors I know very well, such as beverages, because the outcomes are predictable based on previous experiences.

I take considerable risks; however, my preparation has always been over the top. I started reading incessantly from an early age, soaking up books of all kinds. I study every day for hours, reading, listening to podcasts, writing books, case studies, and other business articles. I also spend time testing marketing software and marketing strategies, testing advertising strategies and sales copy. I don't consider any of these things "work"; instead, it's preparation. I still need to finish this book, meet with clients that fly into San Diego, work on Research and Development, and at the writing of this book, launch a line of Hemp cigarettes to disrupt the tobacco industry and take the company public.

Yes, I'm taking my company public. My partner Sandro Piancone and I are taking two companies public simultaneously. We've taken several companies public, even grown one to one hundred million dollars, but still failed several times. My point is that you can take risks and be diligent in what you do. You can fall short and try again, and in my case, again and again.

I admire entrepreneurs because they understand the power of failure, and they value loss as a way of not doing something, not a quitting opportunity. Entrepreneurs have a different way of looking at life, problems, and business. They listen intently, taking the meaning of things differently. When a store manager at Walgreens told me he couldn't buy my beverages and I had to go to corporate to get approved, I interpreted, "I don't want to give you a shot," so I went to another Walgreens store. I had to visit five stores before a manager gave me a shot, and soon after, I was selling to four thousand Walgreens without corporate approval. Many may consider the first four selling attempts failures, but it means nothing for entrepreneurs. It's just another passage in a book.

Falling forward means learning from mistakes, and I must confess I've learned a lot! I'm not afraid of failure, so I constantly try and fail. I bring you the experience of all my clients' projects, plus all the people I've mentored and advised. It's challenging to get an accurate count, but I'll venture to say that I've mentored over one thousand entrepreneurs. My readers' lists alone surpass the fifty-thousand subscriber mark, and I used to host weekly mentoring webinars with up to three hundred entrepreneurs. I usually did twenty hot-seats, where I did rapid problem solving for twenty entrepreneurs per week, and I did this for ten years. That's a lot of issues that I'll help you avoid.

As we did in the last chapter, I'm very enthusiastic about sharing the industry's growth and success and showing you how great an opportunity the beverage market can be. But to be fair to our readers, we also have to talk about the failed products and companies we've seen over the years. Learning to successfully develop and sell your new beverage requires knowing the potential pitfalls that new market entrants may encounter.

I know what you may be thinking; ninety percent of new businesses fail within the first year, so that's normal in any business. Yes, however, there is no need to go through the beverage industry's fail cycle. You can avoid it by reading this book, and that's what makes failure so ugly sometimes. I've found myself speaking with beverage entrepreneurs dozens of times, facing significant difficulties in their quest to grow.

- ✅ **Do**: Take risks after understanding the industry and relying on smarter people with more experience than you to run essential company decisions.

- ❌ **Don't**: Experiment with your time and money, especially with your time. You can always make more money, but you can never make more time.

Winners & Losers in the Beverage Industry

"There's a way you can lose, but you'll have to try hard!"

We can say without a doubt that the number of entrepreneurs that have failed in this business is far greater than the number of those that came out as winners. Don't let this happen to you; it's unnecessary and a rookie mistake. We can take a look at how this can occur in a survey I conducted with beverage entrepreneurs.

I've always had an extensive list of beverage entrepreneurs, and because I'm continually offering webinars and speaking events, the list grows every year. In 2014 I decided to survey beverage companies to measure their success and survivability rate. I asked my team to call three hundred entrepreneurs. What was the initial verdict? All three hundred entrepreneurs said they were optimistic they could create a beverage and succeed in the industry in 2014.

Every month my team called the new beverage entrepreneurs back to check on them and see how their project was going. By the end of the year, two hundred forty-five entrepreneurs were out of business. It took less than one year to go from all in to out of business.

Before we jump to conclusions, let's take a step back to study how committed these three hundred entrepreneurs and companies were to creating a beverage business. When we spoke with the entrepreneurs for the first time and subsequent times, all three hundred told us they were one hundred percent committed to their business; however, many didn't have proper funding or knew how to get it. They ignored how much money they needed to start a business. How can we interpret these statistics?

- ☑ They're not 100% committed, and they have what they think is a brilliant idea.
- ☑ They will create their company regardless of the lack of preparation.
- ☑ They just want a barrier to stop their project.

I'm sure we can come up with many more interpretations but let's stick to these three for our example. We know for a fact that every single one of the beverage entrepreneurs told us they wanted to launch a beverage. The reality was much different. We found:

- ✅ 50% quit after less than thirty days
- ✅ 10% had artwork and samples but no sales or inventory

Of the ten percent, or thirty entrepreneurs with samples, only one had a production run and placed the product in retail stores. The other twenty-nine didn't open any stores or opened and lost the few stores they had opened with samples. Some had investments but misused the funds or produced their product but never got distribution or retailers.

> *"It's not difficult to start a beverage, it's not difficult to sell beverages, but it does require work."*

Energy drink companies continue to flood the market today, but back in 2007, you still had a chance to place a few of them in refrigerator cooler doors. I probably received three phone calls per week from entrepreneurs either starting an energy drink company or going out of business and wanting to dump their energy drinks. By 2010 I spent quite a bit of time convincing people not to go into the energy drink business. It wasn't just because it was overly saturated; everyone wanted to go after the same consumer, retailer, with the same idea. Everywhere I traveled, I could see remnants of these once exuberant energy drink producers; however, many of these products just sat on warehouses, on supermarket shelves, and car trunks of hundreds of sales reps nationwide. I got pitched by every type and size of company you can imagine, including MBA players, NFL players, Boxers, UFC fighters, hedge funds, private label manufacturers, too many to list. None of these is in business now. What was the problem? Lack of imagination.

All new energy drinks wanted to follow the same exact business model Red Bull, Monster, and Rockstar had. They wanted the same distributors and the same shelves in retail stores. I don't need to explain what the problem is. You can't fit all those new brands in the refrigerator. Coke, Pepsi, and Dr. Pepper also have their line of energy drinks, and retailers own their private label brand, so now you're going against ten brands owned by the largest companies in the world. It was easier to sell soda and go against Coke than to sell an energy drink and go against all of the business players, and believe me, I tried. I started, launched, and represented six energy drinks and advised a dozen more; none made it.

You not only have the big problem of going after the energy drinks on their turf, but you also have the other issue of zero differentiators; all these drinks are the same. Sure, one is pineapple, and the other diet or has fewer calories, but essentially, they are the same. What can you do to compete in energy drinks? Simple, don't compete in the same market or have a different selling proposition.

Don't sell your product in convenience stores. I know this sounds simple, but it's the most potent piece of advice I can dish out. Work on MLM, direct response, business opportunities, franchises, or something entirely out of the box.

Managing Risk – Avoiding Failure

We now know that hundreds of drink producers fail every year, but why? Why didn't these products sell? Why did these people—once determined and full of great ideas and ambition—fail?

There're endless reasons why great drinks and motivated entrepreneurs fail with their beverages, but more than anything, these drinks fail because of a lack of essential planning. These developers went about marketing and selling their drinks in all the wrong ways; it's something we've seen so often we've even named the problem—reverse engineering.

Reverse engineering happens when developers start at the end— the end product and assume end sales to consumers—without first creating an essential development, distribution, and marketing plan.

In our business as beverage entrepreneurs, investors, and incubators, we see this all too often. Too many people come to us after having started their beverage without doing the research first. They start with the easy part—developing the actual beverage. Making your beverage is not that hard. People come to us and tell us they have a great concept or flavor; they think their drinks will sell themselves because they have:

- ✅ The best tasting drink, or
- ✅ The best looking drink, or

☑ The best logo or bottle

Let us tell you there are many best-tasting and best-looking drinks out there--and many of them are going nowhere! Let us be the first to tell you that it is not enough to have the best-looking or tasting drink. Many drinks succeed without good taste and good looks. Just look at the big-seller energy drinks that are out there, like Red Bull; need we say more?

We get these calls and emails all the time, and we tell everyone the same thing—it's not just about creating your drink. We go on to ask these people the right questions that will help them sell:

☑ Who are your distributors?

☑ How will you sell your drink?

☑ What POS or advertising will you offer the retailer?

With just minutes of due diligence, we find out that this product is destined to hit the Dollar Store within weeks. Still, these developers insist that they don't need to know this information because their product is so great it will market and sell itself.

Some people go so far as to create drinks without knowing who will buy the product. All of this matters because it determines how you package your drink, where you will sell it, and how you will market and promote it. A drink intended for runners isn't going to be packaged in a glass bottle with a metal top. We try to point out these types of things to our callers and customers to show them how they need to be thinking about their products before producing them.

From here, it gets even uglier because with ignorance and poor planning comes the potential for someone to take advantage of these beverage developers. The suppliers selling producers eight thousand cases of bottles, tops, and labels don't care whether these drinks ever take off, not as long as they already have their cash-in-hand. So, they'll continue to sell the products, services, and supplies these developers will pay for, and these entrepreneurs will continue to get taken.

We try our hardest to educate all callers and emailers to see how they need to start the drink development process initially—to see that mixing a batch of a great-tasting drink is not enough. But with such a great opportunity as this, the calls become unmanageable. So instead, we've decided to put it all down in this book and in our audio course to give you a reliable reference and insight into the beverage world.

Basic Beverage Business Model

"Develop a basic model that outlines who your product is for, how you'll get it to them, and how you'll get them to buy it."

Make sure you have a business model; this is the way you'll execute your business. Your business model doesn't have any of the fluff you might include in your business plan, and it has all of the procedures and business secrets. Your business model allows you to execute, hire and train employees, and to scale your business.

Think about it this way. If you were to build a ten-story building, would you try to do it without a good set of plans drafted by a skilled, experienced architect and engineer? Would you start mixing concrete and hammering nails, waiting to see where it takes you? No. You would start with a definite plan and a well-thought-out, carefully designed blueprint. Once you have your blueprint, you can hire a construction company to execute it. They'll know how to read the plans, buy the materials, hire the employees, and keep to the timelines.

Developing and launching a new beverage is no different. The business is about much more than merely creating a great-tasting product. As a beverage developer without inside knowledge and industry experience, why would you attempt to produce a drink without professional guidance and a solid business plan or an experienced and knowledgeable engineer to guide you? You need to hire an experienced team starting with management or get advice from people who have already succeeded in the industry.

To start, you need to develop at least a basic business plan that outlines who your product is for, how you will get it to them, how you'll get them to buy it, and how you will land and support distributors and retailers. If you want to get more technical, include your Unique Selling and Unique Value Propositions as well. This is a simplified version of what it takes to write a business plan and successfully launch a new beverage. If you do not have such a plan, you will almost certainly fail.

Developing a new beverage is not just about mixing flavors and features; it's about knowing how you will sell that product to:

- ☑ Distributors
- ☑ Retailers
- ☑ End consumers

Probably 99.9% of drink developers forget this fundamental principle. That is why so many of these drinks fail. Developers fail to think through their product and appeal, planning for its delivery and sale from the beginning.

You Need to Hire a Team!

There you have it, the complete picture. Now you know the good, the bad, and the ugly as each applies to developing a beverage. It's not always a pretty picture, but we beg you not to let this deter you from becoming the next successful name in the functional drink market.

It's not that this is so difficult an opportunity to take advantage of; it's just that you have to go about it in the right way. You have to start at the beginning; you have to do your research and planning; you have to know all facets of the industry—the good, the bad, and the ugly; and you need to get professional help for those aspects beyond you.

You wouldn't build that ten-story building without an engineer, and you should not think about launching your beverage without the help of a professional team and a solid business plan. An experienced team will talk you through and guide you through every phase of the process, helping you evaluate and answer the essential questions like "how to" and "how much" as they apply to everything from product concept and development to warehousing logistics to sales and marketing.

When you start your business, you usually focus on the taste and package; this is why I make it clear you should start at the end, with the consumer in mind, then work backward. Invest in design and artwork, but not in formulation and production. Work on a clear and easy-to-read investor slide deck. Make the bulk of your slide deck about your consumer and supply chain, not about your product and the market. You need an emotional connection to the investor, but you can do this with the artwork and your value proposition. Now that you're armed with the right tools raise capital and hire a team to help you.

You have a few options when selecting your team. You can hire a COO, VP, or other employees to help you with your product. You can also hire a consultant while you're in the start-up phase. Consultants will charge you by the project or every month. I take a few intriguing projects per year, more as a way to mentor. I found this works best for entrepreneurs. This way, they can learn to be a CEO in the beverage industry while working on their immediate deliverables: beverage development and business model.

A well-funded business model will usually have a team helping with their financial projections, business model, pitch deck, website, and supply chain. Once the product is in the warehouse, the company will either add an internal salesperson or hire a company to sell to all trade, including Amazon, eCommerce, Affiliates, Mass Retail, and convenience stores. You can also outsource your complete sales and marketing team if you prefer. They can help you with your Amazon sales, sales brokering, and digital marketing.

"I'LL HAVE A CANNABIS TAMARIND MARTINI, PLEASE."

CHAPTER 5

The New Era of Beverage

"I'll have a cannabis tamarind martini, please."

I don't think we've even touched the surface of what the beverage industry will bring into the marketplace. It's all blue sky from here.

We've seen plenty of new drinks hit the market in the last few years. During the COVID pandemic, I worked with a company developing an immune system ready-to-drink beverage and a fast-acting liquid vitamin portfolio. In the past, we've seen new ingredients emerge from The Amazon, and super antioxidant beverages hit shelves and take over convenience stores; however, few of these drinks are unique, and there's no real innovation here.

When I was around ten years old, I walked with my mother in downtown Tijuana, Mexico, when we passed a street vendor selling fruit. My mother bought a coconut, and the young man opened it up for us, poured all the coconut water into a plastic bag, stuck a straw into it, and handed it over to me. At the same time, he cut the coconut into small pieces and placed it in a plastic cup with a lot of chili powder and lemon juice. This wasn't the first time I had coconut water, nor the last, but it never occurred to me to bottle it and send it to the US and overcharge consumers for it. Coconut water is not new; neither is iced tea nor any other new products on the market today. More and more, you'll see all of the ingredients of The Amazon sold as bottled drinks, but that's just the beginning.

There's some innovation happening in the beverage world, and you might be the one that has the trillion-dollar idea. Let's talk about innovation in the beverage industry.

Beverage Innovation

Beverages are a fast delivery system. You can take in nutrients very quickly, such as vitamins, electrolytes, and protein. Abbot sells Ensure for $1.99 for an eight-ounce bottle, and Pedialyte sells for $4.99 for a one-liter bottle. You don't hear about these types of companies much when we talk about beverages because, in the United States, these products sell in pharmacies in the pediatric aisle. If you visit Mexican supermarkets, you can find Pedialyte as a ready-to-drink beverage alongside Gatorade.

Pharmaceutical or pharma-type solutions are an incredible opportunity in the beverage space. One of my clients and great friends launched a probiotic beverage for mouth health, as well as the entire digestive system. I can see a pharma acquisition in their future. As you can imagine, the development and roll-out of such a beverage are not simple. There's quite a bit of research and development and intellectual property to consider, making the company extremely valuable, and it can catapult the company into an incredible Beverage Empire.

Rapid Knowledge Section

Innovation doesn't mean you must have a new matcha-berry ginseng beverage; it can be something else that changes the world. Don't be afraid to think bigger, bolder, and break all the rules.

Your differentiator could be in your new product idea, but it could also be the way to sell or distribute it or the way you communicate to consumers. Imagine having influencers as your only salespeople and possibly your shareholders; you would be disrupting the market big time!

Cannabis and Hemp

As a category, the next big thing will be Cannabis and Hemp. I refer to Cannabis as the THC-rich part of the category and Hemp, the non-hallucinogenic opportunity. Let's start by saying this isn't a new category, but it's still a developing one, and consumers worldwide are only now discovering the properties of Cannabis and Hemp. Entrepreneurs and scientists don't know yet all the properties and benefits of the plant we still call "weed." It seems I'm on a new call every week discussing a new cannabinoid or a newfound use from the plant. I'm lucky to be at the forefront of the hemp industry, working as the Chief Marketing Officer, co-founder, and shareholder of Hempacco. Through this company, I've enjoyed working with executives from the largest public and private Hemp, CBD, CBG, and Cannabis companies in the US and Canada, including Medical Marijuana, Inc., Hemptown, Canopy, Charlotte's Web, and others.

The mainstream consumer might not be ready to buy CBD beverages at a convenience store; however, THC beverages are already successful at dispensaries all over the country. My friend Dan Grim started the company "Good Stuff Tonics" a few years back, and we met after he read my book and hired me to help him launch his THC brand and another CBD brand. Looking at the THC market is a great way to see how the mainstream Hemp market will behave in the future with CBD, CBG, and other cannabinoids. The market is currently not ready, and most large distributors and retailers have unlisted their portfolio of beverages. However, retail is not the way to sell these beverages. I believe the first to cash for Hemp products is selling direct to consumers.

Curiously, the COVID pandemic has helped the Hemp industry flourish, and you can now ship your hemp-derived beverages directly to the consumer without using distributors or retailers. If you're thinking of entering this market, you should consider the direct-to-consumer avenues first and traditional retail last.

Beverage Nutrition

Another opportunity in the future of beverages is nutrition. I don't mean sugary water with Vitamin C; I mean real nutrition with fast absorption. This type of new consumer goodwill requires innovation, but it will sprout a new category of beverages that can forever disrupt the food industry.

When I was a small boy, I used to go to my friend Victor's house after school, and his Mom would throw a peeled banana in the blender, some chocolate powder, a bit of protein powder, cinnamon, and milk. No big deal! My grandmother would also prepare smoothies with citrus fruits, oatmeal, and orange juice. After I saw the movie Rocky, I would crack two eggs into a glass and stir them with a fork in the mornings. No washing or disinfecting the eggs! If there were no time for a meal, I would drink various smoothies and juices at different times of the day with all kinds of vegetables, fruits, powders, vitamins, and superfoods. There's a juice bar only a two-minute walk from my house where I buy fresh beet juice with lime, turmeric, ginger, and cayenne pepper. What's my point of all of this? The beverage industry has been hovering around the refreshing category for most of its adult life. Still, the most significant opportunity is not in the refreshing category, but in nutrition, in shelf-stable beverages that can pack a nutritious punch. Imagine, instead of taking ten different vitamins to get the nutrients fruits and vegetables are supposed to give you, you could drink a healthy beverage that packs your body with these and other nutrients such as iron or fatty acids.

I don't mean to imply that a new Vitamin-B water will be the next big thing because it won't. I'm talking about a nutritional evolution based on nutritional science with futuristic absorption technology that can keep your body running at peak levels day and night. Think about how you'll make this happen and start working on the first-to-market nutritious beverage. Please let me know how you're doing; I would love to hear from you!

The Latin Revolution

Yes, I am interested in this segment of the United States population because I was born and raised in Mexico. I started selling beverages in Mexico at no fault of my own. After I decided to jump into the beverage industry, most of the companies I worked with wanted me to export to Mexico. "Are you Mexican?" they would ask. "Yes," I'd say, "Great, help me export my products to Mexico." Mind you, I had no experience exporting beverages or anything else to Mexico, but they didn't care; after all, I spoke Spanish, I knew my way around, and that was enough for them. Over the years, I made incredible memories working with outstanding people from companies like 5-hour ENERGY, Rockstar, Monster, Miller Beer, and many others. For now, I want to focus on the opportunities Mexico and the entire Latino market can bring into the US market and even the international market.

I researched the prominence of the Mexican American population in business, politics, and wealth while writing my book "The Latino Vote." The same will happen when it comes to deciding what beverages to buy online or at the store. Every beverage marketer needs to get very familiar with the Mexican American way of shopping and discover how to reach this Spanish and English market. If you decide that your perfect consumer is someone like me, remember I'm bilingual, and I go to Sprouts and the Mexican Markets, and I shop at Amazon and Costco. I read, listen to music, and communicate in two languages. Your marketing should match your brand and the way I want to be communicating with your brand.

Mexican Beverage Merchandising

We can all learn from the fantastic job many Mexican retailers' do in beverage merchandising. When you visit any supermarket or convenience store across Mexico, you can see this—even in most Mexican supermarkets sprouting up in southern California, Las Vegas, Phoenix, Chicago, New Mexico, and throughout Texas. When you walk into a supermarket in Mexico, you'll be blown away by how much space beverages have, with pallets of drinks sitting on the retail floor, but this is only one of the opportunities you have to market to the Latino and Mexican American population. The other options are not so obvious.

Marketing to Latinos and Mexican Americans

Yes, technically, Mexican Americans are Latinos; however, they're the most represented segment of the population and the ones with the most businesses. They are among the best beverage innovation and marketing opportunities with a significant crossover opportunity into mainstream retail.

A few years back, I received a call from a Forbes magazine reporter looking for feedback for a boxing and beer article. He wondered why Tecate beer was running all the Spanish advertising commercials during ESPN's Friday Night Fights, a live boxing sports program. The ESPN channel was all in English, commentators called the English fights, and all other commercials ran in English. However, the Tecate marketing team understood something many other beverage brands fail to understand. This goes back to the size of the Mexican American market opportunity for beverages and how to market to them. In this case, we know they like boxing, and they're bilingual. In the end, the reporter understood why Tecate was running commercials in Spanish, and he was nice enough to quote me for his story on Forbes. I still think the opportunity to launch new Mexican American ready-to-drink beverages with crossover appeal is one of the USA's best first-to-cash options.

Beverage Market Indicators

Is there still growth in the beverage industry? Innovation can drive growth in the industry. There are also significant market shifts, like the ones from sugary sodas to natural drinks.

Let's take a minute to recap and consider market indicators from the perspective of business size and the point of view that beverages can create.

- A U.S. beverage market with a potential of at least $100 billion per year

☑ Unaccounted sales not included in Scan Data statistics, which further bolster profits and potential

☑ A wide-open Mexican drinks market, thirsting for U.S. beverage products

We look at this larger picture, and we sense a theme. We sense that the U.S. and Mexico markets are ripe for profit in the new-age drinks market. We feel that this is without a doubt the new era of beverages.

Demand, Profit, Potential

Market indicators are among the first places to start when evaluating a given market's potential. In addition to the proven sales, there is also a significant and growing demand for new beverages. And not only is there a growing demand for these trendy drinks, but there is also a demand for the latest and best the drinks market has to offer. Consumers are looking for a drink that can give them more, more, more…a simple solution in a bottle. Alongside the demand for new and better beverages comes the entrepreneur and more entrepreneurs until we completely flood the market with the same product. The opportunity is then lost, as we saw with energy drinks.

The lesson for new entrepreneurs is this: make sure you're entering a market when demand is new or adopting a product or trend is unique, not when it's ending and saturated. Remember to look at it with your product and your channel. For example, a high-end water retail sale might be challenging to sell, but a high-end water drop-shipped to homes is an easier sell.

Business Values & More

The values of established and successful new drinks companies are soaring, and some companies have made unprecedented sales. We can look towards this as an indicator of the beverage era's arrival and an open opportunity indicator. As you read about specific sales and valuations of beverage companies on the news, keep in mind that these companies' high values and the resulting big-dollar sales can only be taken as confidence in the demand, profitability, sustainability, and long-term performance of beverages.

Essential Resources, All in a Row

Several factors all need to align for an era of beverages to be established truly and considered in full swing. One of those factors is the readiness of essential market resources at all points on the spectrum. Everything from development to production to consumers is aligned, which means that the timing is perfect for entering into this field now.

Let's take a detailed look at these essential resources that you now have at your disposal, ready and waiting for your drink; they include:

- Flavor companies or Ingredient Houses
- Manufacturers
- Bottlers
- Retailers
- Distributors

After COVID

- Drop shippers
- Online partners

And most importantly

- Consumers

The flavor companies or ingredient houses are tuning in to the new possibilities in drink flavorings; they now understand that it's no longer just about artificial and sticky sweetness. They are increasing their lines and enhancing additives to include vitamins, minerals, herbs and botanicals, fruits, organics, and much more. They are also more open now to pursuing new flavor lines that have never been tried before. Flavor companies are ready to partner with you to become innovative leaders in their field.

Manufacturers of drink supplies are also coming on board. They are coming to understand the appeal of unique packaging, the sexy and sleek, practical, and solution-oriented drink supply product. From bottles to caps to wrappers and labels, supply manufacturers are ready to lead too.

Bottlers are in line, happy for the increase in business to mix and package functional drinks. Several bottlers have also expanded their capacity to handle unique bottling needs, including the needs of producers packaging natural and organic beverages and hot- and cold-fill products. No longer do you have to wait for a bottler to develop the processing for your drink. It would help if you located the right bottler who is already capable of handling your drink.

Retailers and distributors are interested in stocking the "hot" drinks, the products that will sell. From experience, they know that the products they can move and make big money on are functional beverages and that without them, their sales will be very disappointing.

Consumers are an essential resource to have inline because, as you know, these are the people who will be buying your drink. Consumers are now educated and accustomed to trying out new beverage products; they've seen what they can get and want more. There is no learning curve for those drinks entering the market today like what the pioneers in the market endured. Earlier products had to wait for consumers to warm up to new beverages, but your drink will come into this educated market readily recognized for what it is. Better still, your drink will go into the market in the next phase, where consumers want the products but want new beverages that will do even more. Now consumers are waiting to see what the next era in new age beverages will usher in to meet their needs and demands better and more tastefully.

Before Time Runs Out

Without question, we're in the midst of the new era of beverage now, but the era will not last forever; or at least, the opportunity in the new era will not last forever. As the players get bigger, it will be harder to capitalize on the opportunity this era presents.

As the industry grows, and as more and more players give the big drink companies (the Coca-Colas and Pepsis of the world) a run for their money, the big contenders work harder and harder to squeeze the industry and block new competitors from taking away from their market.

Big drink companies are learning there is a lot of opportunity for small drink producers. These drinks producers (you!) can mean serious competition with new and innovative, better, unique drinks. They are also starting to block competition by cornering bottling, distribution, and retail outlets.

The demand for these products is not going away; the new beverage wave is swelling and swelling, continuing on the move. There is a tremendous growth opportunity in this market, but you have to get on board now before the big names have their way with it. The time to start a beverage company is now.

✔

Take Action

Are you an innovator? How are you innovating? Here are some ideas you might try:

- ☑ Invent or patent an idea
- ☑ Distribution method
- ☑ Design packaging that has never been seen before
- ☑ Communicate with your consumer in a new way
- ☑ Use a new and improved supply chain
- ☑ Be the first to market

These are not all of the ways you can innovate, and maybe on their own, they're not enough; but combined, they can be a powerhouse. You never know; they can be the next billion-dollar unicorn!

Write down how you can innovate your product or run it through the innovation test if you already have an idea. Does it meet any of the innovation criteria?

For example, you can develop a cool new mold for a plastic bottle that you'll drop ship to homes in a subscription model before going to retail. Your subscription model will also offer free merchandise for every month customers subscribe. The more time they stay, the better the merchandise, starting with nothing the first month, a leather bracelet the second, a t-shirt the third, a hat the fourth, after a year, they get a high-quality hoodie. You get the idea. Here is another view: allow your employees or their families to produce all of the give-away merchandise. Wow, now that would be a good story!

"*THE ANSWER IS EASY, DEMAND; NOW, WHAT'S THE QUESTION?*"

CHAPTER 6

Why Functional Beverages are Hot

Today's consumers have more options than ever before. Anywhere they go, they can choose any beverage they want. There's a beverage to fit every lifestyle, delivered in various sizes, prices, packaging, colors, and smells. Today's consumer will buy what he wants to "feel" how he wants to feel. How else can you explain consumers paying $1.99, $2.99, $3.99, or even more for nicely packaged water, soda, energy drinks, energy shots, coffees, and other beverages? With the new microbreweries selling hard kombucha and your favorite IPA in nineteen-ounce cans, consumers, myself included, pay up to six dollars for one can, wow!

Rapid Knowledge Section

"The answer is easy, demand; now, what's the question?"

Yes, demand is why functional beverages, high-end water, tea, microbrews, or expensive tequila can help Build Your Beverage Empire, but how can you take advantage of demand?

Let's talk about something we haven't talked about this whole time, your consumer's mindset. Even before the COVID pandemic, a movement started slowly in California and other progressive states, aiming towards a healthier lifestyle. Yoga and Pilates studios began popping up everywhere, followed by healthy restaurant alternatives, healthy menus at fast food joints, and, yes, healthy beverages. Here is where you come in with your new drink to enter what was then a niche and is now a mainstream convenience store-ready product.

The traditional Coke and Pepsi war is not over America's sugar palate anymore; the new battle is over who can acquire the most unique, healthy, or alternative beverage companies in the next twenty years. Again, this is where you come in.

The consumer is the driver, looking for new beverages, new menu items, matcha, newly discovered superfoods from Brazil's Amazonian forest, and vitamins that will prevent them from getting sick. This is your consumer's mindset, even before the COVID pandemic. After COVID, there is an even larger mindset towards health and vitamins, now accompanied by an opportunity for a new online sales channel that allows you to drop ship to your customers. You can go to market fast, sell on Amazon, and start making money in about two months; that's incredible! Let's sell and make money by focusing on profit and margins. It will help if you start by calculating how much money you can make in the entire supply chain by selling directly to the consumer using your online store or selling through Amazon, a brick-and-mortar establishment, or going through a distributor.

Beverage Profit Calculator

We already know that consumers are willing to try new and exciting beverages at natural stores, supermarkets, and when the brand is mature enough in convenience stores. To have these fabulous new brands, you also need entrepreneurs, and these visionaries are entering the marketplace with fantastic ideas, accompanied by lots of profit.

Beverage entrepreneurs like yourself have the ideas, but you need a sustainable business model behind these ideas. After all, how will you pay for production, distribution, marketing, and sales? I agree the vision needs to be there, but you knew we needed to dive into the numbers sooner or later.

You are entering the beverage business because there is money to be made, plain and simple. Well, I have good news for you; although there's not much profit in the old beverage model, the new beverage model brings with it the consumer that's willing to pay more for your product, so you can make your margins, and so can the entire supply chain.

Here is an example of a Wholesale Distribution to Retail Model or a Direct to Consumer model where you could drop ship to your end customer.

- ✅ Cost of production per case = $6 to $10
- ✅ Wholesale sales estimate per case = $24
- ✅ Mid-and-high-level retail sales estimate per case = $32 to $50, respectively
- ✅ Direct to consumer price estimate = $1.49 to $2.99/unit

So here again, we see the potential for gross profit in the functional category:

- ✅ Lowest wholesale price per case = $18
- ✅ Mid-and-high-level sales per case = $25 and $41, respectively
- ✅ Direct to consumer profit per case (assuming case size of 24) = $40 /average per case

These numbers are impressive, but it's still difficult to foresee the potential in profit in terms of volume; this number will, of course, depend on how much of your drink you move—how many retail outlets you have for it and how well it sells. Just to give you an idea, however, consider that every truckload of the beverage contains approximately two thousand cases, so for every truckload of product you sell, your gross profit numbers may look like this:

Selling to distributors:

- o 2,000 cases/truck
- o x $17 profit/case

- o = $34,000 gross profit per truckload

Selling to retailer:

- o 2,000 cases/truck

- o x $25 profit/case

- o = $50,000 gross profit per truckload

Selling directly to end consumer:

- o 2,000 cases/truck

- o x $41 profit/case

- o = $82,000 gross profit per truckload

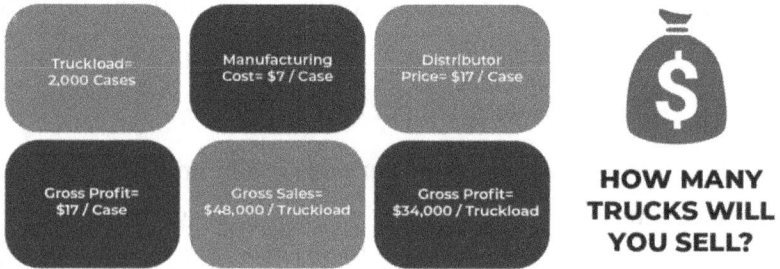

(Profit / Truck) X (# of Loads) = Unlimited Profit Potential

Diagram 1.5 – Profits per truckload

Minimum Gross Profit Potential per Truckload

HOW MANY TRUCKS WILL YOU SELL?

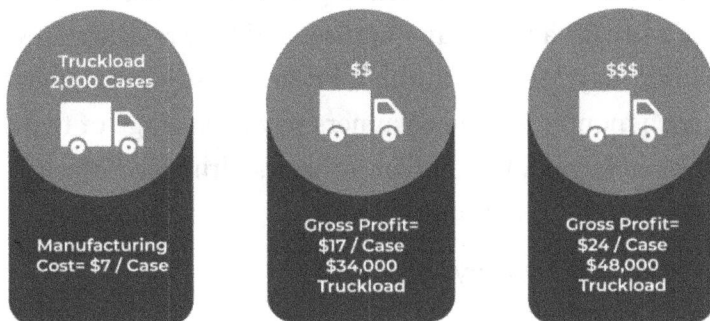

Truckload 2,000 Cases	$$	$$$
Manufacturing Cost= $7 / Case	Gross Profit= $17 / Case $34,000 Truckload	Gross Profit= $24 / Case $48,000 Truckload

(PROFIT / TRUCK) X (#LOADS) = UNLIMITED PROFIT POTENTIAL

Diagram 1.6 – Truckload Sales Numbers

Now that's perspective! The numbers come into focus in terms of profit per truckload, and it's easy to see why profitability is driving this industry to be so hot!

Calculate your numbers! This diagram uses the example of selling to a distributor to illustrate the minimum sales potential of a beverage sold at retail for $1.99. To calculate your numbers do the same exercise selling to a retailer or directly to the end consumer. Don't forget to calculate your gross profit and gross margin for each!

Why Functional Beverages are Hot—Supply

We know that forces of supply and demand drive commerce. This is the incredible reality of New Age and Functional Beverages. The supply frequently diminishes, and someone needs to replenish it. Unlike one-time buys like DVDs, magazines, and other consumer products, a consumer will buy an energy drink, tea, or a new fancy soda every day if you create in them a desire for that product. Let's take a look at this math.

First, let's assume you have a few thousand loyal customers drinking your beverage every day in your city. Let's be even more conservative and say two thousand people buy your drink each day. Let's say it's a workday impulse, and they're drinking your product mid-day Monday through Friday, so say about twenty drinks each month. These consumers pay an average of two dollars per drink (and again, two dollars for some drinks will be a conservative figure) at retail.

- o   2,000 drinkers/day
- o   x 20 days/month
- o   = 40,000 drinks/month
- o   40,000 drinks x $2 each
- o   = $80,000/month in retail sales

Profit Potential for Your City

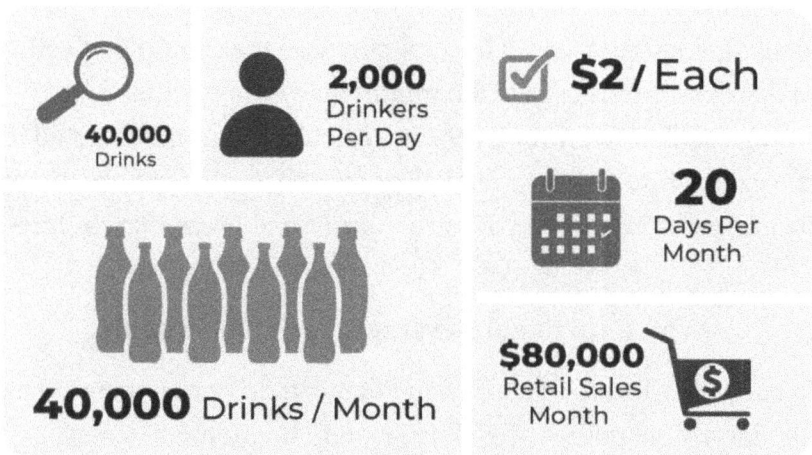

Diagram 1.7 – Profit Potential per City

In the above example, if we figure the production cost to be about twenty-nine cents per bottle, the gross profit margin on these drinks sales is approximately $68,400. There will also be other costs such as promotional costs, marketing, overhead, and sales incentives. Still, as you can see, with just a couple of thousand loyal customers, you can make some considerable money in your beverage business.

After reviewing these projections, it's easy to see how the promise of continual supply can make this a tempting business to be in for you as a drink developer.

Make sure you take these formulas and style of research and add it to your business plan. If you can show how many consumers you'll convert as daily customers, you'll end up with an incredible-looking business plan. Add the number of stores that will cater to your newfound consumers alongside a retention plan, and you're a beverage marketing genius!

Why Functional Beverages are Hot—Demand

Profitability and supply are moot points if there is no market for the product, but this isn't the case for new-age and functional drinks—the demand for this category is very high. Not only do people want these drinks, but they also want *new* beverages that can do even more. That leaves a lot of opportunities out there for innovative drink developers.

Unlike other drinks, new-age beverages are not just about refreshment; they are about lifestyle and living well. People want these drinks to serve a higher function, make their lives more comfortable, and make them look better. As the industry progresses, consumers want drinks that can *do more*, not just good-tasting drinks but *functional* drinks. Buyers wish for drinks that:

- Help them meet their health needs

☑ Fulfill daily dietary and supplement requirements (as is the case with the famous vitamin waters)

☑ Calm them

☑ Hydrate them

☑ Energize them

☑ Help them focus

☑ Sexually enhance them

☑ Enhance their memory

Almost any benefit you can think of is an angle for a functional drink and a potential marketing point. And not least of these benefits is the drinker's perception—that is, the drinker's ability to make the consumer look better; the drink's function as a status symbol of sorts. It's what we call the *Starbucks Effect*. What does that mean?

The Starbucks Effect is what people look for in a product that makes them look good; it's similar to paying top dollars for top brands of mobile phones, PDAs, iPods, and other functional fashion accessories. It doesn't always matter if the product is the best for them, only that it's fashionable. One type of consumer wants the drink that everyone else is drinking; the one the celebrities carry around; the one their favorite players and idols are drinking. These consumers line up for the new thousand-dollar iPhone or three hundred fifty-dollar Nike shoes.

Just like with coffee, consumers could buy their beverages anywhere—McDonald's, 7-Eleven, the corner store—but it wouldn't be *Starbucks* coffee, so that wouldn't be fashionable. When people identify status with your product, you have a drink they will go out of their way to pay outrageous prices for, all because the celebrity drinks it or gives it to their kids. So be like Starbucks, be like Apple, make your brand fashionable!

The difference with functional beverages is that people can buy several drinks per day, unlike durable consumer goods such as cell phones or shoes. Let's say that you provide the benefit of health with your beverages. To maintain the health or wellbeing benefits, your customer needs to replenish their drinking supply every day, which only makes your company and the industry hotter and hotter by the day.

We covered three significant factors—profit, supply, and most of all, demand—and they make beverages a great business. Now you can apply the information to your idea with numbers. Take your vision and put it on paper; imagine not just your product on the shelves but also alternative ways of selling and marketing it. How will you reach your consumers? How could you make incredible contests using social media as your central platform?

✓

Take Action

Start Your Profit Calculator

Run the numbers and see how much profit you can make with the costs and sales estimates you saw today. Here are the channels you should have in a spreadsheet:

- ☑ eStore
- ☑ Amazon.com
- ☑ Direct to Retailer
- ☑ Selling to a Distributor

If you have any other, better, more creative alternative ways of selling, please include them.

To save you hours of work, I created a fill-in-the-blank spreadsheet to download and use for the four business models listed. It also includes a video giving you an overview of how to use the spreadsheet. Go to www.LiquidBrandsManagement.com/beveragebook

"*UNA LIMONADA MINERAL, POR FAVOR.*"

CHAPTER 7

New Beverage Opportunities

Rapid Knowledge Section

You might already have an idea for a beverage, or you might still be looking for the perfect beverage opportunity. Before you decide on the final concept, please read some of the projects I've worked on below and the different categories and options you have available.

Some of the best advice I can give you is to think of your differentiators early on, how you are different from your competitors, and how you will maintain your entry barriers so others can't come in and compete with a few thousand dollars.

There are plenty of opportunities in the beverage industry. Please make sure you're always looking for funding; you'll need at least a million dollars. If you don't have the money, start raising it a bit at a time until you have it. Later you'll need more to grow faster and be first to market.

We'll go over opportunities in functions like energy, vitamins, sparkling, kombucha, and many others.

Beverage Opportunity Categories

Discover new beverage space opportunities, from unique flavors to packaging, categories, microbrews, or ingredients. Let's go over some basic categories and see if you find opportunities to Build Your Beverage Empire.

In this chapter, I don't mean to quantify or list every type of beverage available in the marketplace. It's here to inspire you, to give you new ideas on what new products you can launch. If you already have a product in mind, maybe you could find inspiration in how other products launch or how they came to market and take the same concepts into your brand.

The term "New Age Beverage" is more traditional, and it can include functional beverages. Still, it can also include any non-traditional beverage or packaging, anything of a new invention or presentation. Before, it was just for non-alcoholic beverages; now, it can consist of alcoholic drinks such as flavored tequila or a new triple distilled homemade cherry vodka. For example, water would fit in the new age beverage category but not necessarily in the functional category.

Let's pick on some sub-categories and stretch them out to understand better what they do in the marketplace. Let's explore these:

- Water
- Energy drinks and shots
- Functional drinks
- Enhanced waters
- New sodas

For Alcoholic beverages:

- Ready to Drink Alcoholic
- Microbrews
- Spirits

Water in a Bottle

"Sparkling water takes the gold; it grew over 100% over three years."

Bottled water started selling to provide better quality and convenience to meet consumers' needs on the go and those with access only to poor tasting or poor-quality tap water. In Europe, bottled water has been trendy for many years, not just with Federelle, Perrier, or San Pellegrino but also with many other brands. When I lived in Germany more than twenty years ago, I remember seeing drivers delivering flat and carbonated one-liter glass water bottles to homes. All my German friends had water delivered to their homes in this fashion, and I remember being very surprised.

As a group, bottled waters are the most significant rival to CSDs (Carbonated Soft Drinks). Key industry experts believe the overall water category has what it takes to take that top spot from sodas. As the chairman and CEO of Beverage Marketing Corporation, Michael Bellas, points out, the water category has grown so big that it is starting to splinter into sub-categories. But add those sub-categories back together, and you have one substantial competitive force in the beverage industry. As he says, with the continued growth of the various water types out there, it's only a "matter of time" before sodas are overtaken.

Money in Bubbles

"Una limonada mineral, por favor."

"I'll have a sparkling lemonade, please." I see the most water category opportunity in sparkling water (or bubble water, as I like to call it). I remember drinking Peñafiel sparkling mineral water in Mexico, and even now, I like to order a mineral water lemonade at every restaurant I enter, made with Peñafiel sparkling water. You could also order mineral water lemonade at any Mexican restaurant in the USA.

When I first came to the USA to school, sparkling water was hard to find. I could usually find an expensive glass bottle of Perrier in some up-scale convenience store or supermarket. I also saw San Pellegrino water in restaurants selling for more than I could pay. Bubbles were not immensely popular back then. Even after I graduated college and started making a few dollars, I couldn't find affordable sparkling water to take home, especially not by the six-pack or by the case. I remember I found four packs of Clearly Canadian flavored sparkling water while working in Canada. I took them to my hotel and drank that brand the entire three months I was there. Now, I have cases of Perrier plastic 8.5-ounce bottles in my garage; some are glass one-liter bottles. I also have 8.5-ounce flavored Perrier cans in all flavors. I've tried Bubbly, La Croix, Ice, and private labels from all the supermarkets around my house. Yes, I'm a big fan of bubbles.

It will not surprise you that the Sparkling Water category is growing. Here are some numbers:

	DOLLAR SALES	% CHANGE VS. PRIOR YEAR	MARKET SHARE	% CHANGE VS. PRIOR YEAR
Private Label	$613,883,607	8.7	17.7	-0.7
Sparkling Ice	$553,174,958	19.9	16.0	0.93
La Croix	$435,157,534	-2.5	12.6	-1.99
Bubly	$300,111,786	87.4	8.7	3.44
Perrier	$286,920,838	-0.2	8.3	-1.09
Category Total	$3,464,750,801	12.9	100.0	————

*Includes brands not listed.
Source: Information Resources Inc. (IRI), Chicago. Total U.S, Supermarkets, drug Stores, gas and convenience stores, mass merchandisers, military commissaries, and select club and dollar retail chains for the 52 weeks ending March 22.

The Water Category

What does this mega-category look like? First, we have your run-of-the-mill waters:

- ✓ Still water
- ✓ Springwater

- ⊘ Sparkling water
- ⊘ Naturally carbonated water

These waters are classified in a variety of manners and can come from a variety of sources, including:

- ⊘ Artisan wells
- ⊘ Underground streams
- ⊘ Regular tap
- ⊘ Glaciers
- ⊘ Others

A whole list of other options is used to differentiate waters even more, and these unique characteristics are essential for marketing and pricing purposes. Examples of the differentiating elements are:

- ⊘ Age of source
- ⊘ pH level
- ⊘ Source elevation
- ⊘ Mineral content
- ⊘ Bottle material
- ⊘ Bottle shape
- ⊘ Cap
- ⊘ Other marketing distinctions

This mega-water category also includes enhanced waters and flavored waters, but given the nature of these waters' future, we will separate them and talk about them on their own.

Review the different bullet points above. Each one is an opportunity for you and your beverage. Maybe you can use them in combination with a water idea or add them to your existing drink to increase your brand's perceived value. For example, if you already have an idea for ginseng moringa water to go after the superfood and anti-inflammatory health market, maybe you add naturally sparkling spring water to make it an over-the-top value proposition.

I've worked on several water projects, including:

- ☑ Developing a water company from scratch
- ☑ Water company from New Zealand
- ☑ Private Label
- ☑ Oxygen and Hydrogen water
- ☑ Fiji Water
- ☑ Hemp, CBD, CBG water

The water company I developed from scratch was a fantastic project that included a great bottle I created with two molds, one for a liter, the other half a liter. The New Zealand water project was a lot of fun, and private labeling was not, but I did it anyway! Oxygen water is currently rising, and I've worked with both oxygen and hydrogen water companies. Please remember when you work with oxygen or hydrogen beverages, you can't make any claims to your consumers, no matter what.

I worked with Fiji water a long time ago when they explored the Mexican market and needed help. I remember Cabo San Lucas's hotels giving away Fiji water, a big hit with American tourists. Over the last years, I've advised countless water companies. It's incredible how much you can profit by selling bottled water.

Even Hemp, CBD, and CBG waters are not new. I started working on my first project years ago before hemp was even popular. Make sure you visit www.LiquidBrandsManagement.com often to see my interviews with the latest companies in this space.

Functional and Enhanced Drinks & Waters

Compared to water sales, functional beverages are not that big; however, the opportunity for growth is in this category. Why? For one, it's easier to tell the story, as you have more ingredients and functions. Second, you're not competing with Coke, Pepsi, Nestle, and the other large companies that own the refrigerator.

Here are some examples of sales:

- ☑ 2020 USA Functional Water Sales: $2.8 Billion
- ☑ 2020 Worldwide Functional Water Sales: $23.8 Billion

Compared with:

- ☑ 2020 USA Bottled Water Sales: $61 Billion
- ☑ So who are these cousins to the bottled-water classic that promise to surpass their near relative?

The enhanced drinks and waters segment encompasses a variety of new-age products. Some of the common forms of these drinks are:

- ☑ Isotonic
- ☑ Vitamin enhanced
- ☑ Herbal

☑ Natural

☑ Tea

☑ Functional

☑ Organic versions of the same

Producers strive to differentiate these products for consumers by container and design and the quality of vitamins and enhancers used in drink production.

The most successful and "hotter" enhancers for enhanced drinks and waters today are those that are functional. The hot enhancers serve a particular purpose: to solve drinkers' problems or address health and lifestyle concerns to appeal to consumers. For example, fruits like pomegranate and acai berries are high in antioxidants—one of today's most touted cancer prevention and detoxifying agents. Even existing successful drink brands are coming out with new variations that now include "functional" and "fashionable" ingredients so they can compete with the "do-more" products on the market.

This trend towards increased functionality—getting more from your beverage of choice (or choosing something new that can do more)—drives the functional beverage market. You have created an unstoppable force in this more health-conscious world when you add that functionality to waters' already perceived health benefits.

Your Functional Beverage space opportunities are incredible; I just can't fit them all in this book. Every week I see a new and astonishing beverage that I have to try, and wouldn't you know it, I find it online, not at the convenience store, natural store, or supermarket. I usually find it online, on social media, through my friends, or I get quite a few samples thanks to this book. My point here is that you don't need to sell at Whole Foods anymore to sell a lot. The first thing I do when I'm researching a functional beverage is research online. Let me tell you what I do:

- I go to Google to do a google keyword search
- I go to Amazon to analyze the sales

I'm looking for how many people look for the brand, the category, and buy the product on Amazon or visit the brand's website. I want an immediate snapshot of the brand and their ocean, where they're swimming. This is the post-COVID research, where you don't need shelf space to succeed, you can have one thousand loyal fans ordering one hundred dollars per month online, and just like that, you're a million-dollar company overnight.

It doesn't matter your company's size when you start, or if you have the needed funding, start with Amazon or your online store. Test the market with social media and search advertising, and once you have all your metrics, spend the money to go to retail. This is one of the most considerable advantages you have now that you didn't have before. Test, test, pivot, and test some more.

Energy Drinks and Shots

Energy Drinks started the functional beverage revolution, but they were not the first functional beverages.

Coffee is sometimes believed to have sparked the start of the Renaissance. In the eighth century, the

*Maya enjoyed chocolate, and tea goes back almost
five thousand years in Asia. Energy Drinks are
not new.*

When I wrote the first edition, Energy Drinks took the beverage industry by storm, growing as much as seventy-five percent per year in the sixteen-ounce can category. Entrepreneurs had hundreds of ideas, "Let's make an energy drink that tastes better than Red Bull" or "Let's make an energy drink for Latinos, or African Americans, or without sugar, or with organic honey." Furthermore, these new entrepreneurs wanted to sell their product next to the big energy drink players, in the same stores, in the same refrigerators, not very smart.

I must admit I played a role in the energy drink sales wave. Being an optimist, I thought there was space for at least a couple more energy drinks in the market, so I helped launch and advised at least a dozen energy drinks. The first-ever was Kabbalah Energy Drink. I started with Kabbalah as a distributor in San Diego and Mexico, where I owned three distribution companies, one selling products in San Diego, one selling all over the USA, and one selling in Tijuana with DSD to other distributors in Mexico. Kabbalah was the first beverage I sold as a distributor, and I ended up building their entire marketing structure, routes, sampling schedule, POS material, go-to-market strategy. I sold products all over the USA as well as in San Diego. They hired me as a consultant to show them how to launch their brand, but, like every other energy drink, they could not sustain the marketing spend to capture the consumers in a retail strategy, and they failed.

My energy drink phase continued for a few years. I developed a few energy drinks from scratch, consulted with energy drink brands with big names from the NFL, MBA, Boxing, and MMA. I worked on a big project with Caballo Negro Energy Drink, opening Budweiser distributors and penetrating a very dissent market in several parts of the country. Again, we competed with the big companies in the refrigerator and had a limited budget. We also competed in Mexican supermarkets, but we didn't have a chance. When our promotions ended, the customers stopped buying the product. I was discouraged, spending many of my resources and pulling favors with distributors to get the product into their accounts, only to remove it from the refrigerators because it didn't sell. The dilemma was the same, and I learned my lesson; I hope you learn it too. Maybe you'll be able to place a product in the refrigerator, but if you don't have the money to compete with Coke and Pepsi in convenience stores, you'll be out. It would help if you tried through another channel.

Would I launch another energy drink? Yes!

I'm not contradicting myself; let's be clear. The problem is not the energy drink; it's the product, the target, and the channel. If you have the same product for the same target and channel, you better have the same money, or more, to compete; this means Coca-Cola money. If a company is launching a new Energy Drink and has the money to do it, yes, I would help. However, you can launch an energy drink, or any other beverage, by changing the primary three components:

- ✅ Product
- ✅ Target
- ✅ Channel

If you're launching a Fast Moving Consumer Good as an energy drink or any beverage, change one of the three variables, and you can compete with large companies without having an enormous budget. Let's see how you would do it:

Product: It's not easy to have a product differentiator, I mean a real one. It's not the size, name, or ingredients. The only real differentiator that I've seen was 5-hour ENERGY. Yes, I would change it up a bit, maybe creating a cannabinoid-based energy drink, or tea, like a CBH or CBEnergy or something like that. I would use Hemp related ingredients because hemp is a new and exciting field at the moment. The energy part would come from the cannabinoids, and I would mix it with green tea. Tea releases energy slower than coffee, so you don't feel the effect all at the same time, and you can keep drinking it all day long. The marketing would teach the consumer to feel good about drinking the product throughout the day with no side effects or crashes.

If I wanted to do a shot, I would do a one-ounce shot in a three-pack. For a drink, I would do an eight-ounce sparkling green tea can sold in a ten-pack. This way, my package is different from the single to the case. Now we covered packaging, ingredients, presentation to the consumer, differentiators, and delivery system.

Target: As you can guess by the product, I'm not going after the x-gamers or the convenience store customers with this product. My target is more the office worker crowd which drinks coffee all day in the office. The product is for a woman in particular, as you can tell by the size. Let's be more specific: ladies who work in offices between thirty and fifty years of age prefer not to drink coffee all day long but still enjoy the energy and look for the product's health benefits with CBD, CBG, and green tea.

Channel: The channel is the market, the way you sell your product. Most new beverages launch traditionally, selling to distributors or retailers. We can't compete with an energy drink that looks the same, targets the same people, in the same store, without the same budget, so let us look for a new channel. How would I sell my new energy concoction? Now let me see! I think I will sell it directly to their office managers. Yes, I'll get to them through their office so that they can drink them all day. I would sell it through my new eCommerce store using WordPress and my preferred shopping cart, WooCommerce, and my favorite extensions. Later, when I'm at around a three-million-run rate, I'll start selling at the natural channel, and we'll take it from there.

Alright, enough business modeling for today; let's get back to the energy drink business as a category.

> *"The Energy Drink Category consolidated with Red Bull, Rockstar owned by Pepsi, and Coke distributing and owning a share of Monster."*

Energy Drink Consolidation

The energy drink category continued to grow rapidly but not the way I thought it would. It turned out only a handful of energy drinks survived, the first ones to market. The category consolidated, and Monster, Rockstar, and Red Bull stayed on top without flinching. Not even Coke and Pepsi products could kick them out of their pedestals. Now we see Coke owning 16.7% of Monster Energy and distributing the brand, and Pepsi acquiring Rockstar in March 2020 for $3.85 Billion. All the other energy drinks have insignificant sales in comparison to these three giants.

Energy Shots and 5-hour ENERGY

Energy Shots were another big surprise. The category opened up at a price higher than energy drinks for a two-ounce shot selling at an official $2.99. I've seen it in Orange County and Manhattan for as much as $4.99 and even up to $6.99 per shot. 5-hour ENERGY dominates the entire category; however, as we saw in our previous energy drink example, you can compete in the category as long as you don't do precisely the same thing they are doing. Many tried doing this after 5-hour ENERGY came into the market. Competitors launched copycat products and sold them in convenience stores.

Is there an opportunity for you to launch energy shots? Again, the answer is yes, but not a copycat product.

In 2009 I tested different energy shots in convenience stores in San Francisco. The shots had prime real estate next to the cash register or next to 5-hour ENERGY. I didn't charge the convenience store owner for the product for this test, and they could keep all the profits. What was the result? Weeks later, the store owners called my salespeople to pick up the product. My sales guys could not understand why "It's free product," they told the store owners over the phone. "We don't care, come and pick it up," they said, "it doesn't sell, and it's taking away space from 5-hour ENERGY." I think that sums it all up. I couldn't even give it away for free!

Yes, I still think the category is wide open, and nobody is jumping in. 5-hour ENERGY has the counters in convenience stores, but there's an entire store waiting to be filled with shots. There's the refrigerator, the cooler, the shelves, racks, and there's still space for competition. Not to mention the post-COVID opportunities for eCommerce drop shipping, Amazon opportunities, and more. Go to your local supermarket and head down to your produce area; you'll see ginger, memory, and other refrigerated shots next to the kombucha alongside other wellness products. I think beverage shots can be significant, but you need to think outside the two-ounce shot, outside energy, and go get a boatload of money to be first to market.

So, You Want an Energy Drink

Energy drinks are not the first energy drinks; coffee, tea, and chocolate are probably the first. One of my all-time favorite drinks is expresso with unsweetened dark chocolate and cayenne pepper. Cacao, the bean used to make chocolate, comes from Mexico, and the Maya and Aztecs thought it was a gift from the gods. They drank it hot and cold with cayenne pepper two thousand years ago, and yes, they knew it had a kick.

Here are some caffeine statistics for our general knowledge:

- ☑ 1 ounce of coffee = 11 milligrams of caffeine
- ☑ 1 ounce of dark chocolate = 12 milligrams of caffeine
- ☑ 1 ounce of cocoa solids = 63 milligrams of caffeine
- ☑ 1 ounce of tea = 3 milligrams of caffeine

I hope the cocoa solids caught your eye; they are chocolate without the cocoa bean's fat. It's not a typo; they have six times the caffeine of coffee. Wow, those Maya knew what they were doing! Cacao is also a superfood. Imagine for a moment an iced chocolate energy drink with 240 milligrams of naturally occurring caffeine because that's what chocolate brings to the table. But wait, it's also a super healthy drink, with 132% of your daily needs of fiber, 40% of protein, 77% of iron, and 134% of magnesium. Wow~! All of that from a single ingredient, we haven't added anything else.

My point is still the same as before; you can easily make an energy drink. I just made another utterly different business model than just another energy drink. Yes, you can launch an energy drink, but do it very differently.

Most energy drinks and shots on the market today are something with perhaps slight carbonation, a few beneficial-sounding ingredients, and something to wake you up—usually large amounts of caffeine. These drinks don't have the complexity of enhanced waters and specialty waters, but there are endless options within this category.

What should you do in this category? Let me tell you first what you should not do or what others did and failed. If you enter this category, focus on Unique Selling Proposition (USP) and Unique Value Proposition (USV). Now you have to identify what counts as a USP and USV and what does not. It would be best to have good taste, but the taste is not a USP or USV. Don't focus just on packaging unless you have something with intellectual property in your formula, such as a new substitute for caffeine that works better and only you can use under exclusivity. Your labels will not be your differentiator or even the size of your beverage.

Now that you know what over five hundred energy drink entrepreneurs did wrong, what should you do? Focus on developing a great USP and USV, which can carve a niche not with main street consumers but with niche consumers. The other large piece of advice I would extend is don't go head to head with the billion-dollar competitors in their home turf. What's their home turf? Bars, restaurants, hotels, convenience stores, supermarkets, and pharmacies. If that's precisely the places you wanted to sell, you are not alone. You and every other entrepreneur coming into the business were thinking the same thing. That's precisely the point. You have to find new and alternative channels of distribution. They can be niche, offshore, a brand new target audience, or an entirely different channel, such as direct sales, MLM, mail order, gyms, universities, you add to the list.

For example, the gym that I attend sells local products, and this includes local beverages. They sell water from local companies in San Diego and alternative Energy Drinks. I asked them how many energy drinks they sell to share in the book. It turns out they sell one case per day. That's 24 cans per day. A start-up energy drink might sell one or two cases per month in a local 7-Eleven, so one case per day is incredible. Instead of selling to 20 stores, you sell to one gym. If you open ten gyms, you're already selling up to three pallets. That's not what you would expect from a standard account. Why not focus on this niche instead of spending up to $1,000 to open a single convenience store? You could also make a deal with a gym chain and open 30, 40, 50, or 500 gyms, giving them special promotions, sampling, and more. Selling to gyms is not just thinking outside the box or coloring outside the lines; this is changing the game entirely or playing a different game with your rules and your home-court advantage. As we said before, don't play in their court, they have billions of dollars to compete; you don't.

Carbonated Soft Drinks - New Sodas

Sodas are still big business; let's not kid ourselves. Coke, Pepsi, Dr. Pepper Snapple are still making bank, and it's almost impossible to go in and compete with the big boys. They're not only big, but they're also cheap. They can sell their products for less, and they have an oligopoly on all the refrigerators in America and some other parts of the world.

"Sodas are up after more than a decade of falling sales. What happened? Who flipped the switch?"

I used to do quite a bit of beverage industry analysis for institutional investors. They all asked me the same questions; one that comes to mind is: "What are the threats to the big cola companies?" My answer was always, "None!" Indeed, they could have incompetent management, but no brand will sneak on them and take forty percent of the market share. They have a monopoly, or oligopoly, in the stores. Unless the government closes the stores due to a new pandemic and you can only buy healthy sodas online... well, come to think of it, that might happen.

Big-Soda has an unparalleled distribution channel, and that's their number two asset behind brand recognition. A competing brand needs to create brand recognition, carve a niche in the distribution channel, or disrupt it completely to take market share away. How could you do these two things?

- ☑ Brand Recognition
- ☑ Distribution Channels

Brand recognition can take years, if not generations, to build. I remember the old Coke commercials when I was a kid, both the American and Mexican commercials.

I think a new soda or soda-like beverage will come from China to surprise the market. China has the money, the production infrastructure, and the eCommerce power to skip retail and go directly to the consumers. With a healthy old-world green tea manuka honey combination of caffeine and sweetness, the American pallet could bring it in and feed it to their children. What can we do to compete in the US market with soda? You can work out deals directly with supermarkets to carry the product into stores through the warehouse, without DSD. You can save twenty to thirty percent and sink it all into marketing, direct-to-consumer incentives, social media viral contests, free hats, and cool clothing for our brand ambassadors.

Big-Soda is excellent at producing big soda. They continue to go out with more Coke and Pepsi products. Coke even launched a campaign to convince millennials that it's alright to drink sugary Coke. You can drink Coke and still be cool. The commercials aired at the movie theaters in San Diego and showed a new twelve-ounce slim Coke can.

Big Soda offers everything under the sun. There's a soda for everyone from the extreme sports fan seeking the thrill of the rush to the classy and more sophisticated drinker that prefers a 'healthier' caffeine-free, sugar-free drink in a slim and sexy ten-ounce can. When I travel, I see even more products under the Big Soda umbrella not seen in the United States, such as the Coca-Cola no sugar product in Mexico. It looks just like a regular Coke, but it has a thin lineup on top that reads "no sugar."

To meet this new demand for better functioning beverages, soda producers—both old and new—enhance their sodas. How? With vitamins and minerals, cutting calories, changing their names to more consumer-friendly monikers like "sparkling beverage," and doing things like adding a dash of juice to naturalize their drinks and turning them into semi-functional beverages, or quasi-sodas, or natural sodas, or not-so-bad-for-you-sodas.

Big Soda sales were negative for more than a decade, and now they're back in the black, up four percent year after year. This uptick could be due to new products, not necessarily because people buy old-fashioned Coke and Pepsi.

What Can You do to Compete in this Category?

The soda category is a widely ignored category by entrepreneurs with many possibilities. Just go to your local natural food store to see what sodas they sell and their presentation, usually glass bottles. Think of alternative methods of distribution like small restaurants or delis. Now devise a strategy to penetrate that or other alternative markets with your new product. As always, when developing a product, start with your sales strategy, not just how to create sparkling cucumber water or a berry-berry strawberry soda. I've seen many new sodas pop up in the market in the last few years. Some of them sell for as much as $1.99 per bottle, selling in four-packs. According to the store managers, that's a lot of money for sodas, but they're selling.

According to Beverage Digest, the CSD USA retail market sold $76 billion in 2013, down from previous years. This is an enormous pie, but remember you're not competing face to face with Coke or Pepsi. You want to find new markets, new consumers, new channels of distribution.

"RAISE AS MUCH MONEY AS POSSIBLE AND PREPARE AS IF YOU'RE SELLING YOUR COMPANY."

CHAPTER 8

Raise Capital

Sell Your Company

Business Valuations

Rapid Knowledge Section

There are a couple of essential things in the world of mergers and acquisitions: raising your capital and selling your company. My advice is simple, raise as much money as possible and prepare as if you're selling your company.

Entrepreneurs worry about losing their company's control, and my advice here is also simple, don't lose control. Losing your own company's management should be a concern but not an excuse or obstacle; it's a decision. You decide how much equity and control of your company you give away.

To raise capital, you'll need a good business model, investor presentation, and valuation. Go pitch as many times as you can to the right partners, ensuring your numbers are reliable and your story is compelling. If you want to see a video on how I raise capital, go to www.LiquidBrandsManagement.com/beveragebook

USA Beverage Mergers and Acquisitions

The new-age beverages' sales figures are impressive, to be sure. But making money in the beverage business is not just about how many bottles or cans you can sell—it's also about building a valuable business that can, if you so choose, be sold at a highly handsome profit. Lest you think that we're throwing pie-in-the-sky promises at you, let's take a look at some examples of new-age drink brands that started small and made it big. In this chapter, we'll highlight some fantastic stories of brands that started as little, independently owned companies. Within a few years, they made millions with an 's'; as in, several million dollars were made from a drink line sale. Our first story is about a company that made billions.

Vitamin Water

Energy Brands Inc., more commonly known as Glacéau, makers of Vitamin Water, Smart Water, and Fruit Water, is one of the biggest success stories in the beverage industry. Based out of Whitestone, New York, the company built a very successful beverage company; and, more importantly, a very successful beverage *category* with their "lifestyle" VitaminWater. What is most remarkable about this sale is that Glacéau was formed in 1996, and just a little over ten years later, in 2007, it was sold to the Coca-Cola Company for billions—$4.1 billion in cash and stocks to be exact.

Coke's President and Chief Operating Officer, Muhtar Kent, gave due credit to the pioneering company, saying, "Glacéau's management has been very successful in putting the enhanced water category on the map."

Before the sale, the company maintained its image and grew its distribution through old-fashioned grass-roots marketing. Glacéau relied on independent distributors to carry the product to convenience stores and grocery retailers across the U.S. The company's visionaries used innovative packaging in line with today's market and secured several celebrity endorsements as part of their overall marketing strategy. The company so proved their abilities that Bikof and a few other key Glacéau executives would remain on board for a few years to ensure that the company maintains the same passionate—and successful—way of doing business.

Glacéau was an attractive acquisition for Coca-Cola because it successfully positioned itself in the enhanced water and energy drink categories, two categories credited with making up a significant portion of the beverage industry's growth in North America.

The rest of the stories are mostly measured in millions, not billions, but still, these businesses' values and sales prices are staggering when you consider their roots and their tender age.

Fuze

Fuze Beverage LLC's growing success first became the talk in investment circles in 2004 when Castanea Partners, a Boston-based private investment firm managing a $75 million investment fund, invested in the company. This investment added significant operating cash to the business and valuable working experience from the investor who owned one of Pepsi's largest independent bottlers in the 1980s. But that was just the beginning of Fuze's success.

Fuze Beverage was formally founded in 2001, after getting its start in co-founder Lance Collins's basement. In the beginning, it was just Lance and three others, each with something to offer in business, marketing, and packaging. The idea behind Fuze was to create drinks and teas that were healthy and beneficial, embarking on lines aimed to "slenderize," "vitalize," "refresh," and do more.

Well before its tenth birthday, Fuze sold to Coca-Cola as well, this time for an estimated $250 million, two hundred fifty million dollars for a company that started in a guy's basement in California, and the sale of a company that was only six years in the making.

SoBe

SoBe, which stands for South Beach Beverages, may sound like it was started in the calm, quiet, and relaxation of a warm coastal California beach, but it was actually started in Norwalk, Connecticut. Four partners, including John Bello and Tom Schwalm, all interested in health and fitness and the mission of creating healthier and more functional drinks, started SoBe in 1996 with their SoBe Black Tea's introduction of 3G. The 3 G's stood for Ginseng, Gingko, and Guarana. The first tea was so successful that they expanded the line to include more teas and energy drinks. Today the SoBe line includes Life Water, too.

Like others, SoBe's success caught the big beverage companies' attention looking for a way to expand into the hot NAB market and compete against their rivals. In 2000, just four years after its founding, SoBe sold to Pepsi for approximately $370 million.

Fiji

Fiji Water got its start simply enough. In Fiji, the club owner noted that guests were often lugging in their own bottled water and went off in search of a local source to supply his club with good-tasting drinking water. He found a natural water source deep within the island that he began to bottle and sell as "untouched by man." He marketed his water as superior in purity and excellence and soon rose to be the second leading supporter of imported bottled water in the United States. Ironically, what started as a way to supply his guests with better tasting local water turned out to be a vast beverage export business and most of the water bottled from the source is now exported instead.

Fiji Water expanded its line and sold in 2004 to Roll International, owners of Teleflora and Pom Wonderful pomegranate juice. Industry sources say the sales price for this simple water bottling company was $63 million.

Snapple

In many ways, Snapple was one of the first new-age beverage brands. The company is not young, though; it was started in the 1940s but took off in the 1970s. Snapple was also one of the first big-dollar NAB purchases, selling to Quaker Oats for $1.7 billion in 1994. Quaker failed at managing the established brand properly, and they re-sold the diminished brand to Cadbury for $300 million in 2000. The resale at a loss to Quaker, and the willingness of Cadbury to pay hundreds of millions for a struggling new-age drink, can be taken as proof that the promise of a successful NAB is still a high value for a company with vision.

Rockstar Energy Drink

Russ Weiner, Rockstar's founder, presented the world's first 16-ounce energy drink in 2001, stating it was designed for those who lead active lifestyles—from Athletes to Rockstars. Today Rockstar sells in more than 30 countries with 30 different flavors, catering mainly to millennials. According to Beverage Digest, the Rockstar Energy Drink company had 14% of the US market share in 2009, in third place after its rivals Monster and Red Bull.

PepsiCo signed a multi-year deal in 2009 to distribute Rockstar Energy Drink, making it the master distributor. In 2020, PepsiCo acquired Rockstar Energy Beverages for $3.85 billion.

Perspective on Beverage Valuations

It's essential to include these examples so that readers understand the true potential of their new age drinks line. While the promise of owning a profitable NAB is a great reason to get into the industry, the possibility of selling that well-established brand is equally encouraging.

Having this perspective is vital if you are to understand how you will profit from your NAB business. There is a perception by many drink developers that they will be selling hundreds of millions of dollars worth of their drinks; that is not realistic. The most prominent new-age beverages sell about $200 million per year, perhaps a little more for Red Bull. The others are not as close. Still, these businesses are valued between $100 and $500 million, sometimes more. When you compare the figures, you see that the business's sale price has no relevance to the amount of product sold. It's more related to a brand's potential that has proven itself and what the buyer thinks they can accomplish by purchasing the NAB.

Something else to consider is that there is an excellent potential for investment in this business, as exemplified in the story of Fuze. Keep in mind that in almost all of these cases, entrepreneurs started the drinks based on ideas—not necessarily on access to funds; if you have a good idea and a solid business plan for a good beverage, some investors are more than willing to invest in it. We get inquiries from investors all the time looking to cash in on the NAB craze while the market is still hot. They're just looking for someone like you who can develop the drink on their behalf. The caveat is that savvy investors don't throw their money at ideas; they put their money into planned product development. That's all the more reason you need this book to prove to investors you are well-versed in drink development, and you know how to succeed where so many others have failed.

In the end, for you, as a new drink developer evaluating the potential for profit in this market, the outlook is excellent. The possibility to profit from both product sales and the sale of a product line creates even more enormous opportunities. So business valuation is yet another factor that you need to consider along the way.

Coca-Cola and Start-ups

Coke is not only buying and investing in large companies, like the $2.15 billion investment into Monster Energy Drink in 2015 according to a Coca-Cola press release, or the 17% acquisition of Green Mountain Coffee for $2 billion, according to the Wall Street

138

Journal article dated December 7, 2015. Coke is also buying smaller companies and investing in new companies.

Coca-Cola has been the most active in non-alcoholic beverage investments and acquisitions. They started a new division called Venturing and Emerging Brands, or VEB. Below is the description on their LinkedIn group:

> *"We were created with an ambitious purpose: to find and develop the next generation of brands with billion-dollar potential. We welcome entrepreneurs and other professionals to join our group!"*

Anyone can join VEB's LinkedIn group. I encourage you to join this discussion group allowing you to interact with VEB and other entrepreneurs.

VEB owns and manages Honest Tea, Hubert's lemonade, and Zico coconut water. The company invests in upcoming companies of all sizes and partners with investment groups to reach more investments. Their website is a rich source of information describing what they're investing in at any time.

The VEB portfolio is filled with incredible beverage success stories. Many of these stories describe entrepreneurs that started with no money, no product, and no idea of what they were doing. They managed to work and grow their company to the point Coke was interested in investing and later in buying the company.

PART

02

**DEVELOPING & LAUNCHING
YOUR DRINKS**

CHAPTER 9

Beverage Development

*"You'll spend around two percent of your
beverage business career in beverage development,
and the rest in sales and distribution."*

The best advice I can give you on developing your beverage is to get a team of experts and keep them through your company's entire life. I worked as a beverage development consultant for a few years. I owned a full-service beverage development firm that included formulation, brand development, audience identification, artwork, packaging, and production. Now, I work with a team of beverage development experts that I trust. I've worked with many people in this industry, and I currently only work with a couple of people I trust with my projects. If you want my private Rolodex of beverage development and production contacts, go to www.LiquidBrandsManagement.com/beveragebook. Please note this is not a list of just random links or emails. This link will provide a tailored response to your specific needs, so be ready to answer some qualifying questions if clicking on this link. Please only click it when you're prepared to continue your beverage journey.

I remind beverage entrepreneurs how little time they'll spend in beverage development than the rest of their project. Let's suppose you start a beverage company and sell it in five to ten years. How much of that time do you think you'll devote to beverage development? How much of your time are you spending in development right now instead of focusing on sales and marketing? I think you'll end up spending around two percent of your time on development and the rest of your time on sales, marketing, funding, distribution, and logistics. So don't worry too much about beverage development; hire experts early, and spend more time building your business model.

Rapid Knowledge Section

Don't start with beverage formulation. Instead, decide who your target market will be, your Avatar. Then hire a team to help you develop a product for that Avatar. If you already have an idea, run it through the business modeling test you'll find below. If it passes the test, find your expert partners and get pricing to develop your cost of goods sold and other crucial financial information.

Let's say you have a fantastic idea for a product and all your friends tell you it's brilliant. You want to know if you can make it work and how much it will cost. What do you do? Here are the Top 5 Research Beverage Development Steps.

Top 5 <u>Research</u> Beverage Development Steps

- ☑ What is the value that you'll provide? = USV

- ☑ How will you communicate this value? = USP = Marketing

- ☑ Who is best to benefit? = Avatar

- ☑ How will you get your product to your Avatar? = Supply Chain

- ☑ How much will manufacturing, communicating, and getting your product to the Avatar cost? = COGS + Marketing + Distribution = Cost of Sales

These are the five steps of Beverage Development. Please note there's no talk of formulation, caps, cans, boxes, or pallets; that's all details and logistics. Concentrate on these five steps before you do anything else. Don't despair if you can't find the costs or miss information on one or more of these points. This book has all the information you need. Once you complete the five points, you can then start executing your plan. Now it's time to create your formula, start production, warehouse the product, etc., but not before.

Chapter 6 discussed a collection of spreadsheets and videos that show you step by step how to calculate your cost of goods sold, shipping, sales, and marketing. You can plug in business models for Amazon, eCommerce, Direct to Supermarket, Beverage Distributors, Natural Channel, Convenience Stores, and more. Here is the link:
www.LiquidBrandsManagement.com/beveragebook

Significant Changes in Beverage Development

When I started in the beverage industry, everything was on a large scale. If you wanted to produce your beverage, you needed to spend too much money in cans or bottles to build inventory, track it, and warehouse it. I was lucky if I was able to produce a single flavor of a product for fifty thousand dollars, and some clients reported spending an average of two hundred fifty thousand dollars, all big numbers.

Everything changed; the rise of microbreweries worldwide pushed new and unique production forms, helping the entire industry. For example, today, you can produce a single pallet of a non-alcoholic beverage slim can without a problem, at the exact cost as what I used to pay for forty pallets of the same product; that's amazing!

Significant savings in formulation and development means you can test products on Amazon, your online store, social media, and even some retailers. The game's name is now testing in marketing and then scaling in marketing, following with production. Let me go into an example of how this would work.

Let's say you're launching a great beverage called "Calilla," a ten-ounce iced coffee with cocoa, matcha, ginseng, and turmeric that packs a natural punch while giving you some of the top superfoods in the world.

The business model would look like this:

- ☑ Identify the Avatar and community online
- ☑ Get the Avatar to our website and create credibility
- ☑ Get the sale
- ☑ Repeat the sale with direct response

Calilla is in Beta testing, sold only on Amazon, and mainly advertising on Facebook and Instagram to female professionals who love chocolate and coffee.

We started researching our fictitious business model in Amazon. I then created a female Facebook audience who likes chocolate and coffee, shops at Whole Foods-type stores, Amazon Prime Members, and makes over sixty thousand dollars per year.

We'll market to this Avatar on Facebook, Instagram, and Amazon. We'll sell the beverage from Amazon in a single can, six-pack, twelve-pack, or cases, using advertising as the main sales driver.

We'll send traffic to our eCommerce store through Facebook and Instagram ads. We will have our shopping cart to pay, but we will also include an Amazon checkout for credibility. We will also send people to Amazon to order from there if they desire; however, they'll spend ten percent less if they buy directly from us. We want customers to buy from us because we make more money. We also keep their information, such as telephone, mailing address, and email, valuable tools for remarketing and retargeting with postcards, letters, coupons, emails, and even text messages. Amazon will not provide us with any of this information.

We incentivize our customers to buy at least a twelve-pack; if they buy a case of twenty-four, they can save big and get something extra, such as vitamin gummies. Why do this? Shipping can kill us! We have a big problem, nobody has tasted our drink, but we can't sell one can, ship it, and still make money. We can't even do it by selling a six-pack, and we might make or lose a dollar selling only a twelve-pack. We want people buying a single can or six-pack to buy from Amazon while keeping the case customers or club buyers, the ones who order a case per month, purchasing in our store.

Once we start selling and receiving positive feedback, we expand our advertising and buy another pallet until it's time to go to retail stores in the same city where we performed our test. Marketing will be easier this way. We could send an email blast to our customers, letting them know we're now in neighboring local stores and sandwich shops.

The entire point of this exercise is to give you ideas on how to start your beverage development and your sales and distribution. Take what you like, what you can use, and discard the rest. I want to hear from you. Please tag me on your posts, on your beverages, on your social media platforms. I want to see what you're selling and how you're advertising.

Beverage Development Specifics

L et's go through the steps a new entrepreneur or executive takes when deciding to go into the beverage development process. This section of the book is for you to know what to expect when developing your beverage. We'll go over the steps you'll take and learn what other entrepreneurs are doing right and what missteps to avoid.

"I've spent $250,000 and an entire year trying to develop my beverage, and I'm now discouraged and out of money."

I get these types of calls any day of the week. You would think beverage development is like rocket science if you heard some of my clients' stories. It's really not; it's much more challenging than rocket science, just kidding.

Beverage Development is relatively easy. Launching a beverage is not so easy; that's why you have to start with your launching idea, in other words, with your business model. Beverage development is based on project management best practices, and launching a beverage is based on market timing, distribution acceptance, consumer interactions, your marketing budget, a great management team, and a bit of luck.

The good news is you'll learn those beverage development business best practices in this book. We call the entire process "Reverse Engineering" or starting at the end.

Beverage development is the next part of the book. What you'll learn here applies to everyone interested in launching a new beverage, regardless of your background and entry into this field. You can be an existing beverage company looking to cross over into the energy drink, functional and new age beverage market to exploit this beverage boom. You can be a distributor wanting to produce and distribute a label. You can be an investor searching for worthwhile beverage start-ups to make money or an entrepreneur with a great product concept. Whoever you are, all you need to know to develop and launch your new drink starts here.

A Formula for Success for All Drinks

All types of drinks follow the same necessary process for development through launch. We will outline the process here. This process is fundamental to success with new beverages, as it is with all other beverages, including alcoholic and non-alcoholic drinks. It's a proven process because it is the same process used to launch every successful drink product on the mass market today (whether the developer realized what they were doing). We've used this process for our beverages as well as for clients.

Yes, there are particularities in every beverage project and unique ingredients, packaging, or artwork that will go into your drink, but the best practices, the process, and the formula are the same for all companies and beverages. What happens when you deviate from this plan? You start getting into problems. You spend too long on the artwork, realize your artwork was already trademarked, your bottle does not fit on the store refrigerator, or the most common, you spend too much time and money.

The Ins and Outs of the Industry from Production and Beyond

There are some essential points you need to know before you jump into a beverage development. These include:

- ✅ Target market
- ✅ Research
- ✅ Formulation & Ingredients
- ✅ Warehouse & Transportation
- ✅ Distribution Channels
- ✅ Consumer Communication

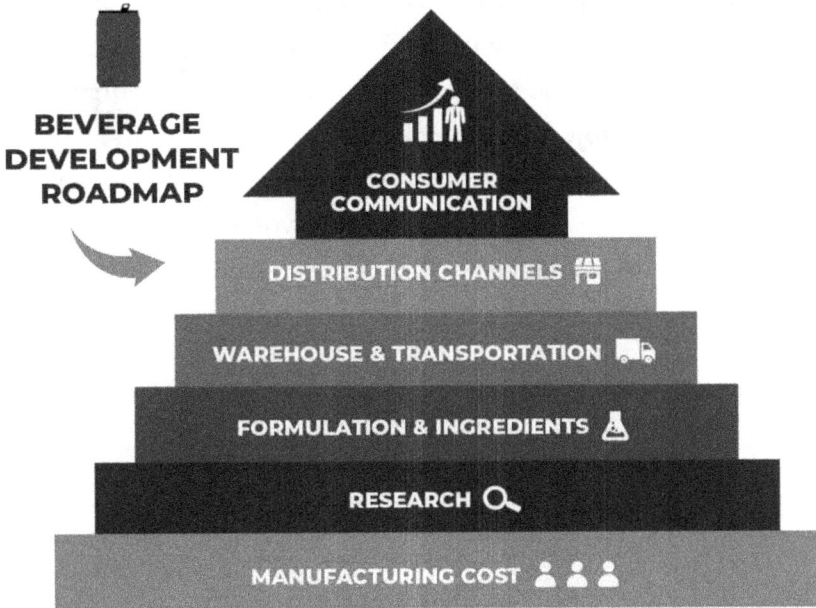

Diagram 1.8 – Beverage Development Roadmap

You'll see me mention "target market" in many of these chapters. It's not because we forgot we said it before; it's because it's the most crucial thing in beverage development. It's essential in sales, in distribution, in marketing, and this book. Target market, or your target consumer, is the fundamental basis of Reverse Engineering Beverage Development because you start with your consumer and move backward through the entire beverage development process.

Beginning at the End—Reverse Engineering

Ultimately the success of your new drink will rely on the end result. I don't mean the taste; I mean the sales or consumer acceptance. This is why this is the most critical part of your entire beverage development process. This is the process you'll use when bringing your idea to life.

Yes, cost analysis is necessary, as is artwork, formulation, and beverage production. But without the process, without your project management having the costs and co-packer, it's just information on a page, what project managers call line items or deliverables. Now it's time to learn how to convert it all into your beverage. For all of this to work, we'll start at the end – you guessed it, we'll start with your consumer.

Why Not Start at the Beginning?

Only by starting at the end, having a clear vision of your product, your market, and your goals can you know what type of product, marketing, and sales and distribution lines are suitable for your product. Only this way can you know how to meet your customers' needs. At the risk of repeating ourselves, if there is one mistake we see made in this business time and again, it is the mistake of developing your product first and considering who will buy it and where second. When you do this, you run a considerable risk of having an excellent product packaged improperly and miserably marketed, one that never gets beyond the discount dollar store shelves.

These are the correct steps for beverage development:

- ✅ Who is your perfect consumer? = Target Market
- ✅ Where do they buy? = Your Retailer
- ✅ Who delivers to that channel? = Your Distributor

- ☑ Channel Pricing = Price to the distributor, retailer, consumer
- ☑ Concept = USP and USV
- ☑ Artwork = labels, design, colors
- ☑ Package = Bottle, can, other
- ☑ Formulation = Color, taste and function
- ☑ Production = Now you are ready to produce

Entrepreneurs usually develop beverages in this order:

- ☑ Idea
- ☑ Google searches
- ☑ Formulation
- ☑ Artwork
- ☑ Production
- ☑ Pricing

You'll notice this last process lacks items related to search and marketing, such as retail, distributor, and other information. Many entrepreneurs realize this only after they have the product sitting in the warehouse and notice retailers and distributors don't take the product or miscalculate their production costs and spend too much money compared to their sales. All of this is part of your initial research.

Channel pricing, retailers, distribution, and finding your consumer are integral parts of your research. So is speaking with as many distributors, retailers, and consumers as possible about your idea before spending a dime. You might discover someone else already tried your vision, and it didn't work.

In determining your perfect consumers, consider who they are, their age, where they shop, how much money they make. Consider if they have a family or if they travel or exercise. Find out everything you can about them. If you don't know everything about them, try imagining it as if you're creating a character. This information will allow you to establish an emotional relationship with your consumer and the holy grail of marketing. The data should reveal where your consumer buys, whether at a 7-Eleven or a supermarket, and how much they spend.

Start first by determining who this product is for. Once we know who will buy your drink, we can work on the overall concept, which will help us determine practical matters like flavoring and product packaging.

After deciding what type of product you will be producing and the packaging, we can look towards finding a bottler capable of mixing and filling your drink, given your beverage's specifications. As you'll learn, there is more to this part of the process than meets the eye because not all bottlers are the same, and not all have the same capabilities for handling the same types of products, bottling supplies, and processes.

Finally, once we have all of this information firmly underhand, we can start talking about distribution and sales in more depth. We'll need to develop some of this as we build your drink correctly, at least in basic terms. We will finalize the deal by showing you how to do the actual work involved with marketing, distributing, and selling.

Case Study Example: Uni:Te

Here is a good case study summarizing what we discussed. We just developed Uni:Te for a new beverage entrepreneur, Larry Gilmore. This CEO had no previous beverage experience.

Here is the tale of the tape:

Name: Uni:Te

Product: Ready to drink and brewed tea (2 separate products)

Unique Ingredients: Date fruit seeds

Intellectual Property: Production process

When Larry first called us, he wanted to sell to small ethnic stores nationwide by creating specialty beverages for each niche. In theory, this is a fantastic idea. In practice, it's a nightmare, not only for him but for us, as we handled sales and distribution. It's a nightmare because each niche has a different sales and distribution channel, not to mention an entirely different customer base. Each time he comes up with a new beverage, we need to do all the work from scratch.

For example, the first product was meant for the Hispanic population, specifically the Mexican-American niche. The task was to find Mexican supermarkets around the USA as well as the distributors serving those accounts. If Larry launches an Asian product next time, we can't use the same supermarkets or distributors. That's a big problem, and it will take a lot of money and time to target all those different niches.

Yes, that was a big problem, but it wasn't our biggest problem. We first needed to convince Larry not to develop his date tea for the Mexican-American market. It wasn't easy. We needed to change the target market because dates don't come from Mexico! It's not a Mexican tradition, and consumers in Mexican supermarkets in the USA will not pay the premium price commanded by this specialty product. It is a great product, but the consumer is not the Mexican-American consumer, and the target market is the Natural Channel, not the "Mexican" channel.

What Happens Now?

Uni:Te avoided several huge mistakes from the start and saved thousands of dollars in developing and producing the wrong beverage, not to mention the time and money saved to sell the product. In my estimates, they saved around $85,000 just by changing their target market.

Uni:Te was developed for the Natural Channel, where the target market is a more affluent consumer willing to try new, natural products and pay a premium for them.

In this case, my team worked on the entire project as full product managers, including research, strategy, formulation, artwork, photography, event coordination, project management, pricing structure, mentoring, and consulting.

After this was completed, the team developed point of sale material, marketing material, website, and everything necessary to sell to consumers, retailers, and distributors.

How does a Beverage Development Process Work?

To answer this question, let's dip into our beverage development best practices. We've developed these best practices over 11 years of product development with more than a thousand different production projects in the USA, China, Mexico, and Europe.

Here are the steps we used for the development of Uni:Te:

- ☑ Initial Consultation by Phone
- ☑ Strategy Session with Client in Person
- ☑ Project Manager Assignment
- ☑ Concept Consultation with Client
- ☑ Retail and Wholesale Research

- ☑ Internal Product Meetings

- ☑ Concept Development

- ☑ Concept Approval

- ☑ Face-to-Face Meetings

- ☑ Artwork Development

- ☑ Package Development

- ☑ Formulation Testing

- ☑ Samples of Formulation

- ☑ Approval of Formulation

- ☑ Approval of Package and Artwork

- ☑ Production

- ☑ Sales and Marketing Collateral

- ☑ In-Person Mentoring

In the end, we developed a ready-to-drink product in a bottle and a bagged product that you brew at home.

Do you have a case study you would like to share? Don't forget to tag me on your social media. I'll share your case study on my podcast or webinar. It will get you free promotion!

In the next chapter, you will discover how much it will all cost. How much money do you need to develop, formulate, and produce your best-selling beverage?

"THE PRACTICE OF COSTING IS ALL IN THE INTEREST OF PLANNING."

CHAPTER 10

Beverage Business Costs

"Calculate your cost of selling and making one store successful, then multiply that by one thousand!"

Rapid Knowledge Section

There's no quick guide on how much money you need to start and scale your business, but there is a formula you can follow to figure it out. Depending on your business model, whether you sell to convenience stores, supermarkets, beverage distributors, Amazon, eCommerce, natural channel, or MLM, you can take the cost of selling to one store, one distributor, one customer, and multiply it by ten, or ten thousand. This is how you get to the numbers you need.

As I write the third edition of this book, I'm in the middle of launching a beverage and a liquid vitamin company for my wonderful clients. I am also launching several CBD products and taking my company public with an entire product line. The goal is to sell in one hundred thousand convenience stores nationwide and sell one million dollars per month in online sales the first year. How do I calculate the costs, production, marketing, printing, hiring, and overhead we'll need to succeed? I first calculate the cost of opening one store, then I scale from there.

For example, if you spend $300 to open one store, and you want to open one thousand stores, you'll need a budget of $300,000. If you're selling online, and the cost of acquiring a client is $20, and you want to get 1,000 customers per month, you'll need to spend $20,000 per month.

Beverage Investment

That is the bottom line, isn't it? If you're interested in the beverage industry as a business or investment opportunity, it may be the only line that matters to you. If you're developing your drink as an entrepreneur, the bottom line figure will be just as crucial in the product development phase because what you can afford is determined by the cost. If you're an investor placing your trust in the entrepreneur, you need to know how much money to give the entrepreneur to get started with a proof of concept, development, and production.

The hard part is finding the answer to this question. There's no real way to give you a hard and fast figure because there are many possibilities and combinations within the industry and between different concept drinks. You'll get a guide that will give you some ideas and the guidance to research your costs more accurately.

This chapter will provide a worksheet or manual that you can use to plug in the costs you know now and determine your concept's feasibility as it is right now and as you develop your drink further. To know your exact cost, we would need to learn at least the basics about your concept, things like artwork ideas, production minimums for your package, co-packing costs for your category, and the ingredients that go into your product. If you use cans, you have to pay a higher minimum than if you use bottles. Suppose you want a custom bottle; that's more money for the mold and the bottle design and specifications. It's essential to research your beverage before investing any money.

Why Perform Research Costing Now?

The short answer to this question is that you have to research your costing right now, in the beginning, to ensure you can afford the production of your drink. But this step has more considerable importance: establishing that there is enough margin or creating enough of a profit margin with sales to make the drink profitable. That also means knowing what your consumer is willing to pay for the product. If your research is incorrect, you can have a fantastic product that your target consumer can't afford.

Many people called our office, often small drink distributors, telling us they had fifty or one hundred cases of a new drink and were trying to sell and profit from with little luck. I had to give them the bad news and tell them there's not enough margin in the product—they either bought it too high or produced it themselves at too high a cost for what the market can support.

I also get calls from entrepreneurs who produced a beverage pallet at $20-$25 for a twenty-four 8-ounce can case instead of the $7-

$12 for a twenty-four 16-ounce case. They couldn't sell the drinks to distributors because the wholesale cost is too high, and they won't profit from it. They'd lose out by selling this drink at a low-profit margin and lose the sales of other, higher-profiting drinks. There are two reasons why we get these types of calls:

The entrepreneur didn't research their costs ahead of time, or someone took advantage of their inexperience; sometimes it's both. How would you know when someone is taking advantage of you if you don't understand the actual costs of producing a drink or new functional beverage?

Having a vision is helpful in this business, but doing your research is imperative. You absolutely must do the market research, market analysis, and cost analysis, and you absolutely must learn about the beverage industry, just like you are doing now.

Before jumping into minute detail on costing, let's do a CEO's view of costing. We can divide the major categories into Development and Sales. Development is everything up to production. It excludes warehousing, transportation, sales, printing materials, travel, or trade shows. It only includes the beverage development process from your idea to the final product in production or co-packing.

You then divide the Development phase into clear and simple points that you can budget and schedule using a timeline and goals for your deliverables. Here is how it will look:

- Concept Development
- Legal
- Formulation
- Small Run & Normal Run Production

Using these four steps as your guideline will keep you out of trouble, out of spending too much money, and out of spending money on marketing or public relations before you have your product ready.

ITEM	Do it yourself	Be Worried	Target Cost
Concept Development	$15,000	Under $10,000	$25,000 to $50,000
Legal	DON´T	DON´T	$3,500
Formulation	DON´T	Under $5,000	$5,000 to $10,000
Small Run Production	DON´T	More than $25 / Case	$15 to $22/ Case
Normal Production	DON´T	More than $12	$9 to $12/ Case

Diagram 1.9 – Beverage Development Costs

The Beverage Development Costs graph gives you an overview of your costs for the major cost categories. Legal fees refer only to costs associated with beverage development, such as label review. They do not refer to any other legal advice, intellectual property, or your corporation or LLC creation.

Beverage Operational Costs

After the product comes out of the production line, you have other costs associated with operating your business. These include things like warehousing, sales, or marketing. Here is an overview of expenses you can include in your research.

- ☑ Warehousing
- ☑ Transportation
- ☑ Marketing

Doing the Research

Doing your research is imperative. It bears repeating. Research is vital for costing but also for everything related to your product. If you don't have the proper research, you will not know if your product has a place in the marketplace. You can study by going into a store, comparing the shelves, or looking at what your competitors are doing. Yes, this is a good start, but it will only tell you what everyone knows. You want to know what nobody else knows.

But what do I mean by research? By research, I mean a variety of things such as:

- Start reading and studying informational resources—such as this book

- Evaluate statistics

- Perform field research at counters and convenience stores

  o Looking at store shelves

  o Pay attention to marketing

  o Find similar products and evaluate their sales

  o Find the product(s) that are missing that present an open market

- Make calls to retailers and distributors

☑ Have a face to face conversation with retailers; primarily focus on stores in the city where you plan to sell first; ask

- o Would you consider taking on this product?
- o What is your purchase price of product "X"?
- o Who is the product's distributor?
- o Gather as much information as you can—it's all part of creating your brand!

Your research should include all of the above points to get the most accurate and complete picture. In your research, you are looking to answer a few key questions as they apply to your drink concept; you want to find out:

☑ Is there a place for your product?

☑ Who is your perfect consumer?

☑ How will your product reach your consumer?

☑ What is the most effective way to communicate with your consumer?

☑ Who are your competitors?

☑ How much money are they making?

☑ How much is the retailer making? The distributor?

☑ What are the freight costs?

☑ How will you sell this product? By the truckload, pallet, or case?

As you progress through the planning and development of your drink, the answers to these questions might change. You may find that your drink does not carry a wide enough profit margin as-is, and you may have to make changes. That's okay; in fact, that's the point of this exercise!

The point is to do the research and make those changes now so that by the time your drink is bottled, you have a meticulously planned product with a clear plan for distribution, sales, and marketing.

The Most Important Research

The most important type of research will not be the one that comes from your local convenience store or supermarket. It will be from speaking with distributors and buyers at retail accounts. Yes, your research comes from conversations. My team currently calls up to 2,000 buyers or decision-makers every month to promote new products. These calls reveal the buyers' needs, trends, and details what works and doesn't work in the stores.

I'm not suggesting that you call 2,000 people per month, but you should at least call 10 to 20 retailers, pick their brains, and gain some insight.

What's wrong with search engine research? Nothing is wrong with researching using the internet. The problem is it will not provide you with the correct information. The same goes for retail stores. It will only tell you what is already in the marketplace and what's successful, not what failed.

Let's paint a picture. You have an idea for a particular type of beverage; let's say it's Orange Tea in a ready-to-drink 16-ounce bottle. You search online for Orange Tea, and you realize there is no competition. You're happy! You visit the stores, and you see there is no Orange Tea in the refrigerators or on the shelves. You're convinced you'll be first to market with a brewed tea packed with vitamin C but low in sugar as a great substitute to orange juice. You now invest in development and production, and a few months later, after spending more than $100,000, you have the product in the warehouse.

It's time to sell your Orange Tea. You call some beverage distributors, you go to a trade show and meet with the buyers from a convenience store and a supermarket that buys for hundreds of stores. You're thrilled. You sit down at your first meeting, and the distributor tells you, "We tried selling this same product 10, 5, and 2 years ago, and after three failures, we're convinced the product is not for us".

You sit with the retailers who explain, "That product doesn't work. We've tried selling it several times, and it didn't sell. Call me when you have something else."

Can this really happen? You bet – it happens every single day with new products. A few calls to the right decision-makers would have told you that the traditional retail channels will not buy your product. It doesn't mean it's a bad product; it doesn't mean consumers somewhere will not embrace it. It means you didn't do your homework. You forgot to research the correct channels beforehand.

If you would like to do even more targeted research, try selling your product to consumers. You can do this by spending a bit of money on a website with sales capabilities (online store). Test your product by selling it to consumers. If consumers buy your product, distributors and retailers will probably take it; if not today, then once you grow your customer base.

The Cost of Concept Development

Your Concept is your number one priority as a beverage creator. It's what makes your beverage different, unique, and sellable. It's your idea and the way you'll market your idea. It's the backbone of everything else.

In this phase, you create your artwork, package, and the entire look and feel of the product, including the beverage's color, the bottle or can you will use; the whole Consumer Experience.

The most important thing about the concept is the Consumer Experience. When you, your designer, or your team talk about the brand, the colors, the concept, always consider what the consumer will do or feel. Doing this will help you answer product size, color, position in the store and shelf, price, marketing, and point of sale material before you even start drawing your logo or your bottle. You don't begin your concept with a graphic designer; you begin by identifying your consumer.

The concept is where you should spend most of your money, time, and effort. Don't spend your time calling co-packers, formulators, or ingredient providers. The concept will tell you all you need to know to develop a product that sells, and that's what you want, not a product that looks good or tastes good, but one that sells.

Concept development can range from $200 to $100,000 or more. I worked with a vitamin company that paid $200 for their drink sample, including the logo and a sample bottle. They contracted an artwork bidding website and received five different concepts. Is that a deal or what? They thought it was great, but they realized they could not use it when they called a co-packer. They still had to pay for the UPC, label legalities, and create the label according to their specifications. In the end, they spent an additional $1,000. That's still a great deal.

You can pay $1,000 for your label; however, it will not be a label that you would want to invest your time and money to produce and sell. If you're going to spend another $20,000 to $50,000 in production plus the cost of sales, why would you spend $1,000 on the most critical part of the process? Remember, the $1,000 was for a logo and label, not for a Concept. A Concept includes all the research on your consumers, distributors, and wholesalers.

Large companies like Coca-Cola and Pepsi spend more than one million dollars on Concept. They use expensive firms and nationwide focus groups. They can even test the product in niche stores to see the consumers' reactions to their new product. We will not go into these scenarios because we want to focus on small and medium-sized companies developing their products.

Spending twenty-five to fifty thousand dollars would be acceptable for this phase of the project if you're working with the right team, not a designer or a private label firm that just produces your label's cans or shots. Even fifteen thousand dollars would be good if you do all the research and concept on your own. By all means, do this if you're already in the beverage industry or product development and have several years of experience in merchandising or marketing. If you don't have this experience, you'll need to spend some time getting it, at least two or three years at a director or VP level. However, if you're not a veteran of the industry, it will be time or money. Spend the money and do it right.

Legal

When talking about legal fees, we're only referring to the costs related to the average production of a ready-to-drink beverage with standard formulation using an FDA-approved formulator and co-packer. By using these FDA-approved facilities, you are guaranteed they're compliant.

This is an entirely different story if you're starting a production plant or have a special ingredient not currently sold in your country. Expect to pay $3,500 for label review, FDA review, and other legalities related to production. This does not include the formation of your corporation or other legal entity or any intellectual property like your trademark or patents. You have to add that to your costs. Before choosing a name and producing one million bottles, make sure somebody else doesn't have the trademark. Unfortunately, I've seen this happen many times.

Formulation

Formulation used to be free a few years ago. Ingredient houses would create a formula for you and make money from selling you the ingredients. This is not true anymore. Too many people call them and ask for a formula never to produce their product again. Now you have to pay for your formulation, and in many cases, you don't own it. Yes, you heard correctly. It comes as a shocker to many people who pay ingredient houses $5,000 and don't own the formula. The ingredient houses' cost is higher than $5,000, and they want to make money with the sale of ingredients. If they release your formula, you can go and buy your ingredients elsewhere.

Don't worry too much. Anyone can probably duplicate your formula at any time if you need a formulator to develop it. Your value, the value of your brand, is not the formula. If that's what you think, you're in big trouble. If you just want to create a product that tastes good, or at least better than your competitor, you'll be out of business before anyone can even taste it. Your real value is in your relationships with the consumers, unique distribution channels, or supply chain.

You don't have to use formula houses to produce your formula. Instead, you can work with independent formulators or laboratories that will give you the recipe. You can then take your recipe to a recommended ingredient house and purchase the ingredients from them. Ask the formulator for a list of ingredient suppliers that will supply all the ingredients before starting the project. If you fail to do so, you might find yourself re-formulating and paying again for the recipe. This happens about thirty percent of the time.

If your formulation is simple, paying $5,000 to $10,000 is reasonable for a base formula. Make sure it includes shipping costs to you for sampling. It might also have an extra flavor using the same base formula. It will not include an entirely different flavor or ingredient base.

If your formulation is not standard and requires unique ingredients or a particular process, you'll have to pay more, up to $20,000 or more, depending on how complex it is. The good news is these are the exceptions. You're probably in the $5,000 to $10,000 price range.

Drink Production Costs

Drink production costs are the expenses incurred from the physical product and packaging. We will go into each of these in more depth in further chapters. Here, we've compiled a quick list of the primary elements you need to consider as you start determining your new beverage costing.

The easiest way to explain this is to ask you to think about your end-product. Envision your drink and look at the various components that comprise it. You'll have the following:

- ✅ Container: usually glass, plastic, or aluminum
- ✅ Top: caps, seals, perhaps an additional safety or freshness seal
- ✅ Label: type and size, design, and artwork costs involved in hiring graphics professionals. There are several options,

and the cost can run anywhere from a fraction of a cent to several cents per label.

☑ Ingredients and flavors: the sky's the limit, and you will find a great diversity of ingredients and costs, but they will be the cornerstone of your drink.

Once your drinks are prepared and bottled, they must be packed for transport and distribution. You can't just send loose bottles onto a truck. Single bottles need to be packaged into cases, which are boxed or wrapped and then bundled into pallets ready for shipping via trucks. There is an additional cost here, too, and you'll also need to add up the costs of whatever it is you choose to use (either a cardboard case, box, tray, a box cut in half, or plastic wraps.

Many people come into this business thinking that they have to set up their bottling facility. That is not cost-effective for anyone but the big, established drink producers. For your drink, you should be outsourcing all production. There are hundreds of thousands of beverage plants throughout the country whose primary business is co-packing. A co-packer is a bottling facility that has different product lines that they produce for others. Each facility handles different products, processes, and packaging (for example, glass, plastic, hot-fill, cold-fill, organic, etc.). You provide them with your product specifications, and they do the rest, delivering you a completed drink product that you now have to manage.

The above covers the elemental costs of drink production that will detail how much it will cost to get your drink produced—to get it made and bottled—but expenses do not end here. You're now ready to start selling your drink, but we still have more to consider.

Small Run and Large Run Production

Don't try to save money by starting with a large production run. Yes, the price of a can, case, or pallet will be less if you produce five or ten truckloads of product. Still, don't do it. It's wiser to spend a few dollars more and produce a small run of production, maybe one truckload or even less if allowed. Test that product in stores, with distributors, and consumers. Open a few stores, and once you have orders and repeat orders, ramp up your production accordingly.

I've seen companies produce ten thousand cases of a drink only to throw them away after they expired. I see this more often than not. Avoiding this is very simple, and it's a great business model. Test your product first. Small production runs can cost up to double, or even more, but in dollars, it could be the difference between $20,000 and $300,000.

You can pay from $15 to $22 for a 24-can case of a regular product without any expensive ingredients in a small run. I suggest producing around 1,000 to 2,000 cases for test purposes before a more extensive production run. Average production runs can cost as low as $6 per case with volume if you're a huge company but expect to pay in the $9 to $12 range per case for start-ups. When do you know it's too much? If you're not making at least 50% margin (100% mark-up), you're not at the correct retail price, or you're paying too much for production.

POS

The costs that come after production costs are called Point of Sale, or POS costs. POS is the material that helps you communicate effectively and economically with the consumer. These costs are part of your initial investment. Retailers expect to get stickers, posters, and other materials to sell your product in their stores. Distributors expect to get t-shirts, hats, sales sheets, and other sales collateral to push your products into stores, restaurants, and bars.

POS costs include:

- ☑ Sales materials

- ☑ Manufacturing costs

- ☑ Point of Sale materials (in-store advertising, marketing, things that help sell products off the shelves)

- ☑ Cost of transportation from manufacturer to distributor to warehouse

- ☑ Warehouse costs

- ☑ Sales costs

- ☑ Slotting costs

- ☑ Other costs such as websites, distributor expenses, incentives, third-party logistics

POS costs encompass a lot, and the cost here is crucial; neglecting to flesh out these costs could spell disaster for your drink before you ever get it into a store.

Warehousing

Once you produce your drink at the bottler, it cannot stay there. Warehousing is often something entrepreneurs do not consider until there's a pallet ready to be shipped. This is a significant expense that you can easily overlook. Your drink will not go straight from the bottler to the distributor or retailer either, and so you must incur the additional cost of warehousing it. There are several costs involved in warehousing that will affect your specific warehousing costs, including:

- ☑ Material handling

- ☑ Equipment

- ☑ Employees

- ☑ Racks

☑ Rent

☑ Space and number of pallets

Warehousing is a cost you will want to outsource and consider. We'll break down the prices and options further in the Warehousing chapter.

Transportation

How will you get your product from point A to point B? You must pay to transport it.

Transportation costs are very much dependent on the volume of the product and how often it moves. It helps if you calculate your transportation costs ahead of time. Still, you also have to keep them variable as movements and changes in trucking and transport costs can increase transportation costs.

The key to accurately budgeting transportation costs is to think them through and have a cushion. Don't just calculate the cost to move your drink from bottler to warehouse and warehouse to distributor. You must think of the minor expenses that are often overlooked and can add up. It includes thinking through transportation costs down to the mailing of single samples.

Shipping costs for mailings and sample distribution is all part of your transportation cost. It's one thing if you are sending out just a few single samples here and there, but once you start sending samples in larger quantities—sending three, four, or five cases to each distributor—and using the US Post Office, UPS, FedEx, DHL, it gets costly. You must consider all of these costs and include them in your business plan.

Sales

Sales costs cover the expenses involved in getting your beverage into stores or venues and then selling off the shelves. Sales costs can cover various expenses and vary depending on the sales channels you use to sell your products.

It might even be that you're following another sales model, one that doesn't require shelves or refrigerators, where you're now selling directly to consumers on your online store or in some other creative way. Calculate your advertising costs, your shipping to consumers, warehousing, agency costs, and other related expenses to sales if you're going off the shelves.

Many beverage entrepreneurs think of sales costs as their costs to support or maintain sales representatives who will sell them. In reality, there is more involved. You may not have a sales representative; you may have a sales rep assigned to your product through the distributor. In any case, you have to plan to go a step further than the salary or cost of the sales representative. You have to spend money to support that representative by providing sales materials and marketing. You often have to give the representative an incentive to make him want to sell your product.

Incentives for sales representatives are essential and also often overlooked by new drink developers. They think it's the sales representative's job to sell their product. You have to remember that sales reps usually have other products they are selling too, and they will promote the product that makes them [personally] the most money. In other words, if you make it financially beneficial to the sales representative to push your product, you will enjoy more sales. You can do this by offering commissions and incentives for a certain amount of products sold. What happens if you don't give the sales representative an incentive? Usually, it means your drink samples are those left sitting in the delivery truck while other, more profitable drinks get all the attention.

Sales costs are not only sales reps, marketing, and support materials, but other expenses taken in the interest of selling, such as:

- ✅ Slotting costs (paying for premium shelf space)
- ✅ Websites
- ✅ Distributor incentives
- ✅ Retailer incentives

Often the costing involved with sales is what can make or break your drink's profitability if not carefully planned. For instance, incentives can boost your sales and the effort a sales rep, retailer, or distributor will put into your product. Still, if you are too generous or have not accurately calculated the profit margin to allow for all incentive costs, there may be no profit left at the end for you.

Similarly, slotting can be a drink's boom or bust. Slotting fees vary by the chain and can be very reasonable or astronomical compared to your profit margin. On the one hand, paying slotting fees is one of the fastest ways to get into the massive grocery chains. Still, on the other hand, they are typically reserved for those with deep pockets, making them sometimes an unreasonable cost that your new drink cannot support. It is worth noting here that we have never paid a slotting fee yet still have launched many profitable drink products!

There are a time and a place for slotting fees for many drinks, but first, you have to be sure the market is even worth it. People who want to get into this business often think that big grocers like

Walmart or Kroger's are the place to be. There are two problems with this line of thinking:

- ✅ It's too difficult to get into the big stores like Walmart unless you've established some sales.

- ✅ You need a large amount of cash flow to carry these large vendors' receivables.

- ✅ Big stores are not necessarily where you want to be.

Developers don't realize that the big sales for functional and new beverages are out in the trenches, not at the grocery counter. People buy NABs primarily at convenience, liquor stores, and minor corner markets, settling for on-the-go refreshments or a quick pick-me-up. It's also important to note that when you sell big in the small stores, the big stores will come looking for you to provide your product to your now loyal customer base.

Delegate and Win

"Rockstar Energy Drink sold to Pepsi for $3.85 Billion in 2020. Rockstar never formulated, bottled, sold, or distributed; they delegated!"

It's not just Coca-Cola and Budweiser that don't develop, bottle or distribute their beverages. It's also Monster, Rockstar, Arizona Ice Tea, and most liquids in the US. Can you imagine? Coke doesn't make or distribute Coca-Cola. They do two things, and they do them well; sell syrup and advertise.

For about 70 years, from 1886 to the 1950s, an 8.5-ounce bottle of Coca-Cola was sold for a nickel. Can you imagine this? It may be the world record for a product having the same price for so long.

Let's transport back to a time where soda was sold through soda fountains. You would go to your local store or pharmacy and buy a soda. The attendant would take a glass and pour the soda from the fountain. This is how all soda was sold. So Coke sold syrup; it was in the syrup business.

In the late 1890's Coca-Cola sold its bottling rights to a third party. This third party had the right to bottle, sell and distribute Coke to stores all over the USA, but they had to buy the syrup from Coca-Cola. Now, Coke was in every corner store in the country. Coca-Cola was still in the syrup business, and a franchise model appeared, where entrepreneurs could buy equipment, bottle, sell and distribute Coke in their small town or city. This model is true to this day. When you see a big red Coke truck driving by, always remember Coca-Cola does not own it. They delegated that part of the business to a local distributor. Coca-Cola started in the syrup business but is now in the marketing business.

Most beverages are in the marketing business, not in the beverage-making business. These beverages outsource their development, production, sales, and distribution. What are you outsourcing?

You should understand others' roles in developing, producing, and selling your beverage from the start. You may feel that your drink is your 'baby,' and you are the one who is best suited to manage it in all ways. That is not a cost-effective costing strategy. The most cost-effective drink production strategy delegates different production aspects and outsources to the appropriate facilities and professionals. Throughout the drink development and production process, you will need the help of many outside sources for supplies and production, including:

- ☑ Flavor house/ingredient house

- ☑ Packaging and graphics designers

- ☑ Bottle/can/package supplier (this isn't usually your bottler)

- ☑ Bottler (who fills the drinks)

- ☑ Warehouses

- ☑ Distributors

- ☑ Sales representatives

- ☑ Retailers

Understanding this from the beginning will allow you to perform an accurate cost analysis to come up with actual costs and expectations and significant money savings by putting drink production in the hands of professionals who can do the job. In the end, outsourcing and relying on your partner companies will turn dividends much in your favor.

Production Costs

We've thrown a lot of different costs and variables at you throughout this chapter, but we probably have still not answered what you want to know: "How much will it cost to develop and produce my new beverage?"

To answer this question, we'll run you through the production process, utilizing the various outsourcing resources you will be using as you develop your drink.

We use the ballpark figure for drink production between $7 and $12 for a 24 can case. Multiply that by your run size (number of cases in the production run), and you have a ballpark cost for your first run. Most bottling facilities have a minimum run of 5,000 cases. But this only covers the actual production and filling of the product. First, you'll need to buy cans or bottles to fill.

People do not know and plan to buy bottles or cans from one facility or supplier and have them bottled with another. Using cans as an example, in the U.S., there are two major can manufacturers. Major American can and bottle manufacturers have a minimum can order of 8,000 cases. You decide on your manufacturer and ask them to produce and print your 8,000 can cases (24 cans per case). Please note, this industry deals in terms of cases, not cans. Once you have your printed cases, you'll ship them to the filler, the bottling company, where the ingredients are added. Either you buy the components directly, or the bottler buys them on your behalf; either way, the cost is yours.

You will note the first discrepancy here. You now have 8,000 can cases, but the bottler will only require you to fill 5,000 cases in each run. You must decide whether to fill all 8,000 cases or the minimum and store the remaining 3,000 cases for the next run. This discrepancy may not seem logical to you, but it makes sense from supply and production. Eight thousand can cases are one full truckload of cans. Five thousand can cases are equivalent to the amount of drink produced in a batch. The batch considers your drink's size (8, 10, 12, or 16 ounces). It usually equals enough to fill 5,000 cases of your beverage.

The occasional bottler will produce less than 5,000 cases, but economies of scale start to affect your budget. In most instances, to keep costs constant, you should go with 5,000 cases for your production runs. By doing this, you start right from the start with reasonable production costs, and it makes sense for all involved—for you, for the container manufacturer, and the bottler.

Going back to the costing example, you bought 8,000 can cases, the ingredients and raw materials that go into the drink, and paid to fill 5,000 cases. Using the 16-ounce drink example, an average size for an energy drink or functional beverage, you might pay $8 or $9 per case. Depending on the vitamin pack and flavorings, the figure could be from $7 to $9. To get the cost of your first production run, you need to multiply the cost per case by 5,000 and then add in the cost of your additional 3,000 cases of unfilled cans.

This gives you an estimate of the amount of money you need to invest in your new energy drink/NAB. Remember, this only covers production, and you also have to account for

- Research and development
- Sampling
- Labels
- POS materials
- Sales sheets
- Websites

All told, the average cost of producing and launching your new beverage will be between $60,000 and $85,000 (partially dependent on the run's size, ingredients, and additives). Yes, we took the long road getting here, but you must understand the big picture and all the unforeseen costs to prepare you for a successful product launch and sustainable future in new-age drink sales.

Take Action

Now you have estimates and the ability to collect more accurate costing figures for your beverage; what do you do with that information?

Once you have a costing figure and an idea of how significant investment will take to launch your beverage, you have to go back and factor that into your planning. As the brand developer, you have important decisions to make.

These decisions go back to the consumer and what they are willing to pay for a drink like yours. It could be anywhere between $1 and $3; you'll know this based on the market research you did initially at the beginning of your costing evaluation. Whatever that figure is, you must make the decisions that make sense to you, the end-consumer, and the retailer. Whatever price the consumer is willing to pay dictates some of your options, including possible changes to the original product concept. You then decide how to further distribute that money across each level (distributor, warehouse, retailer). In the end, the practice of costing is all in the interest of planning.

"THE BEVERAGE
DEVELOPMENT AND
PRODUCTION PHASE
ARE THE EASY PART
OF THE EQUATION."

CHAPTER 11

Beverage Development Recap

Don't let the beverage development and production phase overwhelm you. In my view, this is the easy part of the equation. Now, we'll take a brief look at these various product development components, each of which will be covered in the chapters to come. These components outline product development steps from concept to sales, effectively paving the way to success with your new beverage.

Your Concept

Your drink concept is your idea, vision, goal, big-picture view of your whole company and product. We'll talk about how to focus on your concept, develop it, and use it to build your drink. To do this, we'll go through every step through drink production.

Target Market

Pinpointing your target market is the essential first step into product development and marketing. Target market is a concept many are familiar with as a marketing element. Still, your target market needs to be decided and researched early on so that you can develop a product that can sell. You cannot work on your product concept or packaging until you have decided who will buy your drink.

We have stressed this many times in this book. The most critical point in beverage development is your target market, not your formula or package. Spend the most time here, understanding who your consumers are, your distributors, and your retailers. Develop your Unique Selling and Unique Value Propositions to see how each segment of your supply chain will benefit.

Package & Look and Feel

Packaging may be a convenient and physical component, but it dictates your product's look, feel, and perception. This chapter will discuss how packaging and the look and feel of your drink play into its success. We'll talk about the different considerations for making these crucial decisions and about various options that you have to create your drink's look.

Taste

Great drinks are about great taste, right? Great drinks are, but top-selling beverages are not always. Taste is a vital component in developing a drink that will be long-lived. For the new drinks coming on the market, the flavor will take on new importance as the increased competition and familiarity with innovative beverages will dictate that not only should drinks function, but they should also taste good. We'll walk you through developing the taste of your new product and help you make sure that it is a taste that is in line with the rest of your product's perception.

Production

When you complete your planning, you then need to move your drink into production. You'll learn the production process and outsourcing various elements of new functional drink production.

Most likely, your beverage production will be seamless. You'll contact a co-packer who will do all the work for you. In some notable projects, you'll own your production. Perhaps you have a brewery or a distillery. If you own your production facility, make sure you include it in your marketing propositions and use it to sell your product. You'll be one of the few brands that owns production, so it should be part of your selling proposition.

From Concept to Production

No doubt, by the end of Part II, you'll be eager to go, but we caution you to hold off just a bit longer. You'll be ready now to make a drink, but you won't be prepared to sell it until you allow us to explain the final piece of the puzzle in Part III. For now, let's get into the nuts and bolts of drink production so that you have a firm handle on this vital part of the business.

"AN EXCELLENT WAY TO START DEVELOPING YOUR CONCEPT IS TO ESTABLISH YOUR ELEVATOR PITCH."

CHAPTER 12

Beverage Concept

Beverage Concept Deep Dive

Think about how you would describe your beverage idea to a potential distributor in one sentence. This one sentence is what I call your concept. Your beverage concept explains:

☑ Your drink and

☑ Your company's mission

This chapter is devoted to developing that overall perception that will guide this first drink and any others you may add as your company gains a following and becomes more successful.

More than Drink Flavors

Your concept is more than just the type of drink you want to sell. It's everything about your drink and your company that explains who you are, what you sell, and even how you sell it. Once you've developed your product concept, you'll have answered some fundamental questions, like:

☑ What do you sell?

- ☑ Where do you sell it?

- ☑ What is the drink's price?

- ☑ Who is your target market?

- ☑ What is your goal?

The trick to developing your product and company concept is to start at the end—again, reverse engineering. You need to walk yourself backward through time from that vision of a drink back to the first step in producing it. When you get there, you'll have a full view of what your product and your company are.

The Elevator Pitch

An excellent way to start developing your concept is to establish your elevator pitch. It is a quick summary of your business for those of you not familiar with an elevator pitch. The point is to explain what you do in about 30 to 60 seconds (about the elevator ride span). In the real world, your elevator pitch accomplishes two things:

- ☑ It gives you a fast and reliable marketing tool that you can use at the drop of a hat.

- ☑ It shows people that you are a focused, articulate, and informed business person who intends to succeed!

We ask you to start by developing your elevator pitch to give yourself the same focus and direction. What we want to do here is come up with one quick response that will explain your whole project quickly and effectively. Start by answering a few questions:

- ☑ Who are you?

- ☑ What do you do?

- ☑ What is your product?

☑ What does it do for your customer?

☑ How do you sell it?

Initially, your elevator pitch might sound something like:

"I'm the owner of XYZ Energy Drinks. I produce a healthy organic energy drink for women, which I sell directly through drop shipping. We use public relations and magazine advertising to promote our drink's health benefits and ingredients. We supply healthy, energy-boosting drinks specifically designed to meet women's needs. We currently ship to one thousand customers monthly in the USA and Canada."

When you can explain your concept in one hundred words or less, you can briefly portray your whole idea to yourself and interested buyers and investors. Your elevator pitch serves as the first vision of who you want to be and what you want to do with your beverage company. It stands as the first goal you've set for yourself and your product.

The Vision of Success

The easiest way to develop your drink concept is to start with a vision of your drink. You're the visionary with the motivation and creativity to create this new drink. Imagine someone drinking your beverage.

☑ Who are they?

☑ What are they drinking?

☑ How old are they?

☑ Who's the target market?

    o Is this a children's drink?

    o Is it for young adults or seniors?

   o Is it specifically for male athletes?

Now take a step back and think about where your consumer bought this drink.

- ☑ Did he buy it? Did his mother or father buy it for him?

- ☑ Was it bought at a convenience store or gas station?

- ☑ Is it a specialty product sold only at bars, gyms, health stores, natural foods markets, or vitamin stores?

- ☑ Did a parent buy it in bulk for the family at Costco or the supermarket?

- ☑ Was it drop-shipped from a website?

- ☑ Was it sold through multi-level marketing?

Going through this list, you can see all the many possibilities for marketing and selling your beverage. Deciding on the details ahead of time will help you start narrowing down the distribution, sales, packaging, and marketing possibilities. Now that you have a clear vision of your product, you can use it to back-track through product development until you have the information you need to plan and produce your drink.

Walking Back Through Product Development to Product Concept

Now that we've summarized the big picture, we need to break it into details and plans that will serve as the framework for a detailed business plan—your roadmap to product launch. The several following chapters follow a walk back through the engineering process, starting as we did here with the end-product and then analyzing even further to give us more specifics about your drink's concept. We'll spend a chapter on each of the following topics until we have the complete picture of your product concept. These will include:

- ✅ Problem Solving
- ✅ Package look & feel
- ✅ Ingredients & taste
- ✅ Production
- ✅ Warehousing & logistics

Each of these components contributes to your concept's development. By breaking each topic down into their designated chapter, we guide you through your drink development stages to where you can present it in a business plan and then produce it. In the following chapters, we'll take a step back from the vision of your drink in your customer's hand and look at your product packaging, the look & feel.

> *"YOU ARE NOT YOUR CUSTOMER, SO QUIT ACTING LIKE IT."*

CHAPTER 13

Target Market

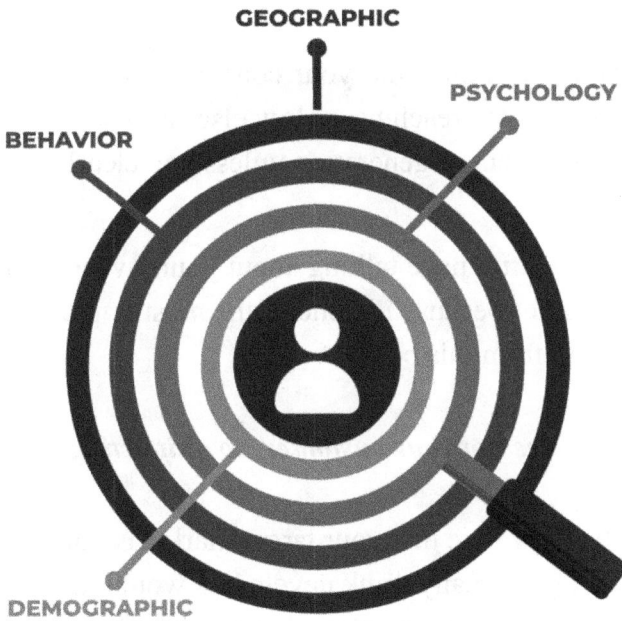

Diagram 2 – Target Market

To define your target market, we need to expand on the idea we developed in the last chapter; we need to go back to that list of questions we asked when you envisioned that consumer drinking your beverage. We need to know who they are, what they like to drink, and how to reach them. We need to know everything we can about your target market to know just how to fulfill their beverage and refreshment needs.

I'm the Consumer

It's essential to know who your consumer is so that you know where and how to reach him. How else can you serve the needs of an entire segment or generation unless you clearly define those needs first?

We spent page after page talking about your Avatar, target market, perfect consumer because it's one of the most important things you can take away from this book.

"You are not your customer, so quit acting like it."

We must be clear here that your target market is not you; it is your consumer. A great many drink developers would never drink their product if it weren't theirs; why? Because it wasn't made for them. We have doctors, attorneys, and investors who would never buy their product simply because it is not made for them; it is made for their target market. This means you cannot just design a drink you like; you have to develop a drink your target market likes. You do this by thinking like a marketer and putting yourself in your consumer's shoes.

I like to run clients through an exercise I call "I'm the Consumer" to help entrepreneurs understand their perfect target audience. The goal is to envision the consumer drinking the product; imagine you are that consumer. Now, put yourself in their place and ask yourself some questions.

- ☑ What do I need from this product?
- ☑ What functions do I want the drink to have?
- ☑ Why am I going to pick this product off the shelf?
- ☑ Why will I buy this product?

Reflect beyond the product's taste and function (although you must give these their due, too) and figure out what this manufacturer is doing that makes you buy this product. Is it the packaging, price, the flavor?

In the next chapter, you'll find out that the answers to these questions dictate a lot about packaging, but it goes far beyond that, too. Answering the questions above is a great exercise you can do with a simple piece of paper. It's a must for any new beverage project.

I like to imagine my target consumer. I imagine their nationality, age, income, where they go to school, what they want from life, goals, and motivations. It's like developing a character in a novel. I try to think like my consumer, paying particular attention to their purchasing power. The consumer's income bracket, where they shop, and how much they spend are crucial to figuring out your retail price. Don't price your product according to your costs or what you think is "a good price." You need to get this from your perfect or alpha consumer.

If your target market is a seven-year-old child, you must also think about the mother, father, brothers, and sisters. Who buys the drinks in the household? Is it the mother? Does she buy organic products or prefer to save money by buying bulk? Develop a "protagonist" in your own beverage story. Get in your customers' heads and see what motivates them.

Where Does Your Consumer Shop?

One of the things the "I'm the Consumer" exercise will tell you is where and how to sell your product. It would help if you thought about what your consumer wants, who is buying the product, and where they shop for beverages. You need to know how to package the product (singles, six-packs, cases) and what distribution and retail channels will get your drink to your consumer. Once you know the answers to those questions, a lot of your work is done, and you can focus on meeting the needs of your consumers and establishing distribution channels to reach them.

You must identify where your consumer shops to gain more insight into your business than just the retail price or consumer background. It will dictate your distribution channel. Once you know where your consumer shops, you know how to get the product to that retail store. Now you only have to contact the distributors that service that particular account. That's simple. You get all of this from basic consumer research, including your retailer and your distributor's profit margins. A convenience store, supermarket, natural store, gym, superstore, or wholesale store make a different margin.

Researching Your Target Market

Researching your target market involves both grassroots efforts and market research. It would help if you looked to sources such as industry reports to study the various drink markets' trends and study the trends for your target market's demographics. You should look at the potential within your market, its size, and the amount of competition. Know, though, that this doesn't mean a smaller market is not the right place to be. Niche drinks in niche markets that serve a specific purpose do very well. All of you should be focusing on a niche, as that is how you will create appeal.

Don't forget what we talked about earlier in terms of face-to-face research, too. Get out on the street and talk to these consumers, find out what they are drinking and why, and what else they might be craving. Again, you can also speak to distributors and retailers, find out who is buying what, and then look into the big sellers for your market.

Later on, in the development of your product, you will take your target market research a step further. You will look to focus groups to gather information and try your product out on them. They'll test your product and answer your questions.

All of this—target market research, demographics, focus groups—is to get your drink as on-target as possible the first time around. There is a good chance that you'll make some changes along the way to meet your target market's needs, but with good research from the start, you'll be able to avoid a lot of remanufacturing and repacking. That is essential to your drink's success and profitability, as every added step and redesign is another factor that will drive up the cost of your drink development and production before you get to the selling point.

Ready to Go On

You now know the most critical piece of information you need to have to move forward with drink development and production—you know who you are developing your drink for. You can keep coming back to your defined target market to make every decision from the drink's size to the cap on top—everything that will make your NAB function for your consumer in the way it should, the way it sells

"ACHIEVING THE PROPER PACKAGING WITH THE CORRECT PRESENTATION IS ESSENTIAL TO SUCCESS."

CHAPTER 14

Package & Look and Feel

Rapid Knowledge Section

Your consumer will guide you to package your drink correctly.
Once you identify your Avatar, you should know your
product's size, color, flavor, and purchase place.

You now know who will buy your product, your target market.
Now it's time to visualize your product. How will it look and feel
in your hand, on the shelf, and in the refrigerator? What size will it
be? Will you use a bottle or a can? Will the bottle be plastic or
glass?

Packaging for Your Consumer

With the vision of who the product is for, we need to choose packaging that will appeal to them and function as per the beverage's intended function. For example, if you designed your beverage to be a drink for runners, it should be packaged in plastic as opposed to glass or aluminum; it should have an easy-access, no-spill sports cap and not a screw-off top so that it can be drunk "on the run."

Let's get a bit technical and explore the different components of your package. Some of them will be too specific for an executive and more suited for a designer or project manager, but it's a good idea for you to see the different options and get a better idea of how packaging works. You have a few basic options for each component of the actual container and cap.

Tops

Tops will vary in cost, and the type of top you choose will depend once again on the intended use and your target market. There are four basic options:

- **Flat top:** this is your basic, standard flat screw top you see on plastic water bottles, soda bottles, and the like; there is a range of sizes, and flat tops are available in just about any color you can dream up.

- **Sport top:** sport top versions of drink tops come in all shapes, sizes, and colors. More elaborate tops can control back-flow and accidental spills, and others are even ergonomically shaped to fit the shape of your mouth. As you can see, the variety is enormous, and the costs will reflect respectively.

- ✓ **Metal top:** these tops, used in conjunction with glass bottles, are either mechanically screwed or pneumatically forced on. An example of a forced bottle cap is found on most glass beer bottles; they can either be removed with a bottle opener or twisted off. Other examples of metal caps and tops are those found on products like Snapple. Metal tops like these are always lined with plastic or other material to keep the built-up pressure inside.

- ✓ **Can top:** tops on cans, as you can imagine, don't vary as much as tops on bottles. The choices have not evolved as much as one might expect, even from the beginning of beverage can production, leastwise not in the authentic look. Today the options would include just a few items like a specially colored tab or a cutout that adds to the beverage's branding. We've recently seen tops that make a sound when opened, but these have not yet created an impact on the overall market. Other than these few, the choices with can tabs are limited.

Containers

We could spend pages and pages going over the variety of containers available for beverages today. There are entire publications devoted to nothing but drink containers. There is a lot of attention placed on containers because drink containers significantly impact the product's overall success. The container is emphasized more than anything else, and it is a massive factor in your cost.

You have three basic options when it comes to containers:

- ☑ **Glass**
- ☑ **Plastic**
- ☑ **Aluminum**

Of these materials, the choices are bottle or can (noting that even aluminum is used for some bottles). There are, however, a couple of options used primarily for kids' drinks and are now catching on:

- ☑ **Pouches** are made from aluminum, lined with plastics and other materials, similar to the Capri Sun packaging. It is popular for kids' beverages and convenient for lunchboxes. These often come 10 or 12 to a box; warehouse stores (Costco, Sam's Club) will often sell four to six boxes at a time.

Pouches are enjoying a resurgence in popularity and are very big in Asia.

- ☑ **Tetra Pack** is made from a cardboard application (similar to traditional juice boxes). Tetra packs extend shelf-life by preserving the package contents and protecting them from the outside environment. Tetra bricks are now being used for grocery items like tomato sauce, too.

Whatever material you choose for your beverage, realize that the packaging will be very influential to sales. For example, glass is hefty, expensive to ship, and breaks easily, making it a poor choice for functional sports beverages or children's beverages. On the other hand, glass can put a product in a different category, often as a more sophisticated drink that sells for more. For example, many new water drinks typically demand a higher price for glass-packed products, and they also ship less; therefore, they cost more to produce. Brands have been able to use glass as a way to differentiate and charge more.

Companies often choose plastic and aluminum bottles to be unique. While it is easy to come up with a unique label, it is much harder to develop your unique bottle. There are different variations of this; many big drink companies will pay artisan crafters to produce their molds, but those are usually used in expensive liquors selling for $30-$60 per bottle. The typical developer may have to go with an off-the-shelf bottle since engineering costs on a custom bottle can be between $30,000 and $50,000.

Even for off-the-shelf containers, you have customizable options within each category. However, every custom addition adds to the cost, and these options are mostly limited to very well-funded beverage companies.

To start, you will want to forgo that expense and go with a ready-to-go product. There are more than enough choices to be unique by working with the standard options and changing them through labeling and design.

We've talked a lot about bottles; now, let's take a minute to discuss cans.

The can category has been expanding quite a bit lately. It used to be that there was only your basic 12-ounce can and nothing more. Today there is a range of sizes and even a few new shapes and variations. One of the unique options in cans is custom shapes, such as the keg-shaped cans produced by Heineken and aluminum bottles. Next to this, the only difference is really in the can's size, and the shape stays the same. A can size fits every drink concept— 4 oz, 6 oz, 8.4 oz, 11.5 oz, 16 oz, 24 oz, or 32 oz.

Each shape and size has its advantages, and you will choose based upon your drink's function and concept. For example, aluminum bottles can't be resealed and used as glass bottles but will be accepted in specific sports stadiums where glass is not allowed for safety reasons. Small 4 and 6 ounce cans are sleek and sophisticated and can give the perception of 'bang for the buck.' You can use the different can options to your advantage as you develop your brand and concept.

In the U.S., there are two major can manufacturers: Ball and Rexam. A limited number of plants can produce the custom-shaped cans, but here again, that is probably irrelevant at this point as you will be better off starting with a more affordable standard can.

Labels

The label is just as important as the container and is a solid differentiating point. Labels communicate to the seller, spelling out quality, price, function, and more.

There are many different labeling options such as:

- Plastic standard wrap—plastic labels are most notably used for their resistance to the environment they will be subjected to, such as refrigerators, coolers, etc.

- Paper—glue-front and around. It has minimal use, although inexpensive. The more colors you add on paper, the more expensive the label.

- Metal/silk-screening—prints directly on the can and is durable against elements; up until now, this has been the only real option for cans. It's reasonably affordable, but silk screening has its limitations. Silk screening is limited in graphics, attractiveness, colors, shades, and tones and requires a large printing run (on average, you'll be required to print 8,000 cases per run).

☑ <u>Shrinkwrap</u>—shrinkwraps are plastic labels that drape the entire container. They are used in bottles or cans. Shrinkwraps can be printed to include almost any graphics, colors, or shades. The printed wrap encases a blank can or bottle, then is heated and shrinks to fit. Designing shrinkwraps is more expensive at first, but shrinkwraps are inexpensive in the long run once set up.

It would help if you chose the right options to meet your drink's functional needs and present the look and feel to appeal to your target market. Achieving the proper packaging with the correct presentation is essential to success so that at a glance, your consumer can see which product has paid attention to their wants and needs and is likely to be the drink they consume.

"YOU WANT TO MAKE
YOUR DRINK AS
APPEALING AS POSSIBLE."

CHAPTER 15

Ingredients & Taste

With your product's look and feel and packaging under control, you can focus on what's inside. Now is the time to start choosing ingredients and flavors and developing your drink's taste. Your ingredients and taste will go back to your drink's envisioned concept and function like the packaging.

Choosing Your Flavor Profile

You may already have an idea for your drink's taste. Perhaps you have even profiled the ingredients and created your drink's recipe. Some of you may even have your drink's profile, taste, and ingredients all in place and have just come here looking to develop the rest of the profile.

If your drink's profile is in the 'idea' stage, you're likely wondering where to go to create it. Even those who have already developed your drink's profile are urged to read this chapter, as essential information will impact your product's concept and help you build your brand.

To develop your flavor profile—the tastes and raw ingredients that go into your drink—you will be working with a flavor house. The flavor house will have access to all of the various flavors and raw materials that will go into your drink and work with you to determine the right balance of each to create a great-tasting new beverage. You will need a clear vision of your drink to guide them and help choose the right flavors and ingredients.

The first step in achieving that taste is selecting the right flavor house for your needs. Keep in mind that not all flavor houses deal with the same types of ingredients and products. For example, if you develop an all-natural or organic drink, you need to find a flavor house that provides rightfully labeled products. Likewise, suppose you are looking for artificial sweeteners such as those used in diet drinks or artificial flavors similar to those used in sodas. In that case, you will want to find the flavor house that works primarily with those types of ingredients. Finally, if you are looking to create a drink with new and exotic flavors, that is what you want to research. By now, indeed, you sense a theme—you need a flavor house capable of servicing your needs; ask questions first, not later, and save yourself a lot of aggravation by considering the options ahead of time.

Choosing the Flavors

There is only one way to know which flavor house can suit your needs. You must select your flavors and ingredients. At the risk of sounding like a broken record, this goes back to the function of your drink.

First, you need to brainstorm your drink, its concept, and its function. Then you have to match that to the flavors that you think will serve that need. If you are unsure, decide on your concept, do more research, find out what similar drinks are offering, and ask the right questions to the flavor houses.

As you choose flavors and ingredients for your drink, think about what your target consumer wants in their drink. Let's take a look at a few examples:

- The health-conscious consumer will be looking for a drink that gives them added health benefits, vitamins, and minerals to meet their daily requirements. Bear in mind this person does not want unhealthy ingredients added, so sugars may not be the way to go. But what about artificial sweeteners? It depends on how far you intend to take the health angle.

- The all-natural consumer will most certainly not want fake sweeteners in their drink. This buyer will look for the ingredients Mother Nature intended and care less about how the product will affect their waistline. Flavors here must be convincing, made up of ingredients that sound 'real.' There are all-natural drinks that can actually be higher in calories but still meet consumers' needs as long as they feel good about drinking them.

- The runner or athlete may think little of these factors focusing more on what they need to perform. That could be an electrolyte pack or hydrating agent.

- The organic buyer will be similar to the natural buyer but may want something on the label that legally certifies the drink's content, so they feel more secure about drinking your product. Keep in mind the organic flavor house has to meet those standards, regardless of the flavor.

- The consumer looking for something hot and sexy will be looking for exotic flavors. These will be more than your run-of-the-mill fruit flavors, something more uncommon and less mainstream.

☑ Today's energy drink consumer is just looking for a jolt; high caffeine has often been the order of the day. But as the category ages, the healthy energy drinker is emerging and looking for natural boosts that are better for them.

Understand that these are just examples to jog your thinking. There are many variations and combinations, creating niche markets for functional drinks or other new beverage categories. You want to make your drink as appealing to your crowd as possible so that it very specifically meets their demands.

As you can see, there are many angles to take towards flavoring and ingredient profiling. It all comes down to finding the right flavor house to be your partner and supplier. Work with them, but always keep your mission in mind, and develop the right balance between flavor and ingredients so that neither will offend your customer. Remember that while taste may prevail as the obvious draw, ingredients are equally crucial to the demanding consumer looking to get the definite advantage of your drink's function.

"THANKS TO FUNCTIONAL BEVERAGES AND CRAFT BEERS, YOU CAN NOW PRODUCE A PALLET AT A TIME FOR LITTLE MONEY."

CHAPTER 16

Bottling

"Thanks to functional beverages and craft beers, you can now produce a pallet at a time for little money."

Rapid Knowledge Section

Production is easier than ever. I recommend you start with the least amount you can produce, test in a few stores or online, and then grow from there. If you can start with a pallet, do that. It doesn't matter if you pay more and lose money on a pallet; that's not the point. You need to prove your concept first.

We have a drink profile; we chose our flavors and package—we know our new beverage's look, feel, taste, and composition. The next step is to get it produced—bottled! For that, we look to the bottling facility.

What Can Your Bottler Do For You?

A s we said earlier in the book, bottling is a job that you must outsource. It is an absolute misconception that you have to have your bottling facility to produce your new beverage. It would be a gross misappropriation of funds to invest in a bottling plant when thousands of them are waiting to co-pack your beverage products for you.

Similar to finding the right flavor house, finding the right bottler takes some footwork. All bottlers do not handle the same type of bottling or use the same kinds of processes. Not all can produce specialty products to certification standards. Different facilities will have additional capabilities; some can produce hot-fill products, others only cold-fill. Some can make natural and organic products, and others cannot. Some can only bottle into cans, others plastic or glass. So you see, not all bottlers can process your hot-fill natural tea in an aluminum can. You'll have to find out first which bottlers can handle which containers and processes.

A Bottler for Every Beverage

Beverage World magazine reported that the rise in new-age beverages, functional beverages, and "craft beers" has contributed to the increased availability of co-pack processers and various processing options. *Beverage World* credited the new age beverage market with changing the co-packing 'game.' They report that small start-up companies have more reason to seek a co-packing arrangement and that the co-pack industry has opened opportunities in new age beverage production that otherwise would be difficult to achieve. They have compiled a list of processers across the U.S. and Canada, complete with contact information, processing capacities broken into the following categories:

- Cold fill
- Retort
- Purepak
- Aseptic
- Hot fill
- Tunnel

This list is a convenient reference for those looking for specific processing needs. You can access it through *Beverage World* or contact us if you need help finding bottling solutions.

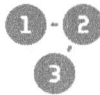

Bottling Process Steps

We'll run you through a swift and abbreviated production process through bottling to give you an idea of how this process will work. For this exercise, let's assume that you've gotten through concept development and research. You are ready to put your order, assuming you've asked all the right questions, and you know that these are the professionals that can meet your needs.

- First, you order your containers and labels.

- ✅ Next, you order all of your flavoring and raw materials (ingredients). Some bottlers can purchase for you after you've scheduled your production run.

- ✅ You call your bottler and schedule a production run. Plan accordingly; it will probably be 30 to 40 days or more before your run is produced.

- ✅ Inform suppliers of production dates and have supplies (containers, labels, ingredients, and flavoring) shipped to your bottler.

- ✅ Produce your drink on the scheduled date.

Be aware that you will need to have storage arrangements in place once the run is produced until distribution. Arrange to warehouse ahead of time.

This is a short and sweet chapter because the bottler of your choice primarily handles your product's bottling. Of course, you have to make sure that all preparations before and after bottling are completed. More importantly, you need to do your due diligence and choose the right bottler for your product. These are the significant points we were hoping you take away from this chapter. Though they are few, they are fundamental to producing your drink. In the next chapter, we will discuss warehousing and logistics for your new beverage.

"HIRE A THIRD-PARTY LOGISTICS COMPANY TO HANDLE ALL OF YOUR LOGISTICS NEEDS."

CHAPTER 17

Warehousing & Logistics

Rapid Knowledge Section

I recommend you hire a third-party logistics company to handle all of your logistics needs. They can receive your inventory, send samples on your behalf, pick and pack online orders, send pallets or truckloads. They can do it all for you.

Logistics Basics

There's a significant logistics component in the beverage industry, and depending on your business model, you'll need to be familiar with some of the terms.

Here are some of the terms used in beverage logistics:

- Drop-shipping

- Truckload shipping

- Less-than-truckload shipping (LTL)

- Direct Store Delivery

Drop-shipping is where you ship directly to somebody; this is often the consumer buying from your website. However, it could also be that you're drop-shipping samples to wholesalers, distributors, and category buyers at retail chains.

Truckload shipping means standard shipping in large quantities or pallet shipments. You ship in large amounts to your warehouse, large distributors, distribution centers of large retail chains, or maybe even to Amazon.

Less-than-truckload shipping or less than load (LTL) is the transportation of relatively small freight. The alternatives to LTL carriers are parcel carriers or full truckload carriers. Parcel carriers usually handle small packages and cargo that can be broken down into units less than 150 pounds.

Direct Store Delivery, or DSD, delivers the product store by store and provides service to the store. If you start your own distribution company, you'll need to do this. If you sell to Budweiser, they do this. If you sell to UNFI, they will not do this. They will only deliver but not sell or merchandise.

Even if you're entirely an online sales and marketing operation, you'll still need to ship products, so you'll need to negotiate shipping rates, warehousing, picking, and packing. It's good to know your options and compare them to traditional business models such as DSD and others if you want to jump on that model in the future.

Traditional Warehousing Options

If you're using any traditional business models, such as selling to retailers or distributors, you'll need this type of warehousing and logistics.

Warehousing can be tricky, and in fact, many drink developers do not realize that there is a need for warehousing at all, assuming the distributor will take care of it. What is not commonly understood is that the product does not go directly from the production plant to the distributor, so you will need to make interim storage arrangements. For this, you have a couple of options, but primarily we will focus on the best solution for new drink developers.

There are three basic options for warehousing your beverages. You can:

- ✅ Build and maintain your warehousing facility (not cost-effective)

- ✅ Rely on small, private storage units (of limited usefulness, but can serve a purpose as we'll discuss)

- ✅ Use a third-party warehouse (the best solution for small beverage companies)

We'll focus mainly on the third-party warehouse, or 3PL, and discuss the role a small storage unit can play in your warehousing needs and why it is not advantageous to maintain your warehouse facility.

The Third-Party Warehousing Arrangement

The most straightforward and inexpensive warehousing arrangement is a third-party warehouse, also called logistics warehousing, third-party logistics, or 3PL. A third-party warehousing arrangement is one where you take your product (have it transported) to a controlled warehousing facility and pay rent per pallet per month.

The average cost of 3PL warehouse storage runs between $8 and $12 per pallet per month. You can get better deals depending on where you are in the country, the number of pallets you are storing, and your relationship with the warehouse, but this is a good ball-park figure for planning purposes.

It's interesting to note that you don't have to be a small company to use a third-party logistics warehouse. Many large beverage companies use 3PLs because they have their office building but no warehouse facilities. This may not apply to you if you are a distributor, as you will likely have your warehouse facilities to store your product at no additional cost. That's a great advantage to you, but most of the visionaries reading this book do not have that kind of access, and that's alright.

3PL & Warehousing Costing Considerations

To accurately plan a 3PL facility's costs, you need to understand what is included in your rental fee. The base fee for 3PL storage covers only receiving your product and its removal from the facility. That fee covers nothing else. Therefore, if you must have a partial order shipped out, have to move or break pallets or cases, have products drop-shipped, or do anything else with your product, you will pay an extra fee. For example, if you have to start sending samples and take cases apart, that could be extra. If you want the warehouse to send one or two cases of samples on your behalf, that will cost extra. Anything that adds more work to the warehouse on top of receiving and removal will add to your basic rental cost.

You cannot assume that you'll ship an entire truckload of product every time you sell to a distributor. You may have 22 pallets sitting in the warehouse but may only sell five or ten at a time. So if there are 22 pallets in the warehouse, you have to pay a fee to receive, move, ship them out of the facility. It's an incremental cost and one that you must account for.

The above can sound like a 3PL could nickel and dime you to death, but you need to put this into perspective. The intention here is not to scare you by working with a 3PL—not at all; it is merely to make you aware of the factors that go into warehouse costing to plan and budget accordingly.

Your only realistic alternative to a 3PL is maintaining your warehouse facility (owning or renting). However, it's not smart to pay rent on your warehouse if you don't need it; it's much more cost-effective to go with a 3PL facility than to try to consume the expense of your own warehouse space. If you only have to store three containers or 5,000 cases of product and are looking at renting, it's much easier and reasonable to save money and use a third-party warehouse. There's no need to pay rent at a rate of three, four, or ten thousand dollars just to call the warehouse your own.

Let us break this down to clarify why 3PL is the way to go.

The rental of a warehouse only covers the actual real estate cost. Many other expenses must be considered, and those get very expensive, very quickly. To maintain your warehouse, you would have to assume all costs, everything the 3PL provides. With the 3PL, the costs are dispersed among all clients; they are all yours in your facility. You would have to hire a warehouse manager to control, open and close the warehouse. You need a security system and purchase or lease equipment to move products on and off trucks and around the warehouse. You also have to incur major operational expenses such as telephone, employees, electricity, climate and environmental control (heating, refrigeration), etc.

These costs make the added costs of 3PL services pale in comparison. Logistics warehousing is almost always the right solution for a start-up NAB producer.

The Role of Private Storage Units

There is one other arrangement we should take a minute to mention. It is by no means a total warehousing solution, but it can help defray the costs of 3PL warehouse fees if you need access to the product for sampling purposes and so on.

Many drink developers rent a small private storage unit and store a few pallets there, especially in the beginning when they need frequent access to small amounts of product. This gives quick and easy access to the product for sampling and drop-shipping without incurring warehouse services expenses each time. The rest of the product is safely stored at the 3PL.

Concept Complete, Moving On

We have completed the discussion on warehousing and concept. We have now reviewed every factor you need to consider to develop your business concept and give you that big-picture view of who you are, what you do, who you sell to, and how you sell your product. We have a few more parts that relate to the concept that we need to explore in-depth, but as these are also essential to the business's sales, distribution, and marketing end, we will take the conversation over to Part III of the book.

Jorge S. Olson

PART 03

MARKETING, SELLING, AND DISTRIBUTING YOUR DRINKS

CHAPTER 18

Introduction to Marketing, Selling, & Distributing Your Drinks

"Develop an emotional connection with your consumer. The internet is your secret weapon against a trillion-dollar oligopoly."

Rapid Knowledge Section

You need big money to go on the refrigerator doors at mass retail accounts and convenience stores. Don't be a victim of the trillion-dollar oligopoly trap and compete with Coke, Pepsi, Dr. Pepper, Nestle, and the other big guys in their own space under their own rules. Instead, make your own rules at your own pace, and don't let them near it.

Your website and online store are your competitive space, and your messaging videos, articles, and, most importantly, your personality is your secret weapon. You don't need a million fans; you only need one thousand loyal fans. You don't need a hundred thousand refrigerator doors; you only need your one thousand loyal customers to order online at retail prices for you to succeed.

- ✓ 1,000 loyal customers
- ✓ 1,000 monthly supply
- ✓ Retail price of $85
- ✓ Sales of $85,000 per month
- ✓ Sales of $1 Million per year

Yes, with one thousand customers buying a one or two-case monthly subscription from you, you're at a million dollars in sales annually. To sell these exact amounts through convenience stores, you would need many more customers and a lot more money.

Sales and Marketing Financial Modeling

Sales and Marketing Financial Modeling is the most crucial part of your business, plan, and daily operations. The good part is that you can do it initially and follow it for the next ten years, adjusting it occasionally with a financially savvy team.

The Sales and Marketing Financial Modeling is explicitly what the numbers say about your sales. For example, say you want to sell on

Amazon and Whole Foods in two utterly separate distribution channels. You would build two different financial models in a spreadsheet, cover your costs and sales, and then calculate what's leftover as your profit. It's easy enough, and the numbers in the middle make up the actual modeling, the essential bits. You already know the cost of producing your beverage; you read it in the second section of this book. It will not deviate a lot from those prices so that you can plug them into your spreadsheet. You also know your retail price or price to the consumer, so you don't need to deviate from those prices. That leaves you with the bits in the middle, how much the retailer and the distributor will make. In the case of Amazon, there is no distributor, but you might use a logistics company to help. The rule of thumb is to give a forty percent gross margin to the retailer (Whole Foods), and the distributors selling to Whole Foods typically make around eighteen percent. We're not talking about a direct store delivery (DSD) or beverage distributor selling to Whole Foods, but a national distributor dropping pallets to stores.

Now that we have the distributor and the retailer's overall costs, we need to establish all the unknowns, all the things in the middle that help sell your product. I'm referring to advertising, sampling, trade shows, sales, shipping, and any other expense that you'll incur in the process of selling your product.

When you start your financial modeling, you don't need to think like an accountant or financial analyst; I don't. Instead, think like a marketer. As a marketer, take the economic modeling approach by building a marketing campaign to obtain one customer, store, distributor, or subscription. Follow your sales model, do one. Remember to complete one spreadsheet for each of your sales models. Suppose you're selling to convenience stores using distributors. In that case, that's one model. If you're selling through Amazon, that would be a second, completely different sales model. If you're selling on your eCommerce store, that makes for a new and completely different sales model and a separate spreadsheet.

I take a marketer's approach when dealing with financial modeling. For example, if I sell to customers through my website using a subscription model and drop-shipping beverages directly to their house, I would start with one subscriber and do the math for that one subscriber. Calculate how much it costs for a Google search ad click, a squeeze page to get their email or phone, an initial sale, a high-ticket monthly subscription item, an upsell, or pre-payment for the year. I also calculate all re-target advertising-related expenses (if they leave the page without purchasing), social media advertising, free samples, mailings, contests, coupons, gamification, free clothing, commissions, and referral discounts. That's plenty of line items you need to consider to get just one customer. Once you include all these in your spreadsheet, your calculation will be complete. So take your time, do it right the first time, and don't forget to include your product's cost plus shipping, picking, packing the box, and other supplies.

Now that you calculated how much it would cost to sell to one customer, you can scale to see how much it would cost to sell to two, ten, one hundred, a thousand, or ten thousand. This way, you'll know how much money you need for one specific business model.

You may want to consider doing the above exercise for other popular business models:

- ✅ Traditional DSD
- ✅ Natural Channel
- ✅ Supermarket Direct

- ✅ Amazon

- ✅ Your Website

For example, in traditional DSD, you would sell to a beverage distributor, the distributor would sell to the retailer, and the retailer would sell to the consumer. Here, your modeling needs to account for how many stores you need to open and how many customers you need to buy from those stores. This is something the majority of entrepreneurs don't consider when thinking of sales and distribution.

When calculating your financial model, you need to figure out:

- ✅ How many distributors you need to get to your sales goals

- ✅ How many stores you need to open per territory

- ✅ How many units you need to sell per store per month

Your goal looks like this so far:

- ✅ Find five distributors in California

- ✅ Open two hundred stores per territory or distributor

- ✅ Sell one hundred units per store per month

You're on your way to selling 20,000 units or roughly 833 cases (of 24 cans) per month. That's half a truckload depending on the size of the truck. It's not much by beverage standards, but you need to work a whole lot to get to those numbers.

Fast Moving Consumer Goods analysts and executives rarely consider how many customers they need to reach their sales goals. They think of distributors and retailers but rarely examine the number of consumers required to walk into a store and purchase their product. Ask yourself, "Did the customer get into a car, drive to a store to buy your product? Was it an impulse buy? Why did they buy it?"

?

How Many Customers Do You Need?

Consider your monthly goal is to sell one hundred drinks in a single store. Do you need one hundred customers buying your drink once or only fifty customers buying your drink twice per month? This is a crucial consideration. It's your job to sell to this customer, and you have a limited number of people who walk into that store every month, so you better take advantage of the repeat business and get them as repeat buyers.

When calculating your costs, please include these marketing expenses:

- ☑ Cost of acquisition of a distributor
- ☑ Cost of acquisition of a store
- ☑ Cost of acquisition of a customer
- ☑ Cost of keeping a customer

The cost of acquiring a distributor includes all costs required to convince a distributor to take your product. Some of these expenses will consist of attending trade shows, mailings, samples, and travel.

The cost of acquiring a store might include commissions offered to the salespeople opening the store, free product, slotting fees, commissions or spiffs, merchandisers, sampling events, point of sale material, and advertising commitments.

The cost of acquiring a customer is tricky to calculate when you're selling to a distributor who then sells to the store because you rarely see your end-consumer. Still, let's try and assign some direct costs with the information we have. These are some sure-ways to market directly to consumers buying at retail stores: social media and online advertising, coupons sending consumers to specific store locations, sampling events, mailings, and geo-targeted television ads. In-store promotions, such as sampling events, could also give you a good boost in publicity and sales. I've found it very time and labor-intensive. It's still a great promotional tool, especially when combined with posting videos on social media and tagging customers.

I ran a successful campaign using a brand ambassador in a convenience store promoting and selling a beverage. He took photos with customers, clerks, and the store owner and posted them on social media. He also took short videos of customers drinking the beverage and giving their feedback. He posted the videos tagging the store and the customers. He then got the customers to follow his brand, the store and share the videos with friends who could become customers. Don't forget to add your location to your post using hashtags, such as #California #SanDiego, when you do these promotions.

Once you calculate the costs of acquiring a client, calculate how much money you'll need to keep that client. Just because you convince a new customer to buy your product on Amazon or your website or with a sampling team in a 7-Eleven doesn't mean you'll keep that customer forever. It's crucial to invest time and money in retaining that customer. Retaining the customer online might be more accessible, at least in concept, as you can follow them with advertising and have more metrics and analytics. This is not so when they buy at your local liquor store. Put on your marketing cap and think about this. It's your job to convince a customer to give you a shot, to buy from you, to establish a connection, hopefully, an emotional connection, and then to persuade them to do it again and to keep buying from you. Try to think of great products you tried while traveling or at a restaurant or retailer, only to forget them and never rebuy them.

On the other hand, think of products you looked for, took a photo of, or made an extra effort to buy them. Did that company sign you to their newsletter, social media, text, or email marketing campaign? Did they make it easier for you to continue to buy from them?

Business modeling can be a daunting task even for financial analysts and accountants because they don't have a beverage distribution or marketing background. Remember, I have tools you can use to get to your numbers faster. I can provide a profit calculator. I also offer entire courses on business modeling, sales, distribution, marketing, and much more. Start by plugging your numbers in the profit calculator:

www.LiquidBrandsManagement.com/beveragebook

Emotional Connection in Beverage Marketing

We move on now to the third and final part of our book. This part of the book focuses on your beverage's sales, distribution, and marketing.

Is there a magic bullet for success in your beverage business? Yes, there is! I know you were expecting to hear, "No, it's hard work, and you need to accomplish twenty things to be successful." There's one thing that just about ensures your success in the beverage industry, other consumer goods, and even in the service industry. Do you know what it is? **It's developing an emotional connection with your consumer.**

If you establish an emotional connection with your consumer, you don't need millions of dollars in advertising, large promotional teams, extensive trade show budgets, and significant national beverage distributors. An emotionally invested consumer will look, travel and buy your product regardless of the price. It doesn't matter if you sell it in a 7-Eleven, on the internet, or out of your garage.

The internet and social media make it possible for you to reach out to your perfect consumer and make connections. It allows you to talk to them about you, your product, and your beverages. Do you ever wonder why Coke brings back old commercials every few years? They're making an emotional connection based on the past. You don't have the luxury of appealing to past consumers with your new beverage, so you have to create new relationships.

How can you create new emotional connections? My favorite way is to tie products to social causes and become a social entrepreneur. Every time you have a new consumer or make a new sale, they make a difference in the world.

You can create your charity or tie your product to an existing noble cause. It's good business and just plain good to do. People will respond to a cause much better than only reacting to a product. It's not easy to make an emotional connection with a product or thing, but it's easier to make it with a notable cause. If your consumers can change a child's life by sending them to school just by buying your product, it's an effortless way to incorporate them into your business model.

Stay in contact with your consumers. If you want to make that emotional connection, make sure you use email, social media, mail, and other tools to keep in touch with your consumer. Don't just tell them you donated 5% to charity; send them a picture of the school or the children you're helping.

Many parts of marketing, sales, and distribution are mechanical and formulaic, but establishing your consumer relationship is not. It takes creativity, planning, good value propositions, and timing.

Where to Invest Your Time and Money

This is the part of the business where most beverage producers and executives fall short. But because we rise to face the most challenging task head-on, this is the part where you get the most value and benefit as our reader, drink developer, executive, or entrepreneur. We show you how to get a drink bottled, but more importantly, how to get your target market buying that drink by the caseload.

All drinks that fail do so in sales and distribution. This is important for you to know. Beverage development is easy, marketing, sales, and distribution, not so much. Most new beverage entrepreneurs and executives have a hard time understanding where their drink failed. They created the best tasting drink the industry has seen; they made the most attractive packaging for their drink; the best look and design, the whole package, but they have no sales.

Most new beverage developers think people will purchase their drink because they read about it or saw it on the internet. They come to the harsh realization that they need to communicate in a certain way with their consumers. "This is my product, this is what it's all about, and this is where I want to sell it." Distributors and retailers alike need to know that an eager market is out there ready to buy your drink. Developers tend to forget that they need to get out there and market this drink to make it a success.

The average drink developer seriously underestimates the retailer, distributor, and other essential personnel in any drink's success. All the brands we see as consumers we purchase because we've been educated about them somehow—we heard about them, read about them, there were sales reps going door to door introducing and pushing them. And it's the people who are doing these things that are making brands what they are today.

Many people forget that what happens after a drink is off the production line makes it profitable. Anyone can manufacture a product on any given day. Anyone can come up with a great-tasting product. It takes a real marketer to get a product where it needs to be on the shelves and get it in the consumer's hands. That's where a drink will either fail or succeed. That's where you will succeed because you have this information now when it matters most.

If the entire process from development to the consumer drinking your beverage were a 10-step process, getting the drink produced and bottled is probably only the first step. There are nine more crucial steps to go through before you have a profitable selling product. That's the span covered in the rest of this book.

The Harsh Reality

The harsh reality of this business is that many of the produced drinks are never successful. There was never an effective marketing and business plan. There was no way to communicate and get the consumer to buy (if that consumer ever actually saw the product at all).

When we consider the number of drink brands that have gone through the development phase, even just the beverage brands that we helped, and see how many have become successes, we begin to see how critical this part of the business is. Sadly, we worked closely with many of these drink developers. We have walked developers through numerous promising, full-fledged products ready for market, only to have the developers insist they didn't need our help marketing or selling the product. Every time, we've tried to impress upon them the importance of the next step. Still, these developers would insist and tell us they had it covered—they had a singer, a friend in the movie industry, or some advantage that would turn their product into the product of their dreams. In the end, only about 10% of the drinks succeed and become profitable. The unsuccessful ones always lack a definitive business and marketing plan.

Stepping Back to Business 101

We've worked hard to impress upon you the importance of a solid plan for your business, sales, distribution, and marketing. The last part of this book is here to help with that. Let's stress again how important it is to have a great sales strategy and answer every question to get from point A to point B.

To develop that plan, we will start with the end consumer and work our way back to your product—just as we did when developing the product. You'll learn about distribution and sales channels and how to get into the right ones. We will also tell you what you don't know about selling your drink, your responsibilities, and what your retailers and distributors need from you. We'll talk about the options and help you identify which can work for you. Essentially, we'll take you through a 101 Business course with an emphasis on the beverage business. We'll show you what others are missing so that you come out of this fully prepared to not only produce a drink (which, again, anyone can do) but sell and make money!

Jorge S. Olson

"YOUR MARKETING PLAN IS EVERYTHING THAT NEEDS TO HAPPEN FOR CONSUMERS TO BUY YOUR PRODUCT."

CHAPTER 19

Beverage Marketing Plan

"Your marketing plan is everything that needs to happen for consumers to buy your product."

Rapid Knowledge Section

What is your marketing plan? It's the roadmap for getting consumers to buy your product. If you're shipping your product directly to consumers, your marketing plan will include direct marketing, drop shipping, catalogs, and price specials. If you're using convenience stores, your marketing plan will probably have consumer marketing, trade marketing to convenience stores and distributors, and logistics. Your marketing plan should specify who your consumer is, your distribution model, and how you'll sell it across the entire supply chain (consumer, retailer distributor.)

Realizing how important your marketing plan is, I decided to spend the time to create an entire course around your marketing plan. However, I also prepared a course explaining your business model, getting funding, selling to convenience stores and distributors, exporting your products, and much more. To see the courses, go to www.LiquidBrandsManagement.com and start your journey into the "Build Your Beverage Empire Courses."

Here is a starting point for the creation of your marketing plan:

- ✅ Outline your marketing plan
- ✅ Secure distribution
- ✅ Define and reach your target market
- ✅ Study your competition
- ✅ Develop your price strategy
- ✅ Understand and develop your positioning statement
- ✅ Complete the packaging (as it relates to marketing)
- ✅ Complete sales materials, including POS material and sale sheets
- ✅ Sales and distribution structure
- ✅ Design promotions and advertising

Be The Decider

"Who is your perfect consumer? Let's focus on that first, and then we can do the cool stuff."

Marketing can be overwhelming because marketing takes the entirety of your business model. In other words, everything boils down to marketing. You're in business to place a product into the market. Let's go back to the early decision-making process and remember who is our target consumer. That's the number one thing we need to figure out; without this, every other aspect of our marketing plan will just not work.

The post COVID era helps the small entrepreneurs play in the fantastic shark-filled ocean. You can play in this ocean as long as you stay on your side of the pool, as long as you don't try and bring a hundred thousand dollars to a billion-dollar game. The name of the game here is online marketing!

Online marketing, mostly post COVID, gives smaller businesses the ability to compete at any level, retail, wholesale, Amazon, eCommerce, and other direct-to-consumer arenas, not just for beverages but other Fast Moving Consumer Goods. Some service businesses, food, and other market-disrupting businesses saw incredible growth, while others, unable to pivot and cope, had to shut down.

Once you find your Avatar, your perfect consumer, pursue them relentlessly by writing articles, recording videos, sending out information by email, Instagram, or other social media sites. Now is the time to communicate with your consumers, have fun with it, use your personality, be part of the photos and videos. Don't try to be corporate about it; market like a small business because you are.

Bite-Size Marketing Plans

Beverage Marketing Plan

When starting your beverage project, ensure you have identified the following:

- ☑ Who's your Avatar?
- ☑ How will you find the Avatar?
- ☑ How much will you pay?
- ☑ What's the price of the product?

The purpose of this document is not to go over these points but to sell a product, maybe write an email, website, or product description for Amazon or an eCommerce site. Without the answers to the above questions, you can't continue writing your plan.

It would help to calculate your Cost of Goods Sold, COGS, value and sales propositions, promise to the consumer, etc. The document grows and grows, and soon you have ten pages. You'll have enough content for a marketing plan, a website, emails, Amazon product description, and executive summary to help you raise capital. My point? Do it from the start! Identify the critical elements from your plan from the beginning instead of focusing only on your product ingredients or flavor.

Your new beverage needs a marketing plan!

Many people think that a marketing plan is not necessary. They think they can just wing it or figure it out as they go. Sometimes they think if they just spend big money on marketing, then their product will sell. You will spend a lot of time and money and achieve very few results.

When faced with the actual expenditure, either 4645 of time or money, developers don't know where to start. Even if you manage to identify your consumer, perhaps even a distributor, it will be too late because there will not be a mechanism to connect these fundamentals.

If you don't have a marketing plan, it will be challenging to put the product in distributors, retailers, and consumers' hands. Remember, your marketing plan is a guide you will use to land those distributors, retailers, and consumers. Your marketing plan is not just your advertising plan; it's not just a TV commercial or promotion. Your marketing plan is everything that involves the positioning, selling, and promotion of your brand, including pricing, sales, and distribution.

The bottom line is this: ensure you have a marketing plan.

Starting from Scratch:

Building Your Marketing Plan

B y the time you complete your marketing plan, you will know:

- ☑ What your expenditures will be per month, or distributor

- ☑ How you will support your distributors

- ☑ How much you will spend on retailers

- ☑ How you will support your retailers

- ☑ How you will ultimately reach out to your consumers and sell your product off the shelves

Your marketing plan includes this very critical information. To answer the above questions, we start at the very beginning.

Your marketing plan's starting point will be your executive summary, a one-to-two-page document summarizing the whole marketing plan. Your marketing plan's structure also applies to your overall business plan; both follow the same standard format.

Your marketing plan will also include information about your product—for example, photos, price points, size, look and feel, why it exists, everything you can think about your product.

Your marketing plan will also include essential budgetary information, all the financials relating to your brand support, including how much you spend per month in public relations, advertising, and marketing. Include all costs involved in supporting the brand, such as sales data broken down by channel, customer, state, city, country, retailer, and distributor. The more financial information you include in your marketing report, the better. The plan becomes a handy tool for all involved, including investors and employees, if or when you have them. These financials will serve as a roadmap for all to follow.

All marketing plans need to include information on the consumer, retailer, and distributor's pricing. You must explain every tier of your pricing plan in your marketing plan.

One often overlooked inclusion in your marketing plan will be information about your competition. Many new drink producers think they will not have competition because they are a unique product or a newly created niche. However, every product has competition. Every successful drink developer will know that and know who that competition is and then include that as part of an effective marketing plan to strategize and compete against them.

Finally, you will talk about yourself in your marketing plan—your background and experience—and also about your distribution channels.

All of this sounds like a lot because it is. You will be including a great deal of information in your marketing plan. And by including it, you will show to others and yourself that you have prepared and thoroughly researched your drink's marketing and profitability. Once you have covered all of these bases, you will be able to look back and see that you have a detailed roadmap for your drink and your business's success.

You don't have to have all of these answers right now. For the time being, you should be aware that you need to know these things eventually. As we progress through this chapter and the last part of this book, we will discuss each of these points in more detail and give you the information you need to research and make decisions to develop your marketing strategy.

Marketing Misconceptions

One reason entrepreneurs fail to create effective marketing plans is they do not understand what marketing is. Marketing is everything we've discussed. It is not just about advertising.

There is a vast misconception that marketing is just about the face of the product. We see projects where beverage entrepreneurs pay a singer or athlete to be the face of their product and think that's their marketing plan. They assume their marketing is complete because they've designed a product with a great name or look or because they market to a specific audience like motocross or athletes.

There is no doubt that sponsoring a high-profile figure or marketing to a targeted audience can be beneficial. We have spent some time driving home the importance of knowing your target market, and that is one way to connect with them. But just putting that famous face out there is not enough. You have to step beyond that and understand your target market.

Having a spokesperson or an identity for your drink is an excellent first step, but it's only a first step. The next step is to look beyond that persona to learn about your target market's actual identity.

Having a sponsor in mind helps give you a clearer idea of who your target market will be (which is not to say that you cannot accomplish that without a sponsor). For example, if you are appealing to the motocross rider, you have an extreme product; it needs specific colors and graphics to appeal to that type of buyer.

A sponsor or angle points out who you are trying to approach with your products and identifies the end consumer. It gives you a starting point because it gives you answers to important questions, like

- ✓ Who is your end consumer?
- ✓ Where do they buy their drink?
- ✓ What activity do they like to do?
- ✓ How frequently do they practice that activity?

Answering these questions starts defining the expenses you will incur to get to that target market. To develop a proper marketing plan, you need to go beyond that starting point and answer these questions. These are the answers that provide details translated into hard numbers, costs, expenses, and profits.

Exercises in Market Identification

"Online custom audiences provide you with instant data on what your Avatar wants, where they are, and how to sell to them, and it's free!"

Here is a relatively simple exercise that you can do to learn more about your target market and get the answers you need.

Google and Facebook can provide you with valuable data on audiences you can target with your advertising, or you can use their data for research, plug it into your marketing data, and advertise at a later date. For example, you could find who is interested in purchasing coffee in a geographical area by age, gender, and income.

Start by saying, "I have a new beverage, and I will sell it in a store." Understand that some beverages may not be sold in a store but instead a bar, restaurant, MLM, or by direct response.

Now you identify the store or location where you'll sell your beverage (if you're going with traditional distribution)

- Convenience store, chain, or independent store
- Restaurant instead of a store
- Supermarket or natural foods store
- Mass retail store
- Pharmacy
- Bar

☑ Night club

Then you start thinking about the type of customer you have and where they shop, start comparing that to where you're placing the product. Answer those questions first:

☑ What kind of consumer do I have?

☑ Where do they shop?

And then go further:

☑ How much money do they make?

☑ How much money are they willing to spend on your product?

☑ Do parents buy products for them?

☑ Are they men, women, teens, aged 16-35?

☑ What kind of car do they drive?

Your list can and should go on until you have the most detailed vision of your clientele and how and when they buy beverages. Everything you do in marketing will attract those consumers and the places that sell to them—the retailers and distributors that supply their drinks.

Here we begin to identify the distribution channels that will be specific to your drink. Once you identify the buyer and the target market, you then go back to your manufacturing point. Let's look at an example.

Let's suppose you are selling tea, green or iced tea, in a convenience store refrigerator. So you must ask yourself, "How do I get my product into a convenience store refrigerator?" There are a few possibilities. You could start at the national corporate level contacting 7-Eleven or Circle K, or perhaps you get a state-wide convenience store chain and sell them on your product.

But then how will the product get to the store? For that, you need a distributor. You have already determined that you have to sell the product to the convenience store and a beverage distributor, wholesaler, or another type of distributor. But how do you decide who to sell to? You have to figure out who already sells to the stores you are interested in.

Your Target Market Profile in Numbers

With the information we just garnered, we can begin to estimate your marketing costs. You have identified your distribution channel, whether that channel is a nightclub, hotel, convenience store, retail store, etc. Your sales outlet determines your numbers. Let's expand on that a bit to give you some idea of what you are looking at.

We are still talking target market. Since you've identified your target market and where they tend to shop, it could be a state-wide supermarket or convenience store chain, for example. Now you require traveling and sending your sales reps to visit these stores. You set up your budget profile and calculate the number of visits per year at an average cost of $2,500 per visit, depending on the city and length of stay. You can see how these travel costs begin to add up and hence why the financials become so important. Your target market helps define how much money you will spend on every sales channel.

Sponsorships may be another marketing expense you have to include. If you choose to sponsor a motocross rider to reach out to that specific target group, you will need a base figure to calculate your annual sponsoring costs. It would help if you kept in mind that you must commit for two or three years to get the valuable space to convert to sales when you sponsor someone. So not only do you have to determine the annual cost, but you have to prepare to pay that over several years.

Club events add another possibility and another level of costs. If your target market is likely to purchase your new drink at clubs, you'll need to include the fees of having club events. You may have to host one event per month at different clubs and cities. When you start calculating the costs of sponsoring those club events with one or two sales reps, you realize hosting events can be very expensive.

As you harvest these numbers, you want to track and include them in your marketing plan. Start very informally and make a list:

- ☑ My target market
- ☑ Where they shop
- ☑ What I need to do to reach my end consumer
- ☑ The frequency of communicating with my consumer

Think of all the possible scenarios and calculate real hard numbers that you can begin to plug into your planning spreadsheets. As we continue, we'll add to those numbers once we start determining costs for things like Point of Sale materials and trade show exhibitions, and so on.

Having accurate numbers is vital for budgeting, but it also serves a planning purpose. Once you know what you are looking at, you might decide that you have the funding to start with five markets simultaneously or that you can only afford to start selling in your city. You may realize you need twenty investors instead of five. These numbers will consolidate your marketing plan, so in the end, you have an excellent plan capable of supporting your beverage.

Competition as a Marketing Factor

People hold many myths about competition. Some do not see it as a marketing factor; they categorize it elsewhere. Others do not think they have competition because they have explicitly designed their product to serve a niche market. Neither of these is ever the case—there is always competition, and it is still a factor that impacts the marketing plan.

Competition is part of marketing because you need to know who the players are and what they're doing, what product they are selling, their price point, and their unique selling proposition. Why are they different from you and your product? When did they start their business venture? How much money do they have? Who is leading in the industry?

The worst mistake you can make is to assume you don't have competition. You have a beverage; even if it is a niche beverage, there are always other beverage choices out there, and consumers can choose to drink your new beverage or a different kind of drink.

All drink types have categories and subcategories. You might have developed a sports drink, tea, energy drink, energy shot, soda, or alcoholic beverage. You could have a variety of different products. All of them have competition, and they are all in competition with each other, ultimately.

Let's look at another example. If you develop an organic vodka and think you have no competition because there is no other organic vodka, you're wrong. Other vodkas are competing with yours. So just being different or having a unique selling proposition doesn't mean you don't have competition.

Now, how can you research your competition?

You can start by going to local markets, clubs, or convenience stores' shelves and looking at the products. Compare the products' size, presentation, labels, colors, and evaluate their positioning statement. What is their pricing? Are they on sale? All of this information helps you see who is out there and what they are selling. Learn from them, from their mistakes, and their successes. It could give you an idea of what you need to do or what you could do better.

At the end of the day, when it comes to the competition, you can generalize or be product or category-specific; but realize that either way, you are competing for two things—shelf space and customer attention.

It doesn't matter what your niche or direct competition is for real estate (shelf space). Real estate doesn't grow. The shelf spaces remain the same as they were ten years ago and will continue to be the same for years to come. You are fighting for the same cooler area as all beverages have been doing all along. It might be a soda or tea, but it doesn't matter what the other product is; you're competing for a single slot. It would help convince the retailer that you deserve that space either because your product is the next up-and-coming drink or because your specific flavor is better-tasting than the competition.

Realize that if your products are trying to go where other products are doing well, it will be tough to get the space you are looking for. Your competition has space, and they are holding on to the market. So when you go out and shop the shelf, you have to figure out who is in your space and who you need to remove. It would be best to see how they are succeeding to know how you can best fill that need and thus make room for yourself.

The other aspect of competition, once you are on the shelf, is the customer's attention. That customer will walk into the store with money in his pocket, thirsty (the biggest motivator in buying beverages), or looking for a particular flavor. Now you are fighting for their attention with the drinks sitting next to you. Whether you think you are competing against a similar product or an unrelated one has nothing to do with it—there is only so much they are willing to spend. Your competition is now every single product in that cooler—no question about it. You must have all your elements strategically aligned to get that dollar.

Channel Pricing

Pricing is a marketing factor, and your channel will be a significant determinant. For example, if you sell your product in natural food stores in the refrigerator next to other functional drinks for double the price, you'll have difficulty selling. Let's suppose the competition is selling for $1.99, and you are selling for $3.99. The customer will look at your product, compare it with the other product, and wonder if there's a pricing mistake. In the consumer's mind, your product is much more expensive in comparison to other similar products. Sure, you might have a unique tea or juice, but the perceived shelf value does not explain that neither does the price fluctuation, and there is the problem.

In contrast, if you direct a customer to your website, where you play a video explaining your product and detailing the unique ingredients, vitamins, or flavor in your functional beverage, you have the opportunity to sell directly to your consumer. Here there are no other beverage videos, no interruptions, no direct channel competition; it's just you and your potential customer. You can try and convince them to pay double the price, including shipping. You might persuade them to buy an entire case or a case every month.

See pricing as a competitive advantage whenever possible. This doesn't mean you need to be cheaper than the competition, not at all. You could be more expensive. I don't recommend you be the least expensive product. Instead, you can sell at a higher price and offer rebates, specials, or coupons, giving the perception of higher value at all times. Consumers always like a good deal. Offer a special of "50% Off Regular Price", or "Buy 1 Get 1 Free", or "Buy Two For One." In other words, you intend to be competitive on price while keeping the perception of a higher value. Your customer perceives they're getting an incredible deal for the best beverage they can buy, and they feel good. When your customer feels good, you're closer to establishing an emotional connection. The above is an example of using price as a marketing tool, not just a financial instrument or an elasticity economic indicator.

Competitive Price

"Pricing includes your profit and that of the
distributor and retailer."

When you think of your competitive pricing, think of your profit margins and the profit margins of everyone involved in your supply chain. How much money will Amazon make? Or your salespeople or the distributor's salespeople? How about the distributor or the retailer? Are you incentivizing everyone in your supply chain with profit? Remember, it's not just the price alone. If you sell more products, they also make more money, so ensure the combination of pricing and turns is there.

Pricing is part of your competition but also part of your unique selling proposition. We will focus on this competitive/marketing aspect of pricing. We will continue to do this again in sales and distribution because pricing is tied everywhere with your product—production, shipping, distribution, retail, and consumer. You need to consider different pricing strategies and how each might apply to your drink or range of drink products.

When we start analyzing the price, we try to conveniently set up a price structure for all parties, consumers, retailers, and distributors. One thing to always consider is the gross margin since it is part of the marketing plan.

If you look at some of the brands out there, they market their product by saying it is very inexpensive to the consumer. Their marketing strategy becomes "we are the every day, low-price beverage." On the opposite end of that spectrum, you have those who position themselves as a premium product. They don't go to the customer and say, "Look how expensive we are!" Their message instead is, "Our product stands out because it is superior and worth more of your money."

In either of the above scenarios, what matters is to get in the distributors' and retailers' faces and show them a product with an attractive profit margin. So the strategy in the second scenario is not just about being expensive; it is about the bottom line to profitability. Here you are telling the distributor and retailer, "See that product on your shelf doing a couple of turns per week? I probably won't do that many, but the returns with my product will be much greater."

We've seen this strategy in the new premium beverage market, giving everyone a premium mark-up for the product so that fewer turns are necessary. The product is more exclusive. It's a trading-up phenomenon where consumers are trading up to get a better product because they can, and it feels good! The real winners are the retailers and distributors. The brands give them more and pump more money into marketing. The retailer and distributor's pricing is great, and they love these premium drinks because their burden is lessened, and they're not being crunched anymore.

This strategy cannot work for every beverage, but there is a place in the market for drinks at all price points. The bottom line is that when you are setting up your pricing, you should remember you have two buying elements to please—the consumer buyer and the retail/distributor buyer. How you do that is entirely up to you, but we will discuss when we talk about setting up price structures later on.

Before we leave this topic entirely, let's take a minute to look at an example of how the pricing for a product might affect how you market to retailers and distributors. We'll use water as an example because it hosts a vast range of prices for very similar products.

The price points on water are fascinating—they're all over the place. Evaluating the different products, pricing, and placement in a store can tell you a lot about managing and marketing your product to distributors and retailers.

Let's consider the waters you might see at the average retail supermarket. You see a deal for a $3.99 case (16-ounce bottle, 24 bottle case). There is a full end-cap with 50 to 60 cases, and each of these cases is only selling for $3.99. That means the retailer is not making much money, probably only making about 15 to 20 points per case.

If you go to the beverage aisle, you might see a single bottle of premium water selling for $3.99. What does that imply in terms of marketing?

It implies that the producer selling those $3.99 cases of water probably has a broker selling directly to the retailer in truckload quantities. It means that in his marketing plan, there is probably only room for a broker and transportation company—there is no margin to support anyone else. In turn, this determines their entire distribution model (which we will talk about in the coming chapter).

Now you look at premium beverages like Fiji Water. Depending on where you shop, they are selling at a margin of a couple of dollars per case or bottle. At that rate, they net ten times the producer's profit selling the $3.99 cases above. Fiji Water is a product with enough margin to accommodate not only a broker and transporter but a distributor, importer, and retailer, too. They all get their "piece of the pie." The product is marked up at a rate of 5% for the broker, 20% for the distributor, and 30-40% for the retailer. There is a lot of margin on a product like that to support all involved. Visualize this example in the following illustration.

Premium Water Brand vs. Alternative Brand

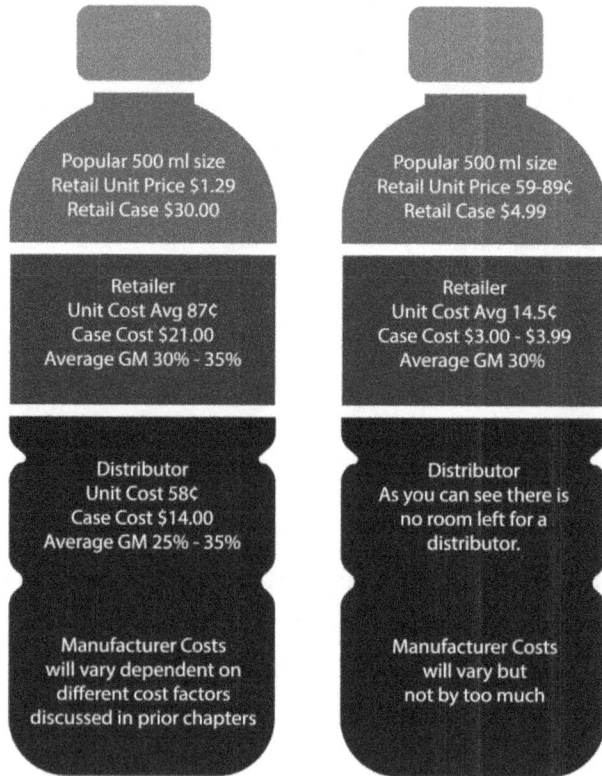

Popular 500 ml size
Retail Unit Price $1.29
Retail Case $30.00

Retailer
Unit Cost Avg 87¢
Case Cost $21.00
Average GM 30% - 35%

Distributor
Unit Cost 58¢
Case Cost $14.00
Average GM 25% - 35%

Manufacturer Costs
will vary dependent on
different cost factors
discussed in prior chapters

Popular 500 ml size
Retail Unit Price 59-89¢
Retail Case $4.99

Retailer
Unit Cost Avg 14.5¢
Case Cost $3.00 - $3.99
Average GM 30%

Distributor
As you can see there is
no room left for a
distributor.

Manufacturer Costs
will vary but
not by too much

Diagram 2.1 – Premium vs. Regular Water Brands

I don't mean to scare you into producing the wrong product but rather to get you thinking about pricing from a marketing perspective. You need to know there are many elements involved in your product's pricing, and you need to accommodate each of them from the very start. Some of those elements could include a

- ☑ Brokers—to help you open retail, wholesale, and distributor accounts (still taking from your margin)
- ☑ Employees
- ☑ Commissioned salespeople
- ☑ Distributors
- ☑ Retailers

Even if you intend your product to go directly from the warehouse to the retailer, you still need to accommodate the margins for all those elements so that you have the room to grow your product and distribution later. If you decide to get more distribution, your pricing should allocate all those margins for the people you need in the middle. Remember, pricing impacts your marketing plan, and it is all intertwined. Pricing is essential to your marketing plan at every single level!

Positioning the Product

"Positioning is how your product fits in the marketplace. If you don't position it, the market will position it for you."

Positioning is another essential part of your marketing plan. To many people, positioning is what the marketing plan is all about—how will you sell your product? How is it different? What is your product's appeal?

When somebody asks you, "Tell me about your product in one sentence," your answer is your positioning statement. As you prepare your positioning statement, avoid saying "tastes great" or "has a great package." It needs to be something else, something more.

This part of your marketing plan will be your positioning statement, your elevator pitch. What you need to do here is explain very briefly why your product is better. This section is not a complete business plan; it's only a summary. Some of the things you want to clarify would be

- ✅ Are you part of a small or vast category?

- ✅ Are you creating a new category altogether?

- ✅ Are you competing based on price? For example, is your positioning statement that you are the lowest-priced drink?

- ✅ Are you competing based on a characteristic? For example, do you sell organic soda?

- ✅ Where will your product sell?

- ✅ What is your positioning?

It's interesting how one thing leads to another. Again, the positioning touches back on your target market—your target market determines your competition, your competition determines pricing, and pricing leads into positioning; and that reflects directly back to that target market. To look at some examples, (again) your positioning might be price-based, or it could be a unique flavor or category or a new and emerging type of ingredient. We see the acai fruit as the emerging antioxidant, so some look for the latest and best antioxidant and try out others to top them, like hydrogen.

For all of these, the positioning must be apparent so that everything that feeds off it (pricing, market, etc.) works. If you position your product as high-end, you have to ensure that your pricing structure is aligned. Position your product similar to your competition to avoid confusing your consumer. You want it to be clear that yours is one of the premium beverages they are shopping for. It would be best if you communicated this clearly in your positioning statement and marketing plan.

Packaging & Marketing Planning

I often see my clients spend the most time designing their packages, in particular their labels. It's good to invest hours on your label, but not months. When I create a label, I write an extensive brief for the designer. I've decided on the colors, patterns, fonts, and images. The designer takes my ideas and turns them into a label, package, display, poster, website, or book cover. The more detail and research I give to the artist, the better results I get back, and the fewer corrections I make.

When you're developing your package, you already know that you're creating it for your Avatar; that's clear. But here is something new, you should also develop your package for the specific channel. If you sell your beverage on a refrigerator door, your package should be designed for your Avatar and for your Avatar shopping in that particular refrigerator door. You should consider the size, weight, feel, and colors when selling at that retail location. The same is true if it sells on a store counter or Amazon or if it's meant for kids or adults. Consider if your product will be packed in cases with trays or boxes.

When I look at a package, I try to imagine it on the shelf. I see it close up and from afar. Imagine a consumer walking down the aisle and seeing your product. Imagine it on a shelf, but not at eye level, instead close to the floor. How does it look down there? Will it make it? Will it sell despite poor merchandising?

One of the things you have to remember in terms of packaging from a marketing standpoint is that you have different product packages and various packaging elements that all work to market your product. It's not just about the product itself but also the bottle size, liquid quantity, type, and size of the master case.

For example, you might choose a six, eight, or twelve-ounce can. You may decide on a large sixteen or twenty-ounce can or bottle packaged in a slick can. It could be glass, plastic, or aluminum. It all depends on your positioning statement and your marketing plan, which depends on your target market. If you target a high-end consumer and use a flimsy plastic bottle with a cheap-looking label, something is wrong with your positioning concerning the packaging.

Another packaging factor to consider is the master case. Do you sell your beverage in singles, doubles, six or twelve-pack, or maybe you only offer your drink by the case? The answer depends on where you are selling it, either in a convenience store, supermarket, bar, or restaurant. Here, you can see how everything ties together with positioning, target marketing, pricing, and the essence you want to give your product. Everything has something to do with that essence.

It's all about staying consistent. Don't confuse your consumer and position your product in a way that doesn't appeal to them. When talking about packaging and marketing, let's take the example of the housewife. More often than not, she may purchase beverages for the entire family. It will help if you package the product to sell conveniently to her, for example, a 24 bottle case or a six-pack. If it is not very economical, you might look at a four-pack. If it's positioned as a sports drink, it needs a sports cap. If it's intended for children, it needs to be spill-proof in re-closable plastics.

Those factors play a critical role, so you go to your packaging once you determine your position and positioning statement. That packaging has to be 100% in line with that position statement.

If you want to review the mechanics of packaging, you can look back to the packaging chapter, but right now, we are talking strictly from a marketing standpoint—*What will people think when they see your product?* Do they know what's inside just by looking at it? Look at all the small details like your font and the quality of your plastic. Should your bottle be made of something more eco-friendly, like glass, bio-plastic, or a new material altogether? Is your bottle part of your best-selling proposition? This all has to do with your packaging, and it all speaks volumes about your product.

Keep in mind packaging is always a perfect excuse to re-launch your product at any time of the year. This is not to say that you can afford to get it wrong in the first place because your sales will not survive that, but it is to say that packaging is an excellent marketing tool with endless potential. But for you to do this, you have to build that cost into your marketing plan from the start.

As you develop your marketing plan in the early stages, include the costs and budget to allow you to revamp and re-launch your packaging based on a chosen time frame, which could be two, four, or six months. Whatever timeframe you think works before your product needs that little added marketing push. In terms of the numbers, you need to budget for the changes you foresee. You can do this incrementally to ensure you always have something new to offer. For example, you might introduce a new and improved version in four or six months or start selling singles, switch to four-packs, and then present an eight-pack. You could introduce a new line, a different color or flavor, or take advantage of your sponsorships, like being an exclusive sponsor of the Olympics or a motocross rider, etc. All of these are great ideas that you need to account for from the start.

Now is the time to go back to your spreadsheet and figure that every two to six months, you may need to allocate more money, time, and research into the packaging, accommodating those changes in a way that will be consistent with your marketing plan. Again, this adds a layer of costs every four months or so, but it will keep your package fresh and innovative and keep your consumers coming back to find out what you will come up with next.

To be sure, customers are always looking for something new and innovative, so your packaging plays a critical role in your ongoing expenses. At a minimum, you will want to make this change and accommodation every six months. If you keep providing that innovation, they will keep buying from you, but they will look for excitement elsewhere when you become old and stale.

Take a look at the list below with some changes to one of America's more popular drinks, Gatorade. Today Gatorade is still the official drink of the NFL. They have made improvements to their product line over the years. These include all types of changes; label (design, material, and colors), container (size, shape, and material), closure (size, color, material, shape, and functionality), and in some cases with none or very little change to the actual product inside. Undoubtedly, you'll recognize many of these product changes and the media's role in emphasizing their success.

The first batches of Gatorade came in glass bottles, but it was soon apparent that the packaging needed to be as tough as the people who drink Gatorade. Plastic coolers, plastic bottles, and powdered drink mixes were developed to help make Gatorade easier to consume.

- Originally came in a 32oz glass bottle with metal closure
- Plastic bottle but the same traditional shape
- Introduction of various bottle sizes
- From paper label to plastic label
- Sports caps (multiple styles over the years)
- New, untraditional flavors
- Catchy flavor names
- More recently, innovations in the form of Gatorade ICE, Endurance Formula, Rain, Xtreme, AM, Fierce, Frost, Tiger, and G2

We've discussed most of the major points that go into your overall marketing plan. We know we have given you a lot of information, but it is crucial for a successful new beverage. However, we are still not entirely done.

As we move on to the following few chapters, we will continue to discuss your marketing plan's essential parts. Like those discussed here, these are both stand-alone elements and integral parts of the overall strategy. In the interest of giving them their due attention, we will start to separate some of these more significant and yet unattended issues. We'll start where we've left off here with the Point of Sale and Point of Purchase material.

Jorge S. Olson

"POP IS NOT A LUXURY,
IT'S A NECESSITY!"

268

CHAPTER 20

Marketing: Point of Sale, Promotion & Distribution

Rapid Knowledge Section

I had a company in San Diego, California, that only existed because of POS, or Point of Sale. The company's fundamental basis, or business model, was Point of Sale, from the products, packaging, and pricing to the training, salespeople, and how we placed merchandise in the store. Everything was all and only POS.

We had no advertising, no social media, no google ads, nothing else, only great signs and positioning in the store. I was a POS maniac and made sure every store was loaded with posters, pricing stickers, clear messaging, and stacked with products. It was all impulse buy products, and it survived because it had great signage.

Retail POS

You need a few things for your POS formula to make sure you have the basics covered in a retail store.

Here is my five-point POS formula:

- ☑ Static-Sticker on the refrigerator door
- ☑ Sticker on the store door
- ☑ Poster on the store window
- ☑ Pole sign in a visible spot
- ☑ Pricing on the refrigerator and shelf

The Purpose of POS and POP

We're moving on now to Point of Sale or Point of Purchase materials. Later in this chapter, we will tie this with promotion. Both are a massive part of your marketing efforts, and so are considerable parts of your marketing plan. This is the first time we've talked in-depth about Point of Sale and Point of Purchase (POS and POP) materials and promotions. We thought to give it just a little more attention by placing it in its own chapter. Along the way, we will continue to discuss POS in terms of the marketing plan as well.

You probably have an idea of what POS materials include, although we can venture to guess that it contains more than what you have envisioned. We will detail what these materials are, but before we do, let's take a minute to clarify the purpose behind using POP or POS materials. (Please note we'll be using these terms interchangeably. These are two different names for the same thing).

POP materials' purpose is communication; it is to communicate a specific message. There are two groups with whom you will be using these materials:

- **Consumers.** The first of the groups is your consumer. Most of the focus of POS materials will be on consumer communication.

- **Buyers.** The second group is buyers and category buyers (on the sales and distribution end).

You cannot be out in the field at all times communicating with people and convincing them to buy your products, so you need valuable POS materials to speak for you. You also need helpful materials to talk to category buyers and plan how your beverage will reach those consumers and help them increase sales. First, we will focus on that larger audience, the consumer, and talk about how you use POS materials to convey a message to them.

What are POS Materials?

Now that you understand who you will be communicating with, we can talk about how you can do that.

There are many, many types of point of sale materials that you might use. These include things like

- Posters
- Price clings
- Racks
- Photos
- Signs

- ☑ Pallets

- ☑ Stickers

- ☑ Static Stickers

- ☑ 3-D cutouts

- ☑ Poll Signs

Many other things could fall into this category, but we are referring to in-store advertising or in-store promotions (those things placed at the point where the purchase is made).

A broader definition of POS might also include the message you are sending or the action taking place within the store. It can be information/activities such as:

- ☑ Pricing

- ☑ Benefits

- ☑ Information and updates

- ☑ Sampling

- ☑ Special events

In this sense, POS would refer more to the message and not the actual materials that deliver it, but you will see that it is all very much related when we tie this together in the end.

Why POS Works

"If POS is your only communication with your consumer, how would you use it?"

The real thing to understand about POS materials is their function and potential. POP materials are one of the best communication tools to target a consumer right when it matters—at the point in time when they are going to make that final decision and make the buy. It is your last opportunity, your last breath, your last chance to tell the consumer, "Reach for this product!" That is really why we use POP; we use it to sell. It's your sales rep at the store, there for you every day when no one else can be.

Although exterior advertising certainly has a place, it's the "in-your-face" in-store POS that proves effective. Many people start advertising outside the store, without knowing that the best advertising goes on inside. If you get your consumer that close [physically] to the product, whether they are close to deciding to buy it or not, you still have that one last opportunity to say, "Buy me!" And you have a chance to tell them, very briefly, why they should buy it. Your poster, sticker, all your POS combined say this product, and you belong together. And it is those materials that present you with that final opportunity.

To fully understand the impact, you can look at the products that do not effectively use POS materials. As you'll see, there'll be other products on the shelf without POS materials, and the chances are if that consumer did not come into the store ready to buy that specific product, they would not buy it. It'll show because these are the products that no one is reaching for, doing no turns, and eventually fading from existence in the marketplace for lack of effective promotions.

Maintaining In-Demand POS Materials

The demise of un-promoted products shows you the importance of including POS in your marketing plan and effectively implementing it. In that interest, there are some things you need to be aware of that will help you as you make decisions about the types of POS you employ, not least of all because this is a cost that can quickly become a costly wasted effort if you continue unaware.

Keep in mind as you budget, plan, and design your POS materials that the competition likes to take it down (and, to a lesser extent, store personnel as they work to refresh displays). It is easy for them to do that, too. You will regularly have your competitors walk into the stores and remove your POS materials as they restock and replace them with their own. You shouldn't let this offend or upset you because it's how the game is played, and it will happen again and again. So your POS is an ongoing investment. You'll pay for it once, and then every time it's taken down (which is at least a couple of times each week), it'll cost you in some way again. At the very least, it will cost the time it takes to have it up again. It may cost you in materials replacement, as well, if the materials are not well-cared for.

This is where the design takes on added importance because if you develop POS materials that are catchy and the retailer likes (the one calling the shots in the store), you'll have an ally on your side. They'll take care of your materials because they are attractive and add to the store's atmosphere.

Good POS design goes even further than maintenance, though. If you create the right POS, you also create a demand for it. Take Budweiser, for instance—attractive neon signs are one of their hallmark POS materials, and retailers fight to get them in their stores. They call up and ask for them without having to be asked to display them at all. Of course, neon signs are a more expensive example, but the same concept applies to more affordable POS materials, too. If you design posters in line with the times and complement the store's vibe, they will fight for those also. They'll happily display, take care, and ask you to bring them more.

Something else to keep in mind is that materials (actual construction materials) can really make the difference. For example, if you have a metal sign—something attractive that stands out—your retailer will help keep that on the shelf, wall, or pole and keep it looking nice. It will indeed cost you more initially, but it can pay off in the end. When your POS is just right and retailers like it, you can count on it being there for quite a while. Long story short, don't be afraid to spend a little more on your POS materials, as it can be the very thing that helps increase your products' sales.

Good material design is the place to start, but there is more to know about effectively utilizing POS. First off, we have to remember that everyone is responsible for POS materials (even though you may have to create the incentive to make them share that feeling). This applies to the retailer, distributor, and you, the manufacturer.

One of your primary responsibilities is to make the retailer responsible for promoting your specials and promotions and running the programs you are running with them. But as we said, the distributor also bears responsibility, as do you. You will need to train your distributors in your specific programs and teach them how to use POP materials properly. Many distributors have their own merchandisers, which means you will need to train them, the salespeople, or delivery people, so they know how to use your POS. You may even have contests with them as an incentive to make sure they follow through.

Ultimately, you are responsible for your POS material. The only way to ensure it is appropriately used is to get out there in the field—visit some stores and see what they have. Consider hiring a regional manager in specific territories so they can go into stores and see if your POS is being used and see first-hand that the material is there and that the message, pricing, and promotion are clear.

A Note about Racks and Displays

One final thing that we would like to add here is a note about racks and displays. We briefly mentioned these in our list as POP materials, but we should also point out the broader purpose they can sometimes serve.

There are all sorts of racks and displays, including disposable cardboard racks, called shippers. These can be very helpful in positioning and identifying the promoted product. They can also help you avoid slotting fees because they do not take an actual space on a shelf—they are their own shelf space. Effectively, they present an opportunity for the retailer to bring in a new product and try it out without losing shelf space to current products (space they may be hesitant or unwilling to give up to a newcomer). Here is a product that comes with its own shelf and promotion, courtesy of the manufacturer. Having racks or displays will often grant you entry into a store as a trial product, allowing you to prove yourself through sales. Shippers can help get your product in the door, introduce the product, and slide into a region or city with a couple of hundred stores without having to change the schematics.

POS isn't only just about selling to consumers; it's also about helping open new accounts. In this way, POP plays a critical role in how you get into a store, even if it's only for a trial period. This opens different opportunities—it could be an in-and-out seasonal presence, or it could be your big long-standing ticket in the door. The reality is that POS is not just a consumer tool; it is also a tool that can get you into stores and selling.

Bringing Together the Message and the Material

So we understand what the purpose of POP is, and we know some of the tools and materials that we might be using in that effort. We can begin to look at how this magic happens by looking at some of its applications.

Pricing is historically one of the more generic uses of POP materials. Still, today that trend has moved away from just laying out your price and conveying your product's message instead. Instead of having giant posters exclaiming the price, you have materials more in line with your product's packaging and positioning. The price may not even be mentioned. Instead, you will likely have materials with lovely, colorful pictures or illustrations showing what product you are selling and its price, all reflecting your positioning. To echo your positioning, you might include your sponsored motorcycle or athlete on there (because that's not something that will go on your can, it's something that goes on your billboards, advertisements, and your POS materials).

Whether you realize it or not, you've seen these types of POS materials a million times. You may walk into a store and see a pole sign celebrating Cinco de Mayo, for example. It could be promoting any event, announcing a sponsorship, delivering a message, such as a new and improved package. These types of materials work as tiny "billboards," if you will, inside the grocery store or the convenience market. Likewise, these can include materials in windows or on doors that consumers see as they come in. Before the consumer walks into the store, they're already being told what to buy.

Budgeting, Financials, and POP

"POP is not a luxury, it's a necessity!"

Understanding how to use POP materials is imperative, but we also have to understand their relevance in the master plan—the marketing plan. In addition to what we've already covered, we have to consider POS materials for the budget.

Before we talk about the numbers, we need to clarify: point-of-sale materials are not a luxury. They are not optional. They are vital, and they absolutely must be included in your budget. POS materials will be one of the first things distributors and retailers request when you walk in their doors. They will flat-out ask you, "What kind of POS do you have? What kind of POS will you send me?" If you do not provide POS, they will not take you seriously, and you will not get accounts.

You need to create a POS budget and include it in your marketing plan and financials. We need to return to your spreadsheet and add some numbers to the financials column to represent POS efforts and materials.

You'll need to allocate a budget or an amount of POS for every case that sells. The traditional way to figure this is to give a fixed amount of POS for every ten cases of product sold. The distributor or retailer gets a certain number of pole signs, posters, stickers, or signs. If you are spending a lot of money in a particular store or chain, you may increase that amount to include more prominent signs to support money spent on shelf space and end caps.

POP materials will paint a significant part of the picture on your budget spreadsheet. You also need to be aware of, and accommodate for, the fact that POS is an ongoing expense, not a one-time cost, so you need to allocate for POS materials every month of your budget.

Promotion, Promotion, Promotion

With POS materials covered, we now need to move on to promotion. As you might expect, promotion plays an integral role in the success of your new beverage.

Promotion is a broad term that covers a wide range of activities to get your product sold. Promotion means one thing and answers one question: How will you sell your product to the consumer?

We've already talked about reaching distributors and retailers, and we will revisit that in later parts of the book, but now we decide how you will get your end consumer. For this, there are many tools as well, including:

- ☑ Advertising
- ☑ POS material
- ☑ In-store promotions or sampling events
- ☑ Club events (depending on your product)
- ☑ Special parties for consumers
- ☑ Events near your target market (such as at a school or university)

The above gives you an idea of *what* you might do, but you also need to consider *how* you will do it.

It would be best to tie in everything we have discussed in these last couple of marketing chapters. You need to know

- ☑ Who is your target market?
- ☑ Who is your competition?
- ☑ What is your pricing?
- ☑ What is your positioning statement?
- ☑ What packaging are you using?
- ☑ What is your sales and distribution structure?

The answers to the above questions will tell you the type of promotion you need depending on your product, target market, and pricing.

If you identified your target market before or have one in mind, go back to it now. That target market has led you to promotions and how you will promote your product. If you have been following along with a spreadsheet, this is the time to take that out again. If you are doing events, add a line calculating

- ☑ The number of events you will do per city
- ☑ The number of cities you will have events in
- ☑ The frequency of the events
- ☑ The size of the events

You should also consider the different types of promotions you might undertake. These could include online promotions, events, or demonstrations, and they each need to be measurable. They need to be budgeted and calculated in a way that allows you to see what your associated expenditures will be; you need to know how much money they will cost, for how long, and the frequency of repeating the promotions.

For example, if you launch two hundred in-store promotions in one month, you can use that as a basis for the next city, perhaps adjusting the number up or down as necessary when you open a new territory. Back on your spreadsheet, those promotions need to be ongoing expenses. Make no doubt about it; advertisements are an investment, but they are an ongoing investment that shouldn't stop. If you stop promoting your products, then your competition may step in and take your sales. This way, promotion is, as it always will be, both an initial investment and an ongoing budgetary expense.

POP – Working with Distributors

Promotions, including Point of Sale material, and Point of Sale promotions, such as sampling, educational, and other in-store promotions, are among the best tools you have to open retail accounts and even wholesale distributors.

Your potential retailers and distributors are all very interested in how you plan to sell this product off the shelf. Like POS, they want to see a reliable promotions plan in line with the product and its target market. Whenever you go to visit a distributor, retailer, independent retailer, or chain, make sure you have a copy of your promotional plan with you so that you can show them step by step:

- How you will help them put the product into the store
- How you will help them sell it off the shelves—by using promotions like events, advertising, PR, and sponsorships

I would like to share one of our recommendations for new drink developers; all drink developers, really. When you draft the promotion and marketing plan, be sure to include pictures so your product, marketing, and promotion look very well planned. Use authentic images of your actual events and preparations showing promoters all in product uniform, people trying your drink next to a table with signs promoting the product. These may seem like simple details, but it is those details that will give your distributor and retailer the proof that you are not just talking; you have a simple, executable, well-scripted presentation that they can rely on and which will ultimately equate to product selling off the shelf.

Final Measurements

You now know the importance of measuring promotion-related costs and budgeting for them in measurable ways. Once you start executing the plan and hosting promotions and events, there is one other measurement you need to attend to—measuring the event's effects.

What this comes down to is this:

- ☑ Documenting everything you do for each event

- ☑ Testing and tracking

It would help if you documented everything involved with each promotion; if something does not work, you will have the information and opportunity to fix and fine-tune your efforts and expenditures. Continually doing this will lead to better and better promotions time after time.

The other side of the equation is tracking and testing. You need to do whatever you can to make the effects of your promotions measurable. Not all results will be directly measurable, but tracking is crucial whenever you find a way to do it—all the information you gather will have value and will be worth the effort to collect. You want to track the success of promotional campaigns and strategies. Whenever possible, calculate how much time and money you spent and how much money or product you sold due to the event. Another way to measure the result is to track how many accounts you landed from that particular promotion.

Knowing that you seek to measure your success can affect which events and promotions you choose to run. For example, one of our favorite events is doing in-store demonstrations. The results are almost instantly measurable and can also include helpful feedback about your product and promotion—information that you can use to further perfect your efforts.

The advantage of in-store demonstrations is that, first off, you are directly up against your competition when you are in the store. A potential customer walks into the store with only a set amount of money to spend, with a decision to make before he reaches the check-out line. He has the product he's bought for years, and then he has your product, the newcomer on the scene. He knows nothing about your product— the taste, smell, or feeling it will give him when he tries it. He's bargaining and doesn't know what he's bargaining for. But here you are to promote your product, and you may just be able to sway him.

Moreover, the results of that encounter are measurable. Your salesperson will know how much product was on the shelf when they got to that store, and they can tell you how much inventory is left after the in-store demonstration ends. Subsequent sales numbers will tell you if that promotion had a lasting effect and created a loyal customer who keeps coming back and buying again and again. In addition to sales data, though, that promoter also has a rare opportunity to speak directly with your consumer and collect feedback from the very markets you are trying to target with sales. They can give you consumer feedback, what promotion elements appear to be working as intended, and what you should change the next time. It is a straightforward way to achieve the measurability and results that you need for your promotions to succeed.

The above is just one example of how a promotion can work for you and how you need to measure those results and turn them into valuable marketing data. There are other ways, undoubtedly, but the end goal is always the same—to help your products sell off the shelves and find measurable strategies for continuing that momentum.

Distribution Structure in Relation to the Marketing Plan

As we wrap up these two chapters on the marketing plan, we need to take a few moments to touch on the sales and distribution structure. The distribution structure is a topic which we will explore further in the next chapter, but it is also one that is elemental to the marketing plan, and so is an issue that we need to address before we can conclude the discussion on the new beverage marketing plan.

First of all, we need to say that you need a distribution model. Like marketing, this is not something you can make up as you go—you need to plan for it in advance. You need to understand what it takes to distribute a product and the different distributors and retailers to decide which is best for your product and target market.

Your specific distribution structure as a whole depends on your product, its pricing, and weight. Not every distributor will ship a heavy product, glass product, or an oversized product. The costs for shipping will directly affect who you sell to and how you distribute your product. Specific options will be open to some products, where others will be closed, and vice versa. If you refer back to those pricing examples we looked at several pages ago, you can learn a bit about how you will set up your sales and distribution structure.

For instance, if you looked at your pricing and figured you need a broker, importer, distributor, and retailer, all of these layers will dictate what the distribution structure looks like and what options you have. There are sometimes places where you can skip a level. Your distribution structure may accommodate for it because you are dealing with a retailer who allows you the flexibility of missing a couple of layers. If your price or product follows a specific distribution structure, your sales will be right in line. Again, the pricing dictates the sales, and the sales dictate the distribution structure.

If this seems vague and confusing now, do not be alarmed; at this point, with the minimal knowledge you have about sales and distribution, it should be. Distribution is probably one of the single most extensive chapters of this book. It will become much clearer after you read the next chapter. Now, know that once you have that information, you need to bring it back here and work it into your marketing and overall business plans. Ensure you realize the importance of the decision-making phase of developing the distribution structure to build the most effective and profitable marketing plan for your new beverage.

*"EVERY PROGRAM
HAS TO BE DESIGNED
TO DRIVE SALES."*

CHAPTER 21

Beverage Distribution Model

"Distributors help you scale; however, you shouldn't see distributors as salespeople. It's not their job to open accounts for you."

Rapid Knowledge Section

If it's not too late, work on your distribution model before you even start your beverage development process. If you have already started developing your drink, stop and focus on this first. It's much more critical.

As I'm writing this book, I'm developing several beverages and already speaking with distributors. I also designed their entire distribution model using a profit calculator to see how they can grow their business, how much money they need to grow, and how fast they can grow.

Landing distributors is not tricky. I've never worked on a project where I didn't use distributors, retailers, or salespeople. On the other hand, I've had plenty of projects where the brand didn't support the distributors properly. The lesson here is that distributors worry that brands will not help them nor keep their marketing promise.

Introduction to Beverage Distribution Modeling

You can find many types of distributors in the USA and other countries. I've owned distribution companies in the USA and Mexico with beverage distribution, non-beverage distribution, and a mixture of beverage and non-beverage products. My point is you can get many types of distributors for your products, and you should not be boxed into any one business model. It will help if you develop your distribution business model even before you start your beverage company. In this distribution model, try to understand the different types of distributors available to you.

When you go down the path of beverage distribution, you'll need to run the numbers. It's essential to know how much your retailer and distributor are making and how much you're making after your cost of goods, shipping, and other expenses. Most of it is math, but before we calculate percentages and margins, we need to decide if wholesale distribution is the way to go for you. Will you sell to beverage distributors or wholesalers? Will you sell to retailers and maybe to bars and restaurants?

You don't need distributors anymore, where you couldn't sell beverages without them a few years ago. Now, with direct-to-consumer options, you could sell directly to retail supermarkets or skip the supermarkets altogether and go directly to the consumers. After all, even if you sell to distributors, you'll communicate with your consumers with social media and live events.

This chapter details the essentials to develop the best distribution plan for your specific beverage. The result is that structure is what you will include in your marketing plan. But first, you need to know how to get it there.

This chapter talks about everything related to distribution—what distributors want, the different types of distributors from the small to the regional and huge distributors. We also include wholesalers, direct store delivery distributors, your independent distribution, warehouse programs, and all the other different forms and options for distributing your beverage.

This chapter will focus primarily on the distribution structure itself. In the following chapters, focused on sales, we will close the loop on distribution and talk about selling to these distributors. Still, first, we need you to understand what the various distribution channels look like so you'll realize your approach when it does come time to sell. You will go away from this chapter knowing what type of distributors you have available for your particular beverage, where they are, and the difference between distributors' tiers. We'll explore all possibilities—from the large, big-name beer distributors to the small, unknown wagon-jobbers and specialty distributors who sell only to establishments like restaurants and bars. As we do, you'll gain more and more insight into who might be a possible distribution avenue for you.

There are many distributors in the USA and other countries, but the best beverage distributors are the beverage-specific, Direct Store

Delivery distributors, or Beverage DSD distributors. These could include beer, soda, and other distributors that only sell beverages. If you can't land these distributors, you go down the line to other available distributors in the specific territory. Yes, DSD distributors are specific to a small region, say a city of two million people.

Suppose your distribution model is not per territory, but per type of store, for example, selling to natural stores across the USA. In that case, you need other specific distributors used by natural stores. If this is you, don't worry about the distributor, you don't need to open or support them, you need to open the account, and the distributor will deliver to the store once you sell to the account. A word of caution, these distributors are also regional. They will not buy a truckload for one location. You'll need to ship beverages to different distribution centers according to your sales.

What Distributors Want

If you know what distributors want, how to connect with them, and what they expect from you, you will make contacts and open accounts far quicker than someone who walks in and cannot fulfill their needs. As you can imagine, distributors are out for their own business' success first and foremost, so they want to deal with people who can give them what they want.

One of the best ways to show you what distributors want is to tell you what they do *not* want. One of the most important things to understand is distributors are not always looking for the best-tasting or best-looking product with the brightest colors. They are looking for innovative products, products that sell off the trucks and off the shelves.

Distributors want the product that is continually selling because it is the right product for the right consumer. Distributors prefer the best-selling product! Distributors only care about what your product can do for their bottom line. Will they earn five, three, or two dollars per case?

How will you support the sales of your product? How will you support the distributors' bottom line? Because in distribution, it's always about the volume moving through the distributor. They want to know: What are you going to do to support sales? Will you come with me and approach all my accounts? Will you open new accounts for me? In the end, that's what distributors really want from you; they want sales and new stores. If your product delivers that, your product is worth having.

The Role of the Manufacturer (You!)

It's almost impossible to approach a distributor and assume they will open their existing accounts to you. It is your responsibility to open those accounts, even if they are accounts the distributor is already doing business with (because he is not doing business with them thanks to your product—not yet, not until you open it). This is the first misconception of distribution and sales.

Many think that when you sell a beverage to a distributor, it is the distributor's job to go out and open new accounts; that is not true. It is *your* job as the producer to go out and open those accounts.

How to Help Your Distributor Sell

There is no one answer to this question; there are many. To open accounts for your product and your distributor, you have to put people in the field. That may be you or your employees, but someone has to get out there and do things like ride-along, where you drive along with the salespeople to visit their accounts. You can also do direct marketing, telemarketing, or mailings to stores in that distributor's region. You can run incentives for the salespeople and give them a dollar or two for every case sold. You can offer them fifteen dollars for every new account they open. Perhaps you can provide a bonus when they place a rack or run contests where the prize is a free trip or a TV. You can do these things to support the distributor and open accounts, and there are more. But these are the types of things the distributor wants to see and hear. They want to know you have a plan to sell your product so they can make money.

The above is a long list of ideas and options you can consider. It is not to say that you will do every one of these things for every one of your distributors. These plans need to be custom-tailored to match your product and your distributors. Your product might not require the bonuses and incentives that you would provide on the retail level. You might find that effort and money are better placed at the distribution level. You might find that specific programs that need more sell-through might require that your program be more aggressive on the retail side than on the distribution side. You need to choose and develop the plans that are right for your sales and distribution model.

In the next couple of pages, you will see some illustrations of some programs we like to recommend. These, combined with this information, will make it so that you can walk into your distributor's warehouse with the appropriate plans for the type of distributor you are working with. We will talk about those types of distributors and how to tailor these programs to the right players.

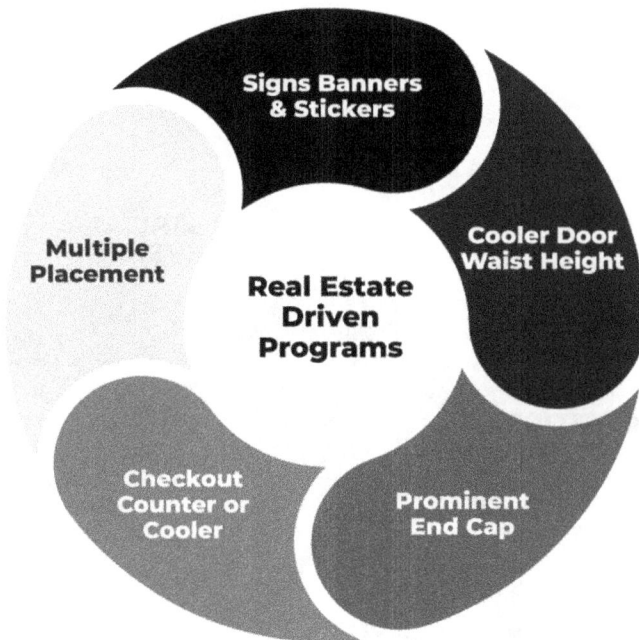

Diagram 2.2 – Real Estate Driven Programs

The first rule is "Every program has to be designed to drive sales."

Successful placement means more than just getting an order and a delivery date. It means getting the product placed inside the store in the best possible spots. How do you do this? You do this by providing the best and most aggressive incentive programs to the distributor and their reps when they perform. Every placement gets them perhaps one dollar for each case sold during the launch period. They will work for you. The worst that can happen is they don't get placement, but you also don't have to pay for lack of performance.

Mix and Match Program for a Single Retailer

Diagram 2.3 – Mix and Match Retail Programs

You can also provide incentives to distributors and salespeople for additional products placed, cases sold, stores opened, POP placed, and much more. For example, I like giving incentives for every extra *flavor* placed in a store. This will drive more than just the regular product on the shelf.

Many retailers have ***multiple store locations*** but will only try you out at one store. Do whatever it takes to get into all of them again by incentivizing. Provide incentives for events; store managers often require vendor support for ***special events.*** Ensure you budget for this.

Retailers participate in ***retailer ad programs*** and are always looking for items to put on special. Be sure to create a calendar with promotional dates far in advance so you can plan together. Specials increase order quantities, and if the product sells, well, they will reorder.

In-Store Demos get you noticed by the store manager and the consumer, create the communication required between the consumer and the brand, and ultimately drive the desired sales.

We just mentioned an instance in which you might want your support programs to be more aggressive on the retail side, but there are instances where that program should be more aggressive on the distribution side, too. Suppose there is resistance on a new product or category that might require extra space on a shelf or multiple placements in a supermarket. In that case, it's a good time to put together an aggressive plan on the distribution side because you will need your distributor's people to go out and fight to get more space for you. In that case, you want to look at the programs we've just mentioned and illustrated, along with others, and tailor your program specifically to your product. Hence, depending on those elements we talked about in the preceding chapters—positioning, target market, etc.—you will develop support programs that are very product-specific and target-specific.

The above gives you a good introduction and summary of what distributors want; now, we need to grasp the different distribution types and the various distribution models you can choose from.

Many Types, Shapes, and Sizes of Beverage Distributors

The first thing to know about distributors is that there are many distributors, and they come in many sizes. Some distributors specialize in beverages, and others specialize in food but handle some drinks too. Others sell everything under the sun, and that might include beverages as well. Any of these might be a good fit for your product, depending on what that product is.

The significant difference between selling beverages and selling other items like candy or snacks is the product size and weight. That is a huge limiter for the distributors, so a significant determining factor in which distributors you can approach. Let me give you an example:

A candy case might have a minimal footprint—maybe six by eight inches—and it may weigh one and a half pounds. A beverage case might weigh 20 to 30 pounds, and it will be much larger than that six-by-eight-inch package. Imagine if you are a distributor with a van that can carry half a ton in weight (1,000 pounds), and each beverage case weighs 25 pounds. You cannot take a lot of beverages in that van. When you sell, if each retailer is buying between 10 and 20 cases, you can probably only visit one or two retailers before you have to run back to the warehouse to fill up again. That means you are probably getting out to no more than two retailers per day, which makes no sense for a distributor.

It would help if you considered that wagon-jobbers often sell from the back of a van or the trunk of a car. There's no way they can carry fifty cases; they may not even be able to hold twenty or even ten cases. So you are limited not only by the distributor's size but also their vehicles. Their warehouse space also confines you.

Suppose a distributor is selling something like snacks, vitamins, or pharmaceuticals, for example. In that case, chances are you can fit two or three hundred dollars' worth in a corner somewhere—in a spare bedroom or a garage. But if you're selling beverages and your distributors need to buy two or three pallets, they need a warehouse to store them. They can't fit that in a small garage, and they can't hold it in a small warehouse because it would take up all their space. It would not be an option for them to order an entire truckload from you, let alone their other suppliers.

What this all amounts to is there are definite limitations on who your distributors can be. You must consider

- The size of the distributor
- The size of their vehicles
- The size of their warehouse

To help you decide your distribution options, we'll break these all down into types in a tier system that we have developed.

Three Tiers of Distribution

The three tiers of distributors are not an industry-wide recognition. We created a division to help our clients and readers better understand the beverage distribution world. It lets you realize what distributor types are out there and where and what you need to get them as your distributor or customer. We break distributors down by size into first, second, and third-tier distributors.

First-Tier Distributors

At the top of the list are the "first-tier distributors" or AAA distributors, the USA's beverage industry's largest distributors. First-tier distributors are typically the largest player in your town, city, or maybe even your state. Often this will be your beer and big-name soda distributors, possibly Coors, Miller, Budweiser, Cadbury Schweppes, Coca Cola, or Pepsi Cola distributor. They will have exclusive rights to those brands for their territory, but they will also take on and distribute other products. The distributors are franchise owners. You're not dealing with Budweiser or the other top brands directly, rather with your city's franchise owner or manager.

These are the best distributors for you or any other product to have, but only if you have the proper funding. The most considerable advantage to tier-one distributors is that because they have these big names and have to service them at all stores that carry them in their area, they make frequent stops to all their accounts. You can piggyback off of that if your product is placed with a tier-one distributor and enjoy the benefit of having your distributor visit your stores several times each week. And not only will your product have the advantage of being delivered two to three times per week, but it also has the opportunity to be merchandised each week.

Now, this may make it sound like a simple choice as to whom your distributor should be, but there is more to consider.

It is challenging to even get in the door to sell a distributor in the first tier. Getting them on a call or confirming an appointment to make your pitch is hard because they are the most sought after.

These producers do not know it is costly to work with first-tier distributors. Many start-up drink producers do not have the funding to start working with first-tier distribution (note, this does not mean you cannot consider them after you have built up your product and sales).

This leads us to the next consideration when targeting tier one distributors in your distribution structure. It usually requires an investment from you to support the first-tier distributor—a significant investment. For example, a first-tier distributor will expect you to open two to three hundred accounts, which costs money. They will also expect you to spend advertising money in their territory—another considerable expense. They will expect you to do contests and spiffs and possibly hire an employee to stay on the premises, perhaps a salesperson or a merchandiser.

All of these might sound like reasonable costs if you can afford them, but you need to realize the potential scale. For example, a first-tier distributor could have anywhere between ten and one hundred sales representatives. That means you must expand expenditures for every sales-related program to accommodate up to one hundred people. If those salespeople need samples, you are looking at thousands of samples for that distributor or territory alone. All spiffs and contests have to accommodate as many as a hundred salespeople. It's not unusual to see a manufacturer have as many as ten to fifteen representatives working with just one distributor for an entire month only to cover the territory account.

So there is an advantage and a disadvantage to utilizing tier-one distributors. To be sure, if you have the money and the workforce behind you, this is the fastest way to gain entry into the beverage market. It offers the most "feet on the street" and the most guaranteed delivery, but that all comes at a high cost that not all new beverages can afford. If you can, however, it is the way to go.

Second-Tier Distributors

Second-tier distributors are medium-sized distributors that may carry just beverages or take other products like food and drinks, for example. A second-tier distributor may be a consolidator, a master distributor, or a large wholesaler.

The second-tier distributors are still large distributors and also cover a large area. We consider them second-tier because they do not specialize in beverages as the first-tier distributors do. There is still great potential to profit with second-tier distributors, but you must be aware of their greatest downfall.

All in all, the second-tier distributor's greatest downfall is not so unlike that of any other distributor. That is, if you gain entry into their distribution or warehouse, you are not guaranteed the sale; in fact, it probably won't happen. You still need to make efforts to support your product through your distributor, possibly more so because it is typical for products to get lost in the crowd of the many various products these distributors sell. These distributors could be carrying anything from candy to pharmaceuticals to fruit and frozen vegetables. They may have a niche or not; they are pretty likely selling name brands like Coca-Cola, Pepsi, or Snapple. If you sell the product to them, it will not rise out of that mix. However, if you go and put a person in their warehouse or out with their sales team, they will probably open some accounts for you and generate some sales. The most important thing to know is if you do not do that, the chances of selling are slim to none.

Overall, second-tier distributors can be very profitable and net you great exposure over a territory—if you are prepared to support them in the right way (which you will learn about in the sales chapter).

Third-Tier Distributors

The final tier is the third-tier distributors. These are modest distributors such as what is known as "wagon-jobbers." These distributors will usually only have one or two vans and sell to one or two hundred accounts. They typically do not carry an abundance of different products, so you will not likely be competing with a hundred other products the way you might with a second-tier distributor. Still, they also lack the scope and reach that the more prominent distributors have.

On the other hand, this can work in your interest because they may be willing to dedicate a lot more time and interest in the product they do have. Going through the third-tier route is often helpful for very niche or boutique-type products, where the focus is less on territory and more on personally serving a few particular types of clients. They may be vital in hitting that niche market. For example, maybe you have a health or natural product, and there is one wagon-jobber servicing two or three hundred spas or health centers exclusively for that type of product. That may mean that the third-tier distributor is your only profitable option.

There are some other factors to consider with third-tier distributors, too. For starters, you have to make sure they can handle your product in profitable volumes. Many of them will not even have the warehouse space to fit beverages. If you can place your product in their warehouse, you will need a very aggressive sale plan to help them sell the product. You may need to build incentives to make the partnership profitable or motivate them to sell your products. You can offer spiffs, commissions, or possibly even stock in your company or a beneficial business opportunity, such as helping them finance a larger vehicle and then wrapping it with your marketing. You may also teach them how to sell and open accounts. There are options here, but you need to be aware that even though they are small and personal, third-tier distributors still require a level of support from you and always at a cost.

The above covers the three basic tiers of distributors. That is a start in knowing where to target your product. You cannot merely assume that the biggest is the best or that the smallest will be good enough. There is more to it than that. Choosing a distributor requires that you look at the specifics of your product and market individually. Once you establish where your product needs to get to, you need to find out who makes those stops. That's how the selection process starts to find the best distributor for your brand.

However, we are not done with distribution yet. Even within these three basic categorizations, there are other classifications and programs yet to be discussed.

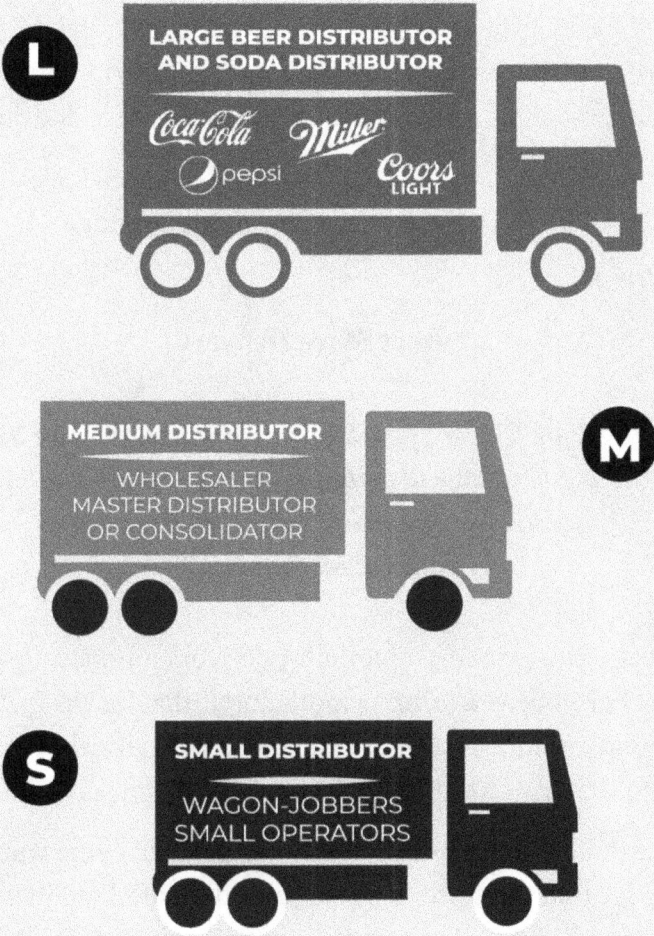

Diagram 2.4- Three Tiers of Beverage Distribution

Classifications of Distributors

All of the distributors that we just went over in the tiers can be further classified into different *types* of distributors. Any of those small, medium, and large distributors can be classified as either a

- ✅ Direct Store Delivery, or DSD Distributor, or a

- ✅ Wholesaler

Direct Store Delivery

"DSD or Direct Store Delivery distributors can be the big beverage distributors, or the small wagon-jobbers selling candy and sunglasses to convenience stores."

The Direct Store Delivery distributor delivers products directly to the store. For you, as a drink manufacturer, that means that the first, second, or third-tier DSD distributor will deliver your product directly to the retail location for every one of your accounts.

DSD distributors don't just pick up your product at the warehouse and drop it off at the store; they actually do more than that. How much more will depend somewhat on their systems. DSDs will usually operate a one, two, or three-step system. An example of a typical three-step DSD system looks something like this:

☑ Order taking. The DSD or their representative will go to the account on a given day (say Monday) and take the retailer's order. They will go into the store, see what was sold in the past week, and recommend a purchase order to the retailer, owner, or store manager. They might suggest they order five soda cases, five water cases, and other products for a total of 20 product cases (one of which will be your product). Then they either enter the order into a wireless device or onto an order sheet and submit it to the warehouse for fulfillment (they may either submit it electronically or carry it back to the warehouse themselves). Back at the warehouse, the order is "picked" or placed on the truck for delivery.

☑ Delivery. The next step is the delivery of the ordered product to the retail location. This is usually within one, two, to three days, with one-day delivery being the best. Delivery means the product physically arrives at the retailer, then is placed in their on-site warehouse.

☑ Merchandising. The third and final step in the system is merchandising. A DSD employee or the DSD himself visits the retailer, moves the product out of the warehouse, and stocks it on the shelves. They will place racks, apply pricing labels, and all your POS materials.

DIRECT STORE DELIVERY

ORDER TAKING

DELIVERY

MERCHANDISING

Diagram 2.5 – DSD or Direct Store Delivery

Some DSDs will have a system requiring fewer steps, but the same essential services are provided; you still get the order placement, fulfillment, and merchandising. If that DSD has only a one-step system, this may all happen simultaneously. They arrive at the store with the product on board, inventory, and order, then fill the order from the truck or van right then, even merchandise before they leave. That is a classic one-step DSD delivery, such as what is typical of your small wagon-jobbers. A two-step system could be any combination of these steps. Larger DSD distributors will have a similar structure. Still, they may have a more extensive sales and delivery force carrying it out (a team instead of a single representative or delivery person).

Wholesalers

A wholesaler has a much more simplified function than a full DSD distributor. A wholesaler just delivers products from their site to the retail warehouse. They have an expansive reach and can service accounts on a regional, national, and in some cases, international level. However, there are some marked differences between DSD distributors and wholesalers.

First off, wholesalers do not go site-to-site evaluating and taking orders. The order is taken either verbally over the phone by someone at the wholesaler's office or submitted through some electronic media; only very rarely do you have people walking into the store to service the account or provide stocking and merchandising services. A few wholesalers will provide these services, but they are additional and come with a fee. The advantage is they perform fewer services and may have lower prices, broader delivery capabilities, and carry a more extensive product line.

The other major characteristic of a wholesaler—they are not restricted in product to just carry beverages, and they tend to take a far more comprehensive range of products. They do not specialize in drinks, in other words. They can also consolidate orders, so retailers do not have to order 20 beverage cases they're not ready to take. They can order two soda cases, four new beverage cases, and one water case, along with other products like soap, candy, or frozen foods. They will deliver it all at once, consolidated into pallets picked and filled for that single retailer.

Who's the Best?

By now, you are probably wondering which of these is the best option to choose. You can see advantages to both, and truthfully both do have their benefits. As you might expect, there is no "right" answer to suit all beverage producers. We are not entirely done with the different options, but we would like to interject that the best type of distributor will depend on your market and placement. However, this should start to give you an idea of what your distribution structure might resemble.

It is also helpful to know that emerging drinks often use a combination of these or start their DSD delivery and then use a wholesaler to handle their products outside their local territory as the product grows. We will talk about starting your own distribution shortly.

The best type of distributor is still an individual decision and may not be a single decision. Below is a list of the Top 10 DSD and Wholesale distributors by tier. We encourage you to visit these distributors' websites to get an idea of the services each of them can provide for you and how that might fit into your distribution model.

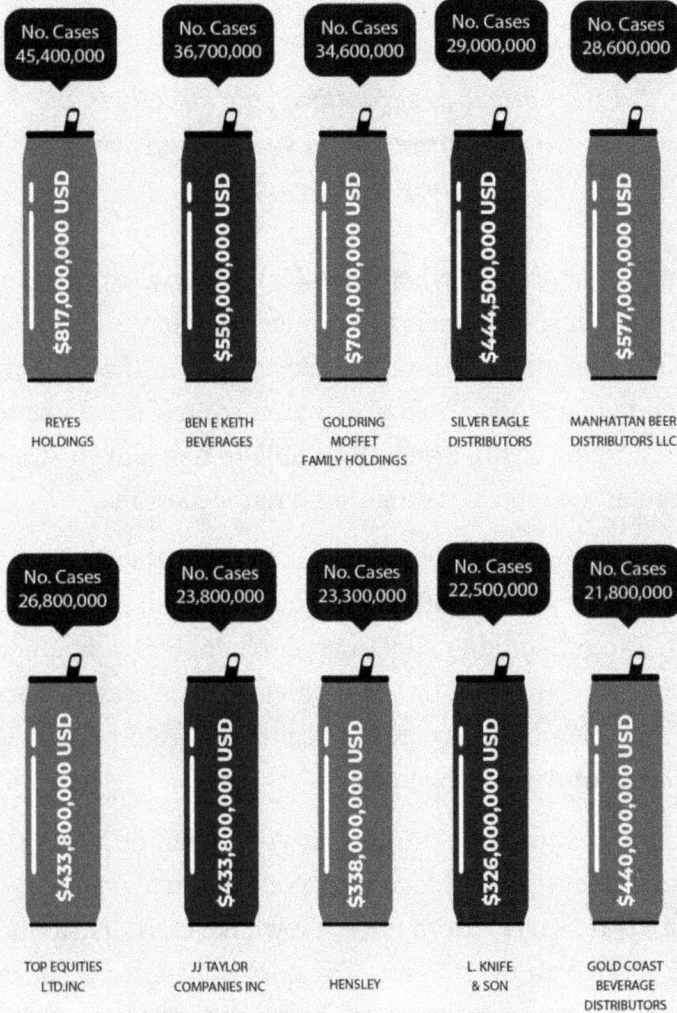

TOP 10 U.S. BEER WHOLESALERS

No. Cases	$ USD	Company
45,400,000	$817,000,000 USD	REYES HOLDINGS
36,700,000	$550,000,000 USD	BEN E KEITH BEVERAGES
34,600,000	$700,000,000 USD	GOLDRING MOFFET FAMILY HOLDINGS
29,000,000	$444,500,000 USD	SILVER EAGLE DISTRIBUTORS
28,600,000	$577,000,000 USD	MANHATTAN BEER DISTRIBUTORS LLC
26,800,000	$433,800,000 USD	TOP EQUITIES LTD.INC
23,800,000	$433,800,000 USD	JJ TAYLOR COMPANIES INC
23,300,000	$338,000,000 USD	HENSLEY
22,500,000	$326,000,000 USD	L. KNIFE & SON
21,800,000	$440,000,000 USD	GOLD COAST BEVERAGE DISTRIBUTORS

Diagram 2.6 – Beer Wholesalers

309

Other Direct Sale Distribution Options

As we've alluded to, there are still other programs and options that you can choose to use either entirely as your distribution model or in combination with others as a means of covering all territories and targeted retailers.

Warehouse Programs

"A warehouse program is a sale directly to the store, usually a large chain, such as supermarkets or pharmacies."

A warehouse program is when you sell through a large chain's warehouse. You ship to their warehouse, and they ship to their stores. That doesn't happen very often anymore. Most chains want you to send your product to a distributor, even if it's a wholesaler type of distributor. Still, you will be able to negotiate a straight, direct to retail warehouse program on rare occasions.

A warehouse Program is when you, as the manufacturer, deal directly with the retailer, often a large chain retailer such as Walmart, Kroger, another supermarket chain, or a convenience store chain like 7-Eleven, or some other account that you manage directly. The distribution (getting the product from point A to point B after the sale) will be separate.

The key to the warehouse program is you do not need to manage distribution to every retail location. You negotiate and ship only to the chain's warehouse. From there, they have their distribution that works to service all their stores. The only transport you have to handle is from your warehouse to theirs, and orders are fulfilled from there.

Warehouse programs, as with all programs and distributions, have their advantages and disadvantages. The top benefit is once you are in one of these chains, you go wide, often nationwide, in a short time frame ("overnight"—although there is no such thing as "overnight success" in beverages). The most significant disadvantage is, like all distribution, getting it to the store warehouse is never enough—you have to get it on the shelves and sell it once you've achieved that. There are several ways to do that, though.

The best way to clarify this and show you the advantages, disadvantages, and options to overcome them is to run you through a typical example of a product that has made it into a warehouse program. For illustration purposes, we'll take utilizing a warehouse program with a supermarket chain as an example.

Suppose you decide to sell to a supermarket chain with five hundred supermarkets, and they've agreed to take your product. Usually, they will not agree to try your product if it is new and unproven or may only decide to try it in a few stores or a specific region. Now that you have the supermarket chain account, what happens next? How are you going to get your product to their five hundred stores?

Here is the warehouse program's beauty—you do not have to get your product to five hundred different stores. You only need to get it to one warehouse. You do not need to contact a distributor, either, because they have their own distribution. The supermarket has a warehouse and trucks. All you need to do is ship your product in pallets or truckloads to one warehouse located somewhere in the U.S. In turn, the supermarket will pick it up from their warehouse and deliver it to the five hundred stores. Depending on the deal you made with them, they may transport five cases per store, ten cases, a pallet, or any number.

Since distribution is taken care of, a more significant concern for you is what happens now that the product is in the retail store warehouse (on location). You need to make sure that the product finds its way onto the store's shelves. Often, producers think that is the store manager's job. In theory, it is, but that is not the case in practice—not if you want your product to sell and thrive.

In reality, store managers have many products and only one goal—to increase the store's profit. They do not care which products do that, and you will be competing against other beverages that have full-service DSD distributors, and all of you are fighting for space. In the worst-case scenario, your product will stay in the warehouse and never make it out to the floor. The most likely scenario is that maybe ten or fifteen bottles or cans will make their way to the floor but not the best location.

What are your options, then?

- ☑ You can hire a merchandising company to help you merchandise your product and ensure it is out on the floor.

- ☑ You can do programs with the store managers or district managers to ensure your product gets onto the shelf.

- ☑ You can call store managers and offer support, keep your name on their minds, ask them if there is anything you can do for them, answer questions, so they know how to merchandise your product correctly.

- ☑ You can contact the category buyer and do a program with them. Many big supermarkets have specific beverage category buyers or even particular beverage type buyers.

These are all real options, and there are more, too, but you get the point. With a warehouse program, you benefit from a simplified distribution process, but then you need to attack it from the other end, too, to make sure your product sells.

Warehouse programs also work for convenience store chains, but they don't typically have their own distributor or warehouse when you sell to convenience stores. Instead, they will refer you to their preferred distributor. An example of this would be McLane, which is a large distributor that services 7-Eleven stores. If you sell to 7-Eleven through a warehouse program, they will agree to take your product, then instruct you to contact their distributor, and McLane will service them from there. But as with the supermarkets, McLane is not a full-service distributor (not a DSD), and so you also need to support the convenience store from the other end to make sales, much in the same ways we discussed above.

Drop Shipping

The drop shipping I'm talking about here is not the one you ship to your client or consumer. That is when you sell from your online store. There's another type of drop shipping, wholesale drop shipping, or selling and shipping directly to retail locations.

These programs are exactly what they sound like. You are drop shipping directly to every retailer's accounts. You pick up your product directly from your manufacturer's warehouse and ship it directly to the retailer. The retailer takes full responsibility for the product unless you have some programs in place (and again, we will talk more about what those programs might be when we discuss retail sales methods).

Drop shipping sounds simple and inviting enough, but it is not for all beverages because shipping beverages is just so expensive, especially when you're drop shipping cases to retailers. It would be best to consider your price, margins, and cost to manufacture your drink when running a drop-ship program.

Jorge S. Olson

To give you an example, if you are working with a $3.99, 24-count water case, it will cost you about $20 to ship one case from one city to the next. No one will make money on that product. But if you are producing an energy shot, a single two-ounce unit selling for $2.99 retail, perhaps at the cost of $1.49 to the retailer, there's enough margin for you to pay the shipping. If you ship one hundred shots and sell for $149, you still make a decent margin. In that instance, drop-shipping can be pretty profitable and has the potential to become an integral part of your business plan.

Your product's weight will be one of the most significant limitations on drop shipping because, for the most part, shipping rates are determined by weight. So, where you can ship a two-ounce energy shot affordably, a 20-ounce drink case probably cannot. There are some other determining factors to mention, too. The consistency (physical makeup) of your product and packaging is one. Suppose you package your product in skinny cans, for example. In that case, they could puncture—something that will not be well-received by anyone involved and will only serve to anger the shipping company and your retailers. Glass is similarly vulnerable and carries the added disadvantage of being very heavy. If you have a smaller can or a tighter non-glass bottle, or something little like an energy shot, then absolutely drop shipping provides an opportunity to sell and ship directly to your accounts.

Assuming that drop shipping is an option, the next question is, what do you need for a drop shipping program?

You have different options here. You will still need a sales mechanism, even though you probably will not require a traveling sales team. Instead, you might have a friendly call center to field client calls or an interactive website with all the programs and literature. You should also have all the electronic media to provide your information to the different retailers.

You will not need to include a third-party distributor, but you will need to contract services from a delivery company like UPS or FedEx. There are a few downfalls to consider there as well. Typically those companies drop the product, get the signature, and you will usually not know where your product ends up. If you're lucky, in a few days or weeks, someone will find it in the warehouse and maybe even stock it on the shelves. To combat this, you'll need a plan in place—perhaps implement a sales program or follow-up sales calls to make sure the product is pulled from the warehouse and placed on the floor (ideally both).

As for actually opening those accounts, there are a few different ways of going about this. Sometimes this comes about because of a client's preference. Maybe you close a deal with a store chain, but the chain doesn't want to do a warehouse program, so they provide a list of their store addresses and leave it up to you to get the product there. Now you cannot hire all the different distributors around the country to service that account, so you decide to drop-ship the product instead. You do the math, and if you can pay the postal service, FedEx, UPS, or DHL to deliver the product, then you are in business.

You don't always have to sell to large chains. You can choose instead to sell directly to individual stores. You can use a direct marketing program that includes telemarketing, direct mail, or direct advertising through trade magazines. Trade magazines are publications retailers read, and you can advertise in them, offering a free shipping incentive to purchase a master case. There are several options for you to sell directly to retailers, and if you can do that, drop-shipping may be a very profitable option for you.

In one of my distribution companies, I drop shipped energy drinks to supermarkets and pharmacies all over the USA. I tried using every shipping method available, and I could make a bit of money with UPS Ground, as long as I could ship a pallet. The challenge was convincing the stores to take an entire pallet. The lesson for me was that you could sell beverages as you wanted, but it's better to have a winning distribution model and stick to it. That's what I wish for you, explore everything, but develop a winning model that works for you. It might include drop shipping to stores, DSD, or a hybrid.

Your Own Distribution

I've owned a Miller Beer distribution company. If you're planning on having self-distribution, you should know that it's a great learning opportunity, but you won't make money. You'll learn a whole lot about the beverage industry, but you don't have enough variety of products to make a profit. This is why distributors might have twenty or thirty different products in their portfolio, including a big-name beverage. If you only make one hundred dollars per store per stop, you'll lose money every day.

Self-distribution is an option for every beverage producer to consider. Many clients come to me looking for help to do precisely this—both produce and distribute their product themselves. These people have experience in sales and enough capital to get a few small trucks or vans to get started.

Self-Distribution is setting up your own company to distribute your product locally; in other words, buying your trucks or vans, hiring employees, renting a warehouse, and selling to retail accounts, restaurants, and bars. Naturally, there are drawbacks and considerations, but this is not something we would try to persuade you away from if you can manage the factors involved. For one, being your distributor allows you to find out what customers and retailers have to say about your product—what consumers are telling them—and it lends itself to becoming a great case study for any product. You wouldn't hear from a distributor across the country telling you what did and didn't work as you will when you are the distributor. This is a great way to start a business and a great way to build up your own direct store delivery program while ensuring that your product will get the support and attention it needs.

There are many factors to consider. One of those factors is capital; the cash outlay is significant. However, there are also many investment and borrowing options. In and of itself, the need for capital investment should not be the limiting factor that keeps you from doing this; there are always banks and financing options.

What is more critical to consider is that to be efficient as a distributor, you need to have a portfolio of products—you cannot survive on distributing your single beverage alone, even if you have multiple flavors. To survive as a distributor, you need to increase your dollar amount sold per store; you need more products to do this. These other beverages don't need to be your own; you can distribute beverages for other brands.

Sooner or later, making a delivery to a single store with just one SKU or a couple of flavors gets extremely expensive and inefficient. It's always a good idea to find a few other items—may be very lightweight, low-cube items with a high ticket price that will help offset many of the costs associated with making those deliveries. With fuel costs the way they have been and knowing they will continue to be a factor into the future, it is a part to consider very seriously to make it as profitable as possible to justify handling your distribution.

There are pros and cons to being your distributor; however, many of these are more considerations to take under advisement than actual positive or negative points. Collectively, those points would be:

- ✅ You have 100% control over your distribution and market.

- ✅ You have the best possible opportunity to get to know your customers very well.

- ✅ You get to know every retailer, store manager, and many if not all of a store's employees.

- ✅ You have the chance to speak with employees and end consumers (your target market).

- ✅ You most likely live in the area, so you are very close to the operation and sales.

- ✅ You can easily make special deals, personally.

- ✅ You make more money because you cut out the "middleman"—an extra 10, 20, or 30% on the product.

- ✅ You need to spend money on infrastructure (warehouse, employees, additional insurance).

- ✅ It would help expand your product offerings to make the business viable by developing your portfolio or carrying other products (not necessarily drinks).

- ✅ Your effort is no longer 100% focused on drink manufacture—you now have two businesses to run.

- ✅ National distribution would be costly and probably unrealistic on your own.

- ✅ You are now responsible for collecting payments from every single retailer.

- ✅ You get to know key people—such as accounts payable representatives—because you are in close contact with and managing your collections.

☑ Your representatives and efforts will directly support your retailers and your product, and not middle distributors.

☑ Your expenditures (investments) become more focused on your products.

☑ Focus often results in more sell-through.

This is a lot to consider, but the most extensive consideration is making your distribution efficient so it pays. Look no further than the biggest and most successful drink producers of all time—the Coca-Cola and PepsiCo's of the world. These are technically self-distributed products. But as we all know, they do not only distribute Coke and Pepsi, but they also have very extensive portfolios, and they are continually increasing those portfolios.

Coke and Pepsi also franchise their business, so they franchise out into different cities, states, and countries even where they do not own all of their distribution. There is a lot to be learned by studying the big names, particularly if you are interested in managing your distribution.

One final thing to understand about starting your distribution is it does not need to be the be-all and end-all of your distribution plan. In many cases, developing your distribution is your avenue into the market and works very effectively, especially in a small territory. If you can start your self-distribution and make it profitable in your home town, that's fantastic. You can duplicate that into the next city, train other entrepreneurs, or show more prominent distributors that you can do the same for them and leverage your success into much bigger accounts.

I've done beverage distribution with a van and a mini-storage unit. You can do the same or train others to do it and grow your business that way. You may expand by supporting another small or start-up distributor looking to develop a three or four SKU portfolio. That will result in many small jobbers distributing your product either alongside you or on their own. The natural next step becomes an entry into wholesalers and warehouse programs and expanded regional and national sales.

The point is that when you begin with your successful distribution, you plant a seed for your product; you establish a foothold that can thrive and grow from there. When you are ready to approach these large warehouse programs or wholesalers or larger tier distributors, you have a lot to back you—you have an intimate product and market knowledge, proven sales, effective pricing, positioning, established retailer relationships. You will have a complete successful case study that will pique anyone's interest whose attention you are trying to attract. The progression into the larger markets happens naturally. When that happens, and you turn over your accounts and step back from that end of the business, you then net the advantage of their many thousands of stores that you have yet to tap into.

Your self-distributed beverage is a way to get you in the door, fully trained, and leveraging opportunities. It's not easy to run your own distribution company, and when you have your brand and your distribution, you're running two companies.

Specialty Distributors

The last type of distributors that we need to talk about is specialty distributors or specialized distributors. Some distributors only sell to bars and restaurants and only sell beverages or even just alcoholic beverages. Others only sell to bars and restaurants and distribute food but may also include beverages. Others sell only within a niche market, such as those specializing in natural channels or natural food stores.

Considering these examples, you might go back to your product and see if there is a place where it would fit with a specialized distributor. For example, suppose you have an all-natural drink with no artificial colors or flavors or an organic beverage. In that case, you might consider specializing with a natural foods distributor and entering the market through natural food stores, vitamin stores, supplement sellers, etc. That might prove the best opportunity for hitting your market target without losing your product identity. Also, something to note is that you don't need to go out and look for many specialty distributors, as only a few specialize in natural foods channels. They have already established a relationship with the stores you want to get into.

That being said, it does not mean they are going to do your work for you. It means you have a way of getting your product from point A to point B, but you still, as with any distributor, have to go and support them, help them open accounts, and do all the other work we've already discussed.

One of the other specialized distributors is the foodservice distributors. These are companies that specialize in selling food, and yes, beverages, too. But they are not beverage specialists— they are food specialists. It may be a big company like Sysco that goes around and services restaurants and bars, selling them everything they need, from flour to water, to utensils and vegetables and potentially your beverage, too!

The final specialty is distributors specializing in bars and restaurants but are not food service providers; they're called "on-premise" distributors. (In beverage, when you sell to a bar or restaurant, you don't say food service; you say on-premise.) These on-premise distributors specialize only in selling to bars and restaurants, including hotels and other institutions. Many specialize in alcoholic beverages. Southern Wine and Spirits comes to mind.

They go to bars and restaurants and sell mostly alcohol, not beer, but maybe wine and spirits. They will also sell energy drinks, water, and other nonalcoholic beverages, so it's a promising opportunity avenue to approach to get into many of these accounts.

The benefit of using these specialty distributors is that many of them are very large. They can still buy locally in one city, but they are national distributors who have a presence in more than one state—they could be in five or ten states or more. Hence, they are a way of achieving rapid distribution.

But, and this probably won't surprise you by now, you cannot forget that just because they carry your beverage does not mean they will sell it. Even more so than specialty beverage distributors, these distributors who are not specializing in the mass retail or convenience market require even more support because they carry more products. If you are a food service distributor selling everything a restaurant needs, you might have two thousand different products. In contrast, if you are a beverage distributor, even the large distributors will only have a portfolio of twenty different products. As you can see, there is a big difference between twenty and two thousand, so you will need more contests, more spiffs, more commissions, and more people helping to sell to accounts, and more people doing promotions in the bars and restaurants to make sure your product sells.

Classifications of Distributors

WHOLESALERS

DISTRIBUTORS

DROP SHIPPING

Diagram 2.7 – Classification of Distributors

Summing Up Beverage Distribution

This wraps up all the different options for drink distribution. There are many different distributors, but keep in mind that all of those we've just mentioned—food service distributors, alcoholic beverage distributors, natural foods, on-premise—fall under the more extensive wholesaler classification or DSD. For instance, the natural foods distributor is a wholesaler who could engage in all the different programs we mentioned. Then you have food service and on-premise distributors who are naturally DSD distributors as well. To help clarify this, we have included some different matrixes outlining the different kinds of distributors and their classification on the next couple of pages.

You now have the information you need to start constructing your distribution model. Only one part is left to complete the picture and launch your new beverage—the final piece, sales. In the upcoming chapter, we will talk about all aspects of sales to have that last piece in place, and you will be armed with the knowledge you need to develop and sell your successful new beverage.

"NEVER GO TO A TRADE SHOW WITHOUT CONFIRMED APPOINTMENTS."

CHAPTER 22

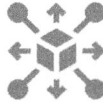

Selling to Distributors

Rapid Knowledge Section

I love selling to distributors. I love the distribution business, one of the oldest businesses on the planet. Wholesale distribution is responsible for creating wealth on earth before the Middle Ages, debunking the monarchy's concept as the right to wealth.

I love distribution so much that I wrote a book called Wholesale Distribution MBA, and it's all about selling to distributors and retailers. I've also owned distribution companies, beverage and otherwise, in the USA and Mexico, and I've sold to distributors all over the USA and Mexico, and I still do. I also love training distributors on opening stores, selling, merchandising, and growing their business.

What's my point in telling you this? I try and get to my distributors, to give them value, to understand them. If you only send samples and hope for the best, it won't work. When I send samples to distributors, I include a copy of my book. If it's a beverage distributor, I send them this book. If I send out samples of my hemp cigarettes, I send them my Wholesale Distribution MBA book.

You must give distributors value, get to know them, understand their pain points, wants, needs, and fulfill them.

Selling to Distributors

The chapters on marketing and distribution are about sales. Instead of exploring and defining distribution channels, as in the last chapter, we'll focus on the techniques used in selling beverages to distributors.

If you're following a traditional beverage distribution strategy, in this case, Beverage DSDs, you'll need a distributor in every city or metropolitan area. This means you're partnering up with distributors who are essential to your business. As one distributor used to tell me: "You marry a distributor."

We mentioned before that we don't have to sell to distributors. We can choose to sell directly to retailers; we might even sell directly to consumers. However, scaling a beverage fast and into every single store in a territory uses DSD beverage distributors. If this is your business model, it's the start of your sale cycle:

Distributors, Retailers, Consumers

Selling to distributors is quite different from selling to consumers. You'll need far fewer distributors, you can contact them often by phone, mail, email, and you only need a handful of distributors to be a successful brand. Spend time marketing and selling to distributors. Don't get discouraged if one, two, or ten say NO to you, or NOT NOW. In my experience, you can call them back in a few months when you have some traction and try all over again.

Let's talk about locating the players, approaching them, and what you need to provide to make the sale. We will do this for each of the three types of players—distributors, retailers, and consumers. In this particular chapter, we will focus on selling to distributors.

Sales Organization

I take sales optimization and best practices seriously, and you should too. If you're taking the path of selling to the trade (distributors and retailers), you'll need sales organization and best practices or procedures. If you like sales and sales calls, you can do it; if not, hire someone to do it or outsource it. Your sales process guarantees success in sales and revenue. If you're following best practices, it's hard to fail. Let's see what this entails.

The smallest team would be one salesperson armed with CRM software to enter leads, take notes, and organize the follow-up process. Your salesperson would start with a distributor list and call them one by one in the territories you would like to sell. After calling, the salesperson would send samples, sell-sheets, pricing and convince them to buy a pallet.

Here is a typical sales process:

- ☑ Call distributors
- ☑ Call, call and call again!
- ☑ Send an email with artwork and information
- ☑ Send samples
- ☑ Start with an order

- ✓ Visit distributors to open stores
- ✓ Train distributors' salespeople
- ✓ Arrange for in-store promotions
- ✓ Advertise in the territory

Yes, you can do all of this with only one salesperson; however, while your only salesperson spends two weeks with your distributor, he does not call back other leads or reach out to new leads. This is not entirely bad because if you only have the funds for a sales team of one, maybe you shouldn't open more than one territory simultaneously.

The scenario of opening a distributor and supporting them to open stores assumes you're opening DSD beverage distributors per territory. You could simultaneously replicate this exact scenario in two, three, or more regions if you're fully funded. Suppose you're using a different sales method or a hybrid of any kind. In that case, you should still have an organizational sales plan that details how you want to contact customers, the call script, leaving voice mails, sending emails and samples, and every interaction with prospects, leads, and customers.

Where to Find Distributors

"I buy distributor lists. I've done this for twenty years. I then call and sell them beverages. It's that easy!"

Finding distributors is the big question for new entrepreneurs, but it need not be. Distributors are not hard to locate—we deal with all-tier distributors daily. The problem is not finding distributors; it's selling them on your product. How you go about doing this will depend on your business plan and your budget.

I buy distributor lists and have my team call them on the phone, then follow up with samples, pricing, sell-sheets, brochures, and more phone calls to close the sale. It's a very normal sales process, nothing fancy, just consistency. If you follow this simple process, you'll get deals in every industry and channel.

Trade Shows

"If you're new to the industry and are not well funded, trade shows might not be for you. I never go to a trade show without confirmed appointments."

Trade shows are one place where you can begin to make contacts in an industry where you have none. There are many trade shows; you could start with one of the largest, NACS—the National

Association of Convenience Stores, or FMI, or one of many niche trade shows specializing in natural products. Trade shows are held locally, regionally, and internationally.

Don't spend them on a trade show if you're new to the beverage industry and have limited funds. This is not the way to go for you, don't even go to the show, save your money and get more funding. However, if you're funded and can make appointments before going to the show, trade shows can be fantastic. They are so great, my partner Sandro Piancone and I organize our own shows! So far, we've had a few in Mexico and two in the USA for the Hemp industry.

When you attend a trade show, you can purchase a booth space or walk the floor and attempt to make contacts that way. But a myth needs to be dispelled regarding trade shows, which will be essential to understand if you are to benefit from them. One of the most common misconceptions is that you can go to these shows and look for distributors or retailers at their booths, but there are no booths for retailers and distributors; only drink manufacturers have booths. So if you opt to walk the show floor, most of the people you will meet are vendors looking for information and product. That may seem like just who you want to meet, but if you are not buying, it will be difficult for you just to walk the show. Still, in the absence of a bigger budget, it is a place to start.

To maximize trade shows, you need to make those contacts, but you need to do it in a memorable way that provides vendors with information. For that, you need a booth. But even having a booth is not enough to make trade shows worth your while because if you just sit there and wait for people to approach you, it will be a very frustrating trade show, and you will only conclude that it is not worth the expense.

However, if you can get vendors to your booth, get the word out about your product, and generate some sales, you will think it was cheap no matter how much you pay. What we would suggest, then, is that you do some work ahead of time (beyond your presentation). Find a list of distributors, email, call, fax them; contact them, and invite them to visit your booth. Undertake a direct marketing campaign and entice them to meet you at your booth. You can also implement giveaways like free t-shirts or host a "party" complete with invitations; perhaps hold a contest requiring distributors to visit your booth to enter or pick up a prize. Make your presence at the trade show well-known, and get those targets to come to you where you can get your product and your package in front of them.

Direct Marketing

You use direct marketing when you target consumers on Facebook and Instagram. You use it in Google search advertising and when retargeting traffic to your eCommerce site. Direct marketing is not new; it didn't start with the internet, it's an old way of marketing and selling, and right now, we're going old school, back to calling and mailing distributors. Direct response means you need a response from your marketing, proof that you're targeting the right audience, and being successful means someone says, "Yes, I'm interested in your product." If you send a mailing to one thousand distributors and twenty call you back asking for samples or ordering your product, you have a successful direct response.

I prefer you send a mailing out to distributors than see you spend twenty-thousand dollars advertising in trade magazines. Why? Because in all my years in selling to distributors, with all the brands I've represented, I've never had one single brand get a single phone call from a distributor because of a magazine advertisement. On the other hand, I've had every distributor pick up distribution because of a mailing or telemarketing campaign.

You could also do an email campaign, ensuring you use a good write-up, article, or collaboration. But if it's only advertising, then no. When I talk about a "mailing," I mean a direct response mailing campaign with a letter from you, a handwritten note, a handwritten envelope with a stamp. The kind of letter everyone opens because it's personal, not machine-made. This letter has a follow-up, a personal voice mail, called a voice drop, or a phone call from you, making sure they got your letter. If they didn't, then you send it again. This has proven to work.

What else can you do? Here are some of my favorite direct marketing campaigns:

- ✅ Mailing campaigns—this could include postcards, letters, brochures, etc.

- ✅ Faxing

- ✅ Telemarketing

- ✅ Voice Mails

- ✅ Texting

- ✅ LinkedIn InMails

- ✅ Emailing—do note you should only use email as a direct marketing method if it is "opt-in"; that is if the client has signed on through your website or email to receive emails from you. Otherwise, your emails are considered SPAM. However, if you deliver quality information that clients will want (articles, newsletters, tips), they will likely opt-in to receive more.

LinkedIn is now my favorite way to contact distributors, retailers, buyers, investment bankers; you name it. I have quite a robust list of followers and manage large groups on LinkedIn, so getting the contact or sending a direct message to someone on LinkedIn is easy. The question is automation. Can I get to my target audience with automation to do less work and more contact? The answer is yes, I can do that, and so can you. LinkedIn offers direct response campaigns that allow you to contact thousands of prospects at the same time. I've used LinkedIn for funding, to get distributors, retail buyers, brokers, even for events. I don't usually pay to play anymore, as my groups are large, and I have so many followers that I can just send a blast to my list, and I get the results that I want.

I didn't grow an extensive list of LinkedIn followers overnight; I have worked at it since LinkedIn started. I recommend you do the same, regardless of your industry. Spend half an hour a day on LinkedIn, create a group, build your network, provide value, and you'll see high-level contacts following you and connecting with you overnight. For example, I have a Venture Capital Group on LinkedIn with over forty thousand members; when I need capital, I send a blast to all of them.

Feel free to follow me and subscribe to my companies and groups on LinkedIn, so you can see what I'm doing. You can also follow me on Twitter, Instagram, Facebook, and other networks. I often post beverage and market-related content that you can use to market yourself.

Referrals

Referrals are an excellent—one of the most valued—ways to locate distributors. As with any referral or "word of mouth," it is always one of the most trustworthy forms of connection.

The beverage industry is very small. Everybody knows everybody else. It doesn't matter if it is a large Miller distributor, a medium, or a small distributor, every one of them has friends in the industry. Therefore, if you sell to one and do an excellent job, they will help you get in with their friends. This works from distributor to retailer and vice versa. Please a distributor, and they will recommend you and your product to retailers. Please a retailer, and they'll be happy to tell their distributors where to find the next great opportunity in a beverage. It's not complicated, it's a good business sense, and it works.

Advertising

"Don't advertise in trade magazines. Advertise to get the consumer to buy your product."

Advertising can work, but you would need to think outside the box. Beverage entrepreneurs make the mistake of advertising in trade magazines that other beverage entrepreneurs read. This is a horrible idea as you're advertising to other people that want to sell beverages to you! If you're looking for distributors, advertising in beverage trade magazines is not the place to go.

Now that the easy way of trade advertising is out, where else should you spend your advertising dollars to attract beverage distributors? Spend your money on Direct Advertising. Direct Advertising is a form of direct marketing. The premise is simple; you need to measure results. If you spend one thousand dollars, you need to know how many leads you got and how much those leads cost.

You can target your advertising dollars on LinkedIn by owners, sales managers, and buyers at specific distribution companies; you could also send them InMails. You can also build a Facebook audience with the emails you get from them or the emails you buy from a list broker; this way, you don't spam your list but run ads targeting them. This is Direct Response Advertising 101, and you're going to experience it.

The Follow-Up

Once you have made some form of contact and connection, you still have work to do. The most important work lies ahead, and that is the follow-up.

You want to achieve visibility for you and your product, but the distributor wants to see how you can help them. They want to know where your product might fit into their business. A good action plan might be to email a sales sheet and then follow up by mail and send your product information. Follow it up with a phone call to ensure they've received it and provide more product specifications and pricing information.

As we said, though, the distributor wants their needs filled, so start a conversation about their portfolio of beverages and find out where the "holes" are. Distributors regularly lose drinks due to market consolidations, closings, and competition, thus creating a need for new products like yours. You just have to find out what the need is and show how you can fill it.

Whatever you do, do not forget about the follow-up. Once you contact a distributor and start talking with their buyer, make sure to send them samples, information, and your distributor package (which we'll talk about soon). Deliver the goods the buyer needs to be able to do business with you.

Contracts

Some distributors will require you to sign exclusivity contracts; these are primarily large DSD distributors such as the beer distributors. These contracts are open-ended; in other words, you need to buy them out because they never expire.

Large beverage DSD distributors work primarily in a system of territories. Each distributor has an area they operate in, and they will go out and open that specific geographical territory. That costs them a lot in resources and effort, so they need a protection system so that others cannot just come in and sell to their accounts and undercut that money, time, and effort they have expended. Distributors want to be contracted with you, assuring that any money and effort put into promoting and selling your product will not be a loss if someone else comes in with a cheaper offer or better options. The most common way to afford that protection is for the distributor to enter into a mutually agreeable contract with you.

Another way that a distributor might be secured is through channel protection and not geographical protection. In this case, distributors are divided into vendor types. One channel might be for supermarket chains, and your contract might restrict your sales through other distributors to supermarkets. Another might be pharmacies and chain stores, and perhaps another hotels and bars, or on-premise accounts. Often you might find that there are two or three distributors in one geographical area, but each serves a different channel. And so, to cover the entire territory, you might contract with all three of them, with the contracted stipulation that one does not cross into the sales territory (channel) of another.

There are a few other clauses and issues that are commonly addressed in distributor contracts, including:

- ☑ **Buy-out Clauses.** Buyout and termination clauses protect distributors from losing contracts. However, a smaller distributor sometimes has to yield to a larger one and accept a contract loss. When that happens, they need to see some return on their investment, resulting from a payoff. That payoff may be in the form of sales commissions, buyouts for the amount of product sold over some time (such as the last 12 months), a lump sum, or other fair compensation for profits and potential profits lost.

- **Contract Term.** Every contract is written for a specific period for which it is valid. Typically, the original contract will be for one year and will renew automatically; the term can be as long as five years with automatic 5-year renewals. Each contract term is accompanied by specific clauses that determine whether extensions are granted or not. Those are often tied to performance, requiring that the distributor's performance be such that it merits renewal. If the distributor does not meet performance goals, their contract will not renew and go to another distributor.

- **Trademark or Trade Dress.** Use of trademark or trade dress is an essential inclusion in a contract, giving the distributor the legal right to use your logo, trademark, and brand dress so they can sell and promote you according to your outline. It does occur that distributors sometimes use trade dress in a way not consistent with your marketing plan or message, so you want to control that. Ensure you clearly define how distributors can use your trademark and why in their marketing and promotion.

- **Support Programs.** Support and spiff programs should also be addressed in the contract. This serves the dual-fold purpose of providing an incentive and solidifying your product and distributor commitment. A well-drafted document will require product support and will often be tied to distributor performance. For instance, for "X" number of cases sold, you (the manufacturer) will invest a certain amount of money into the distributor's marketing plan or perhaps match their investment. We'll talk more about support when we outline the Distributor Package.

This concludes the significant provisions that should be included in a distributor contract. As a last note, you should be aware that not all distributors will require a contract. It is primarily the large tier one distributor who will require exclusivity and territorial protection contracts. That's fine because when you are working with a large distributor, you won't need anyone else, so granting them exclusivity for their area is not a problem.

What these distributors are trying to avoid through a contract is diverting. Diverting is when another distributor comes into their territory and undercuts them, thus absorbing the accounts they've worked so hard to open. Without a contract, diverting does happen, so an agreement will provide your distributor with protection and peace of mind.

Pricing Models

We've reviewed pricing models in other parts of the book, and we come back to it briefly here. This may seem unlikely to address this, but pricing is essential to distributors' sales, as it determines their profit and motivation to sign with you. The pricing model is also vital on the retailer's side, but to a lesser extent, as they control the price to the end-consumer, so they have more direct control over their profit margins.

As discussed, you have to build your pricing model before launching your product and before talking to distributors. You also have to leave room in that model for large distributors to turn an attractive profit. This is true even if you are just starting, and even if you think you will manage your distribution, your ultimate goal is to go national with your product at the end of the day. That is not a level of distribution that you can manage on your own, and so at some point, you will be looking to recruit distributors. Even if you could distribute on your own to all the major supermarket chains, you have not gone national. To do that, you need to hit all the hundreds of thousands of independent retailers, pharmacies, convenience stores (chains and independents), and to get those accounts, you will have to deal with distributors. You will need the margin to pay them.

Regardless of where you are today, you need to consider all the different pricing levels you will ultimately require. Let's look at a typical scenario and then lay out the pricing levels you need to build into your model.

Many small startups enter the market opening local stores in their backyard. The temptation here is that, because there are no other levels involved, they only need to make 30 or 40% to keep their drink alive, and they price their beverage to accommodate a 30 to 40% margin for themselves. In reality, if you are distributing your product, you should be making up to 70 to 80% margin. But selling for less and being more affordable is all too appealing, and so they fall victim to that temptation. After all, if you were selling through a distributor, you wouldn't be making that money, and the consumer loves an inexpensive product, right?

That may be true, but decisions like that will always come back to haunt you because you are too big for yourself next quarter or next year, and you may need a distributor. When you approach that distributor, he will want his margin, from 20 to 35%. If you are only making that yourself, or only 5% above it, there is nothing left for you, and worse, nothing left for the product support that will be necessary to carry your product through larger markets. Even if you toy with expanding your distribution, you'll soon find how impossible that is because you do not have the margin for transportation, hiring a co-packer, and supporting the retailer. Not writing in the margin for distribution now will destine your product to be restricted to your immediate area forever.

To wrap up this discussion on pricing models, let's give you an idea of the margins you need to consider.

- ☑ **Distributors.** The margin for your distributor will depend on the distributor's size and your product. Still, to access tier-one distributors, you will need a minimum of a 20 to 25% margin and upwards of 35 or 40%. The industry standard set by the top three tier-one distributors is 30%.

- ☑ **Retailers.** It's hard to pinpoint retailers' margins because each retailer will set its own price. For chains and franchises, the price will remain consistent. You will have to negotiate with the retailer to find out what their expected margin is and what their pricing will be. You can start with your suggested retail price with a margin of 30 to 40% built into it for the retailer, which they may accept or decline, and whatever number you land on with them will determine their profit margin.

- ☑ **Brokers.** Brokers are one of the more overlooked entities in pricing models. We'll talk about brokers in the next chapter, but you will want to include a margin, so they remain an open option to you; for that, you can count on a figure between 2 to 5%, and possibly as high as 10% if you are dealing with a strong, aggressive brokering company.

You will need to consider other items and margins to support your product—you need to account for those too. One of the best ways to do this is to start on the consumer side, look at your product and determine a price that can work. Then you start calculating, deducting these margins for all the necessary levels and players. Here is where you may need to adjust that price model. What is left becomes your margin for support programs, which is no less critical. If the numbers do not add up and leave enough profitability for you or your support programs, you'll need to make adjustments again.

When you find a suitable price model that makes sense for everybody, you will recruit the distributors because they can see that your business model makes sense and has profitable potential. The price model lends itself to every little segment of your business, including, not least of all, sales. It is what determines whether or not you can go to those trade shows, afford to direct market, advertise in the trade magazines, and land the referrals because of your solid model and significant profitable margins.

Support

Support is vital to distributors—how will you support them to promote your brand and establish and grow your sales?

There are several things you can do that support your drink and your distributor. Whichever of these you choose, you will need to include, in detail, as part of the distributor package. Some of the support they may need includes:

- A representative in their territory who does ride-along in delivery trucks, opens accounts, visit stores
- A mailer sent out to all the retail stores in the territory
- Point of sale material—posters, stickers
- Samples and sampling
- Merchandising

ⓥ Support programs (spiffs, commissions, etc.)

The "little things" are also a means of distributor support—throw parties for them, stay visible by giving out freebies like pens, t-shirts, briefcases, and so on. These aren't the things you'll include in your distributor package, but they are small tokens of support that build relationships and keep your presence and support known.

Some of the other methods of support are not 100% the responsibility of the manufacturer. You can put support systems that guarantee that the distributor will match all or a percentage of the money you invest in support. These can apply to co-op programs or co-op events, sponsorships, or mass-media marketing. Cooperative support programs can also be things like slotting.

In basic terms, co-op support programs ensure that the distributor will make an equal effort to yours and incentivize them to do so. It's effortless for a distributor to ask you to spend money sponsoring events and advertising. Still, when they realize that they, too, will have to invest in the program, they will be more discerning and take more care to choose profitable marketing avenues. So there are two ways to look at co-op programs; on the one hand, as part of the distributor package, they say, "I'm willing to help you bear the cost of marketing," and on the other, they give you some security, too.

This list is just a start in terms of support. The bottom line is that if you keep in mind that you do need to support them and bear that ultimate responsibility for sales, you will be more than halfway there.

The Distributor Package

The Distributor Package ties in directly with distributor support; all those essential support items must be included and communicated in your distributor package.

The distributor package is the actual "sales pitch" you give to the distributor. The distributor package is your personalized sales proposal specifically designed to show them how you will support and convince them through your efforts.

A distributor package can include many things, and each one will be a little (or a lot) different because it will be tailored to your product and business plan. Some basics should be included in every distributor package, though.

- ☑ **Spiffs and Commissions.** Distributors like to see you support and motivate their salespeople and sales managers because they know this is how they make money. So although spiffs/commissions are targeted directly to the sales team, they are very enticing to distributors. These programs reward sellers or managers with a sales percentage or a set amount per case sold. For example, each salesperson may get fifty cents, $1, or $2 per case of product sold, or $15 to $20 for each rack placed at a retailer. You may reward them with $50 for opening a new account or $X for selling more than 100 cases in a week. You can design the program however you choose, and it is a definite inclusion in your distributor package.

- ☑ **Point of Sale Material.** You'll already have this planned; you just need to include it here, so the distributor is familiar with it. This section includes stickers, sales sheets, posters, pole signs, event photos, press releases or media coverage, product photo renders, and product specifications. Specify how many items are in each case, including case and product bar codes, cases per pallet, pallets per truckload, etc.

- ☑ **Contests.** Contests are similar to spiffs and commissions in that they are targeted to the sales force more than the distributor, with the key difference being there are only one or a few winners. Whereas with commissions, everyone who sells wins; with contests, they need to compete to win. The prize will often be a trip with their spouse or family, an electronic device, or a TV. The reward should be sizable and enticing, though, or no one will bother to participate. Like spiffs, you can design your version; the contest could award the top seller or could be a drawing-type where anyone who sells more than 100 cases enters a drawing for a new TV. There are many, many possibilities for contests; get creative.

These are the basic types of things that should go into your distributor package, but let's also talk about the distributor package's physical format.

Ideally, you should arrange all of this very nicely in a quality folder with your logo on it. All of your sales sheets, press releases, POS materials, specifications, and everything else will be inside, including a business card and prominent contact information, thus creating one complete, concise presentation that broadly speaks for itself.

A Step Further

It is often the added effort that sets you apart from the crowd, and that is just what you want to do to sell your distributors. So while a basic distributor package will get you in the door and get you some attention, a more informative one will put you on the top of the pile.

If you want to impress potential distributors, use it to tell them precisely what you will do to open accounts for them. This is the thing that separates the small guys from serious players, and it conveys you know your stuff and are serious about successfully selling your drink.

This part of the package does not need to be overly long. A brief marketing plan will suffice. In it, layout exactly how you will go out and sell the product from their warehouse to their retailers. If you do that, yours will be the best distributor package they've seen. This is our strategy, and it has proven successful time and again. We have received calls from distributors who have dealt with specific products and liked them but could not sign them for their lack of a sales and distribution plan and impressive package. They call us and ask us to look at these brands and work with them to develop a sellable plan.

The one thing to remember with your distributor package is that it has to have some meat. It cannot be just for show, and it needs to go much further in-depth than "here's my product, please sell it." It has to be the means to that end. Given the beverage market's high valuations today, many entrepreneurs are jumping in and developing new beverages. Distributors are fielding many calls daily, and when you approach them, you have to be different—and prepared!

Finally, limit your outreach to what you can handle and what you can afford. If you do not have significant funding, start on a smaller, more localized level and build sales and revenue from there. If you are well-funded, you can simultaneously approach several distributors; but only approach one or two if you are operating on a smaller budget. Don't just blanket all the distributors you can find because if you get lucky and sign with you, you don't have the money to follow through with product support or delivery. Remember, you have to duplicate all your efforts for every distributor, which replicates your costs.

Create Your Budget

We'll wrap up this chapter on selling to distributors with a section on budgeting to support those efforts.

For all of the support programs that go into the distributor package, you need to create a budget before implementing them. You cannot just take opportunities as they come along; you have to plan for them so you can attend to all expenses and facets of product support, production, and sales. What you most need to know ahead of time is how much will you allocate per city, distributor, or case? If you don't know this, you will quickly lose control of your funding.

Suppose you allocate 30% of sales back to the distributor. That means that 30% of the sales made by distributor "A" will be allotted to fund *that distributor's* marketing and support. If you sell $18,000 worth of product to distributor "A" in a month, $9,000 will go into marketing and support for distributor "A." Working together, you and distributor "A" will decide where that money should go—such as into events, advertising, or sponsorships.

Of course, you cannot expect that your sales will fund 100% of your marketing budget. When it comes time to open a new territory, you will need to invest money that is not yet reflected in that area's sales. For instance, you may spend $100,000 to open a new market, and that money will not come from your ongoing budget; it will be money invested from other funding. It's a formidable dollar figure that you are committed to, and you need to know where it is coming from. Likely, it is coming from another region's profit. In time the money you make in the new territory will fund your next level of sales, and so on. Still, it is an actual amount and not a percentage of sale revenues.

When you do create your budget, you need to be aware of all expenses. Manufacturers often budget for the high costs but forget that everything they send out has a price, so you are budgeting big things like spiffs, commissions, advertising, and the little things like t-shirts, stickers, and posters. It is imperative to identify all of these line items, allocate a dollar amount, and ensure you include them in either the launch or the ongoing budget.

It is difficult to say precisely how much money you will need to fund this budget. Your budget will depend on your drink, your production costs, the type of company you have, and what you want to achieve, as well as the distributor that you wish to contract. It will cost you more money to go after the tier one distributors. In contrast, you can support a smaller distributor with less funding (but of course, we've already talked about the difference in sales potential).

To place something of a guesstimate, we can go back to that 30% figure. The big three distributors have made this industry-standard, at least for the tier one distributors. That's a good rule of thumb to start with as you begin to take a look at your numbers and funding. Again, this is for your ongoing budget, though, and does not reflect the costs of launching and opening new territories.

This ends our chapter on selling to distributors. The next logical step is to sell to retailers and then on to consumers. This will be the subject of the final chapter of our book as we complete the path from production to end consumer sales.

"YOU MUST HAVE A KILLER RETAIL PACKAGE TO SELL IT OFF THE SHELVES."

CHAPTER 23

Selling to Retailers

After the Covid pandemic, this is the most critical chapter of the book. Before Covid, selling to distributors was hands down your most important job. For a beverage executive or beverage entrepreneur, opening distributors and working with them was the number one thing on their agenda day after day for years. Now, the power has shifted to the consumer. The consumer can dictate what gets into the store; the consumer can even choose to buy something directly from you without ever going to the store, holding power in their hands. As an entrepreneur, you can focus your attention first on the consumer and the retailer second. Remember, the retailer could be a brick-and-mortar retailer, such as a supermarket, or an online retailer like your eCommerce store or Amazon.

Selling to Retailers

There are various types of retailers, and how you sell to each one will differ, too. We will break the types of retailers down into categories much as we did with distributors, so it will be easier to plan the sales strategy you will need to service each one.

Let's outline the different types of retailers. They are:

- **Supermarkets**—which we can further break down into independent and chain supermarkets

- **Pharmacies**—again, both independent and chain pharmacies

- **Club stores**—such as Sam's Club or Costco

- **Convenience stores** (or "c-stores")—these can be independent or chain stores and this category also includes gas stations and liquor stores

- **On-premise**—hotels, bars, restaurants

- **Institutional accounts**—large kitchens in schools, colleges, universities, or government buildings

- **Vending**—a combination of a distributor and retailer account, as the one will serve both functions

- **International**—exporting outside the U.S., with Mexico being one of the significant markets for U.S. beverages. (We created the largest export group into Mexico, the

Mexico Sales Alliance, which does business with every account in Mexico).

✓ **eCommerce**—your store, Amazon, Etsy, eBay, or online stores or supermarkets, such as Target.com

Now that we have identified the players let's talk about your game strategy for each of them.

If you sell to distributors, they will already have retail accounts. That does not automatically mean you have "sold" those retailers; you still have to work to open those accounts. You do this by

1. Building a margin into your price model so distributors can profit from the resale, and

2. Supporting the brand and personally opening accounts

How do you reach retailers through your distributor? We'll go through the different categories separately to find a variety of answers to that question.

Selling to Independent Retailers

A distributor may have independent accounts, including independent c-stores, supermarkets, clubs, restaurants, and bars. Each one will have one decision-maker, the owner or manager, who has the final say over which products are in or out.

One way or another, you need to reach and convince this decision-maker that your product is the right one for their clientele. If the distributor doesn't do the convincing, then it's up to you. You will want to approach this retailer personally, either by telemarketing, visiting them, or through direct mail (or a combination), and open the account yourself (or through one of your representatives). When it comes down to it, opening independent retailers is very simple—you just have to go out, present your product, and sell it.

Simple doesn't mean easy, though, because this is an effort that will have to be repeated many times for each independent retailer.

Selling to Retail Chains

Chains can refer to the large, well-known regional or national retail chains like 7-Eleven, Circle K, Kroger, Walgreens, or Walmart. It can also refer to small chains where a single owner may own between two and twenty stores. Regardless, you sell them the same way.

With chained retailers, your target is the buyer. It may be a category buyer who only buys beverages or a buyer who purchases all of the stores' products. In some cases, the buyer may even be the chain's owner. Introduce yourself to this buyer (either alone or with your distributor), sell them on the product, and let the distributor take over from there. Of course, this is an oversimplification of the process, but that is the primary selling method to chained accounts with a distributor. Each chain, though, may have its own buying patterns. Some are centralized, while others are regionalized, and some have district structures. You may deal with one buyer for an entire chain or several across all the territories you are selling.

For example, Walgreens breaks its chain into districts, with each district having around thirty stores. Additionally, they have special managers allowed to buy for several stores. This structure opens more opportunities for you to sell to the Walgreens chain, though. A worst-case scenario might be you present to the corporate office, which controls about 6,000 Walgreens stores, and they reject you. You can then approach each of their 200-300 district managers and sell individually to them. If that fails, you can go to the local buyers who control five to ten stores. If you are still not making sales, you can resort to approaching each store manager. It may sound like an act in futility, but we have done just this with success. It's not the easiest sales route for a retail chain, but it can produce results in the end.

The basic selling method to chained accounts is to locate the buyers responsible for the stores you want to be in and start selling on down the line.

Selling to On-Premise Retail Accounts

The other entity to address in regards to retail sales through distributors is on-premise accounts. This is another case where you need to do a lot of personal selling or selling alongside your distributor. The distributors will regularly sit down with these retailers, with a buyer, chef, or bar manager, present products, and do product samplings. You will need to either accompany them yourself or with a sales rep, or at the very least, provide the samples and information needed to make the presentation. Maintaining contact with these accounts is indispensable because both the retailer and distributor deal with hundreds of different products. It is very easy to get lost in the crowd. Thus, the personal approach—visits, contact, ride-along—take on greater importance.

Selling to Retailers through Buying Clubs

You also have the option of selling to retailers through your distributor through buying clubs.

Many convenience stores, supermarkets, and independents belong to a retail club. Membership in the club gives them buying power in the form of discounts, bonuses, and specials. To reach these retailers, you need to approach the buying club, present, sell to the club, and service through your distributor as with the other retailers. This gives you access to hundreds and thousands of retailers through a single club, with only having to sell to one buyer.

Selling to Retailers Without Distributors

Using the warehouse programs we discussed before, you can also sell to retailers without working through a distributor. To recap, this is where you sell to a chain, usually a big-box store or large chain, directly through their buyer. The procedure here is to approach the beverage category buyer who decides for all of the stores. This is somewhat similar to the process for selling to retail chains and clubs, in that you sell to only one representative but access hundreds of stores; only in this instance, you are on your own without a distributor by your side. When you make the sale, it will be immense—truckloads at a time and only one delivery point to manage.

In addition to the pros and cons outlined before, the payment contract is something to be aware of. Different warehousing programs may attempt to contract their purchases through a scanning program. This means that instead of a straight sale and payment in 30 to 90 days, you only get paid when a product is scanned—basically a consignment arrangement. Instead of receiving payment in a month or two, you may not get paid for four months or more, and if the product doesn't sell, they can return it and have lost nothing; you will be the only loser. You want to avoid scan programs at all costs.

Warehouse programs are also a possibility for chained convenience stores like 7-Eleven and Circle K. You will not hear directly from the retailer unless pushed because they want the free labor that a DSD or distributor provides, but it can be done. The basic process is to sell to corporate and arrange for delivery to their warehouse or distributor. Again, you must personally introduce and sell your product to them, but there are specific criteria your product will have to meet based on your product's weight. If your product exceeds the formulation, no matter how good a retailer package you have, it will not be considered for a warehouse program.

There is a catch to successfully selling convenience stores this way, and that is this—you *must* have a *killer* plan to sell it off the shelves; in other words, a *killer* retail package. Along with funding (because you must turn revenue to continue to produce large orders for these warehouse programs), a stellar retail package is a requirement for even considering sales to c-stores through warehouse programs. With that in place, though, it can be done, despite what you may have heard otherwise.

One final point to mention, since we're talking here about selling direct to retailers without distributors, is utilizing drop-shipping as a means of selling to retailers. We've already gone through drop shipping in detail, but you should include this selling method to retailers on the list. You'll recall this has specific criteria and requirements attached—your product will need to be smaller and lighter so it can ship affordably, and you will have to maintain the sales team to open accounts. The process for doing that will require you or your sales representatives to contact the designated buyers, either on a corporate or singular store level, present and make the sale, then ship the product through a third-party company like UPS or FedEx.

The above tells you how to approach each of the different types of retailers, but as with distributors, you will need one essential piece, no matter who is doing the selling or what kind of retailer you are selling to. That is the retailer package.

The Retailer Package

The retailer package is fundamentally the same as the distributor package; it is the presented plan for support and marketing that speaks to the retailer to show them how to sell your product and how you will support the retailer.

The retail package can be a physical document, similar to the distributor package. It can be a brochure, binder, or it can contain multi-media (a CD, audio, or video); it can also include photographs and text. However you choose to present it, your plan tells the retailer what they want to hear—how you will help them sell your product.

Like the distributor package, there are some basic things that you will want to be sure are included in your retailer package, and you can customize and add to it from there.

- **Sampling & In-store Promotions.** Sampling and in-store promotions are primarily marketing tools used in grocery stores, supermarkets, larger retailers, and club stores. To recap a bit, these are the events that occur on-site. A trained representative presents your product to the consumers in a store and offers free samples; they also monitor store inventory before and after the event and collect consumer feedback. You will need to plan for samplings and in-store promotions and include them in your retailer plan as a show of support. At first, this may be very basic, but over time with a few events behind you, you can communicate more about your plans and include photos and summaries of your specific promotions.

In-store promotions also encompass sales specials and programs (such as buy one get one free promotion, special pricing, etc.). These are ideal to couple with a sampling event. You should plan for these, too, and also present them in your retailer package.

- ☑ **Merchandising.** Merchandising is where you have someone—a representative or your full-service DSD distributor—go into the store, stock shelves, and place promotional posters, stickers, and other points of sale material. It is vital to include this in your retailer package for two reasons: to communicate how to promote the product in-store and outline who is responsible for the promotion.

You may include incentives for the merchandising team here. Just like with salespeople, you can run contests and reward programs for merchandisers, where any team that places an end-cap, side-stack, or gets additional placements in the store earns $2 per case for the order. Incentives drive sales in a couple of different ways because these require more product, resulting in more cases purchased by the retailer and getting the product on the floor where it is more accessible (not hidden in the warehouse). Extra placements also provide new opportunities for merchandising.

- ☑ **Pricing Specials.** Pricing specials are just what they sound like—specialty prices for a limited time designed to drive sales. Your standard pricing special would be a buy one get one free or a lowered sale price. These are targeted primarily to the retailer as a way to get them to take on more inventory. They are not as consumer-focused as they might appear (because we don't want to do anything to cheapen your product—we want to keep you as close to

357

your suggested retail price as possible for the sake of reputation and value). More than anything else, pricing specials are a tool to get the product on the shelf in large volumes. They are a part of your retailer package that shows them what tools you will give them to do that.

☑ **Distribution Options.** Remember, your retailer package is a comprehensive account of all that the retailer needs to know to feel confident you can deliver the goods and help them make sales. Retailers understand product distribution is elemental to that. So one of the first questions to answer is how your product will reach them and if it's a reliable plan. You need to explain this in the retailer package, too. You need to include all the distribution options so each retailer can find a suitable solution, proving you have covered every aspect from production to sales and have a solid business plan to support the product.

☑ **Point of Sale Material.** Point of Sale Material is what matters most to retailers. Every retailer will expect to see POS material included in your plan. It would help if you had all of the sales collateral ready and done when you walk into a store. You need to list the various POS you will provide, show photographs, and offer samples and examples. The retailer needs to know the physical materials they need are in place and there for them.

Now is a good time to think about other promotional items (like lighters, t-shirts, pens, and other gadgets) even though they are less point of purchase and more for general promotion and promotion to the retailer. This isn't necessarily something to include in the retailer package, but nice to have if you have the funds.

☑ **Rack Programs.** A rack program is pretty much in line with point of sale and point of purchase. They are an added tool to get shelf space and move inventory from the warehouse to the consumer. These are a better alternative to slotting programs because they do not take up fixed shelf space, and do not come with the fees.

Rack programs provide a movable rack to be placed and stocked with your product, thereby creating your own shelf space. These require a more considerable investment and do have some drawbacks. They are costly and require upkeep and care, so they do not get lost in the warehouse or taken by owners or managers. Rack programs are not a good idea if you do not have a DSD arrangement with a representative looking after them on your behalf. An alternative to racks is cardboard shippers, which cost about 90% less than racks (around $10 to $15). They have 90% of the lifespan, too, but are a more effortless loss.

Suppose rack programs are in your budget and marketing plan. In that case, they should be in your retailer package, giving your retailer options and avenues, especially for those with more limited space and a full line of beverages in place.

☑ **Contests.** As with distributors, retailers enjoy fair competition, too. For retailers, these are usually held between chained stores or within regions or divisions. There is a lot of communication and competition between stores to prove their worth in the company's grander scheme. You can capitalize on this by running contests for things like the top-selling store, the store selling the most through a promotional campaign, or the store with the heaviest sales volume for a time. You will need some enticing prizes (one thing that works well is electronics, like free iPods). Having contests in your retailer package provides more of a show of support for them directly and capitalizes on that age-old question, "What's in it for me?"

Contests can be accomplished for independent stores, too, although you'll need to be a little more resourceful. You will need to run the contest through their cooperative or a similar organization to get enough stores involved to make it a real competition that raises sales.

- ✅ **Advertising to Drive Traffic.** Retailers do not need you to tell them advertising drives sales, but they need to know you understand this and understand it to be your responsibility, not theirs. Retailers will be looking for your plans to accomplish two things—drive traffic to the store to get your product and sell once the buyer is in the store. Your plan will focus on outside advertising bringing people into those retailers who carry your product. These are things like co-op advertising (in mailers and flyers) and frequent shopper discounts (additional discounts to loyal shoppers in that store—contrary to popular belief, funded through product/producer support and not through the retailer).

Advertising to drive traffic to the store is essential to your retailer package; it is not optional. The retailers will choose your product over others if they see you plan to sell it off the shelf. They expect to know you have accounted for advertising in the form of print, radio, outdoor advertising, TV, vehicle wraps, sponsorships, or events.

The above should give you a good foothold on getting those managers and store owners to accept your product and sell it to the consumer. That is a subject that needs addressing, too, but before we have that final discussion, we want to tell you a bit about working with brokers and how they can fit into the sales game for sales to retailers and distributors.

What are Brokers, and Where Do They Fit In?

What are sales brokers, and why are they important to you? Brokers are groups of people who specialize in representing other people's brands. They are a big part of the beverage business; some companies rely exclusively on brokers to sell their products. You can think of a broker as an outside sales agent, but their responsibilities are limited.

If you find a good broker and have a great relationship with them, they can sell your product to the country's largest retailers. If you haven't already, go to www.LiquidBrandsManagment.com and take the Build Your Beverage Empire Course. The course includes an entire section on working with brokers.

First off, let's talk about what a broker is not. A broker is not an employee; therefore, you do not have to pay Workers' Compensation insurance or any other benefits; he is an entirely independent agent. He is also not liable for product sales. That may sound contradictory, but you cannot hold them accountable beyond discontinuing business with them. A broker is not a collections department, either. There are definite limits to what you can expect from a broker.

A broker is your brand's representative for as long as you agree with them, but that same broker can also represent other brands. A broker is hopefully a well-connected agent who facilitates the sales of products.

There are different sizes and different types of brokers. Some very small brokers may work out of a small office or even out of their homes. There are also large brokerage firms with brokers doing upwards of $500 million or even a billion dollars in sales in the U.S. and abroad. In the U.S., there are several substantial brokers like Acosta or Advantage Sales and Marketing (the largest broker in the U.S. right now). Advantage has expanded into Canada as well by buying out a brokerage firm there.

How Brokers Work

Hopefully, you now understand more about brokers; now, you need to know how they work.

There is very little that you need to do for a broker that you are not already doing. Once you locate a broker and reach an agreement, they will add your product to their portfolio and begin presenting it on your behalf to potential buyers—distributors and retailers. The broker then collects the orders and turns the buyer over to you.

Some brokers will offer additional services, and some will offer them, but for an additional fee. For example, some brokers will take care of all the paperwork required to register the brand, the pricing, and the many forms needed to sell the product into the retail account. As described above, others just secure the target and turn it over to you with all the documentation, terms, and agreements. However, they comply with the customer, stay in constant contact with them, and handle their orders. You would receive a fax or an email with a purchase order the broker has represented, and they earn their commission based on that sale.

Contracting with a Broker

The broker agreement is similar to the contract that you might sign with a distributor. It is a legally binding document that lays out the broker's function and responsibility and details payment and compensation terms. It is a commission agreement to pay a 2.5% and 20% commission on the product's sale price to the retailer or distributor.

A broker contract is a protection document, too, just like the distributor contract. It offers protection for you, the broker, and the broker's account for months or years. The industry norm includes a 30-day cancellation clause, which gives you the right to end the arrangement with 30 days' notice. After that time, what happens to those accounts will depend on the agreement and the broker's savvy. An experienced broker will include provisions, so they continue to collect commissions on the accounts they opened for several months or years, and sometimes indefinitely for as long as you sell to that client.

The agreement will also list payment terms, which are on average 15 to 30 days to the broker after receiving the buyer's funds (retailer or distributor). If payment is not received, it is your responsibility or your accounts receivable department to collect it. In some cases, you can leverage the broker's relationship with the buyer and ask for help collecting payment.

The larger brokers will not come free; they will charge a fee to get listed with them. That fee can be as high as $20,000 for the bigger brokerage houses. The fee helps them cover the costs of getting sales moving and is designed to protect the broker, ensuring you are serious about your business and maintaining a relationship with them. Working strictly on commission with nothing binding you to the broker would put that agent in a tenuous position and make it all too easy for manufacturers to come and go and leave them without a source of income. Additionally, there may be additional fees for additional services, so you will want to know what your money is paying for upfront and what remains your responsibility. The fees charged by smaller brokers will be less or maybe nonexistent, but paying broker fees is common and reasonable in this industry.

What a Broker Needs from You

You cannot assume that just because you have a product, a broker will willingly represent it. Like distributors, brokers can have their pick of products with all the beverages that are out there. Like distributors and retailers, the broker's job only goes so far—you are still, always, ultimately responsible for the support that closes the sales.

To make those sales, the broker will need you to provide sales literature, front-line pricing, brochures, and all the information included in your retailer and distributor packages so they can represent that and convey to buyers that this product has the necessary support. These are not things you can expect the broker to develop for you, except for a few inexperienced brokers. Some offer it as an additional service because they know how to put the package together and know having it helps their cause. By and large, though, brokers do not create the retailer and distributor packages.

Samples are not the responsibility of the broker, either. Instead, the broker will make his contacts and provide you with a list of clients expecting the product to sample. You must mail samples out to them—which means you continue to bear the work and the cost. It's one more thing to be aware of and include in your plan.

If you do not support or fund your product or do not follow through with your end of the bargain, you will find that your product just lies dormant in the broker's portfolio. Before you go out and contact brokers, you need to have all of these pieces in place, including proper funding, or they will either a) outright refuse you or b) accept your product but go nowhere with your sales.

You may have noticed there can be a lot of variables when working with brokers. It is essential to make sure each of these is clear to all parties and give your broker the tools to make your sales by holding up your end.

Why Use a Broker?

Brokers often become brokers after having some other experience in a related business, such as a category buyer for a chain or a large store (many smaller brokers, in particular, get started this way). The result is the broker builds an extensive network of connections with other brokers, retailers, and distributors, lending a great deal of outreach to your business. The larger firms have an even greater outreach if working with one is within your budget's funding.

That outreach is one reason to go with a broker. Another would be the work they perform on your behalf, which you do not pay for unless they provide results. For smaller start-up companies, brokers are a great way to start and get into retailers and distributors that otherwise will not talk to you. Many brokers have worked with these contacts for many years and can walk products into accounts and get their feedback. The added benefit is that these brokers have trustworthy, open relationships with the buyers who won't waste their time. They'll be frank about which products have potential and which don't. Buyers trust the brokers' opinion and trust they will not lead them into a product that cannot profit.

On the downside, there is an additional level of cost involved when you work with brokers, and a bad, unskilled, or unmotivated broker may sit on your product without ever pushing it, costing you sales. Choosing carefully and clearly defined contracts help ensure a profitable arrangement for all involved.

Choosing the Right Broker

There are brokers for all kinds of products. Like distributors, some specialize in beverages and run an entire portfolio of diverse and sometimes unrelated products. Those brokers will not generally do a great job selling your drink because they are a Jack-of-All-Trades, master of none.

Also, much as a prominent broker may seem the obvious way to go, there is potential for failure there, too. Many large brokerage houses have all the top brands listed and will focus 80% of their attention on them, possibly leaving your product to collect dust on a shelf.

Another problem is that some large brokers work with the biggest retail chains and accounts and focus on those big-name retailers. But when it is time to fill in the gaps and sell to the smaller stores and independent accounts, they are unwilling to devote their time to what they view as less profitable avenues.

These are things to be wary of as you structure your agreements with these brokers. Many will expect the same kind of exclusivity that a distributor will. Still, you have to build in a safeguard so if they do not move your product and do not go after all the accounts, there is a built-in window to bring in other brokers to service them and net those sales.

Brokers can be an excellent sales mechanism for your beverage if you know how to manage the relationship and attend to all of your responsibilities. It is definitely to your advantage to know about brokers and know all of this ahead of time so you can consider it as you build your business plan and your business empire!

The Ultimate in Sales Success: Selling to Consumers

Finally, we've reached the pinnacle of success for your new beverage—successful sales to the consumer market.

It may seem that we've come a long way and that your work is nearly done, and it is true we've learned a lot, but as work goes, you are never done until you have made that sale to volumes of end consumers—to your all-too-important target market. Selling to retailers and distributors is only the start of sales; the real work comes in selling off the shelves to consumers. Do that, and your work with retailers and distributors will be easy. They'll love you, they'll love your product, and they'll buy it by the truckload.

"NO PROMOTION WITHOUT DISTRIBUTION!"

CHAPTER 24

Selling to Consumers

Rapid Knowledge Section

I'm in my office looking at the artwork for a brand-new product we're launching. It's a Hemp related line extension for the industry's most significant player, a player that shall remain unnamed per their request. The entire marketing team is on Zoom to review their artwork, the VP of Sales asks me about our distribution channels, and their Marketing VP wants to know how our Influencer campaigns are going with our products. They seem to all be talking simultaneously, as it sometimes happens with these video meetings.

"Who's your Avatar?" I ask. "What do you mean?" asks the graphic designer. "Who's your perfect consumer?" I ask again. "Who's buying this product?"

After a few silent seconds from all the participants, one of the higher-ranking executives asked me, "Who do you think should be our consumer?"

Please read and re-read the abridged excerpt of the Zoom meeting and see if you get the nuances. I need to figure out many things from this call, and they're not sure of their answers. They need to commit to something because I need to figure out:

- ☑ Who is the Avatar = perfect consumer

- ☑ Where will I sell this = where the Avatar buys

- ☑ Who will take it to this retailer = distribution

- ☑ Where does the Avatar congregate = how will I market

- ☑ What does the Avatar like = packaging, size, colors, pricing

- ☑ What are the psychographics = what motivates the Avatar

I wasn't getting any of these answers during the meeting. The team wanted to talk more about the package's colors than the distribution channels or the Avatar. How can I know if this product goes into a Convenience Store if I don't even know if it is for a male or female audience?

The quick knowledge takeaway for you is to always start with your Avatar and work backward from there.

"Your main job is to sell to consumers; everything else is the supply chain."

Avatar, Your Perfect Consumer

We've been talking about selling to wholesalers, distributors, and retailers. We did chat a bit about selling to consumers and finding your perfect consumer. We talked about this at the beginning of the book. This is especially important because it's the basis of your entire business model, your distribution model, and now more critical than ever. After all, we're talking about selling to the consumer.

Your perfect consumer is your Avatar, the person who you target with your product. Still, not just any customer; this is your ideal customer, the one that's willing to buy a case of your product, give it away to friends, post it on their social media and be your product's ambassador. If you think that everyone will love your product, you're wrong, and you're mistaken as it relates to your go-to-market strategy. When you're a start-up, you need to use your limited capital to target only this Avatar, which will make your start-up successful.

Especially in the post-COVID world, understanding your Avatar is extremely important, and knowing how to target them online should be part of your business model, regardless of whether you sell online or not. You see, by finding your customers online, you can direct them to your 7-Eleven, Circle K, CVS pharmacy, or your corner store or local independent supermarket. Knowing your Avatar allows you to use direct response to find and sell to your Avatar, online and offline.

As the brand owner, you have many more opportunities to find and sell to your perfect consumer than ever. Internet analytics, Facebook, and Google Advertising audiences give everyone advanced tools to target who you think will buy your product and start testing your hypothesis, headlines, labels, and messaging in around thirty minutes. You can then decide if you want to sell on Amazon.com to take advantage of Prime and free shipping to consumers. You can determine if you're selling on your website and cut the distributor and the retailer but pay for shipping. Perhaps you prefer to send your customer to a brick-and-mortar store to buy the product there.

Beverage Advertising

"Online direct response advertising changed the world and lets you compete with the big boys, especially in the after-COVID economy."

I'm running several Facebook, Instagram, YouTube, Google search, and retargeting advertising campaigns, sending people to brick-and-mortar stores in different territories around the USA where I have distribution partners. This was part of my distribution and retail programs going in to sell the product, and I'm keeping my word and sending traffic to the stores. Additionally, some consumers buy these products from websites, which is all part of the new economy. One of my friends strictly advertises on Instagram and has people send him money using various phone Apps, and never sends people to an eCommerce or a brick-and-mortar store. The world of advertising and sales has changed, and now you can track every dollar spent online and online related stores without the guesswork. It's a brand-new ballgame.

The new age of advertising, combined with the post-COVID economy where consumers feel comfortable having other people shop for them and deliver their food, or even their beverage cases, is a win for you. Today you and I have no problem selling a fifty-dollar beverage transaction online, where before COVID, it was unheard of for a beverage start-up.

> *"There is a big difference between advertising and direct response advertising. Make sure you're using direct response advertising; otherwise, you might be throwing money at a wall."*

No Promotion Without Distribution!

If you don't have the product, don't start selling it unless you're running tests. I test all the time. A test might be where you have a small campaign going on Facebook to see if your target audience likes a new packaging or flavor. If they click and buy, you have an answer. This small-scale testing is sufficient, but if you're not testing, don't promote until you have a brand.

You shouldn't spend any money on the promotion if potential clients can't find your product, and the way people see your product is by having it in traditional and online stores.

But how do you get around this when creating your distribution and retail networks? Didn't we just spend the better part of two chapters emphasizing the importance of product support and its importance to distributors and retailers? How can you create a retailer or distributor package without advertising in place?

For starters, make sure the advertising is local to the territory you're opening with your DSD distributor. It also needs to know limits; if you don't have the proper distribution in place, you need to limit the amount of advertising you do. It would help if you were very conservative because you can quickly spend advertising dollars with no results. It can get out of hand very quickly.

You should be aware that you will begin to get calls for advertising as soon as people see your product listed. It would be best if you resisted the temptation to jump at every opportunity before you. Those opportunities come at a high price.

Is it possible to tie your advertising into your business plan and sales revenues? The way to do this is to allocate that percentage of sales and allocate funding reliant on sales targets being met. In other words, once you sell "X" number of cases, you will begin advertising campaign "A," and once the next sales target is met, campaign "B" will kick off. You might set a target of opening 150 accounts, and once that target is met, you will roll out radio advertising; with another 100, you will follow up with TV ads; 200 more and you do print ads and outdoor advertising; with the distributor's first order you agree to wrap their trucks, and you go on from there. Those sales targets should be tied to a predetermined number of sold cases, delivered, and paid (not just delivered, because stores can return them, and you could still have no revenue to pay for the advertising).

As long as you approach your distributors and retailers with a definitive, well-structured plan like this, they will have what they need in terms of advertising. Advertising is a necessary part of the plan, but performance measures have to be set.

The above explains how and when to implement your advertising to consumers. How do you know when to use each advertising type? Not all kinds of advertising are appropriate all of the time, nor suitable for all target markets. Radio, for instance, is appropriate for reaching some market segments and not others. For this, you need to know your consumer and how they spend their time. Some spend a great deal listening to the radio and hence radio ads, while others are primarily a print or TV market. Your local advertising agency will help you define those targets (don't rely on the medium themselves—a TV producer will always think they are the way to go!).

Print is another option, but you usually want to rely on it more for those promotions and sales. Print advertising for beverages is most common in sales flyers or includes a coupon that promotes a special in one form or another.

Outdoor advertising—like signs, freeway signs, and billboards—is one of those formats you want to reserve for after distribution is in place (one to tie to a specific number of accounts) because the audience is mobile. That distribution needs to be significant because 60% of that audience will not be local to you. Unless they are pulling over right now to buy your drink, they will not find it in the stores once they get home. You may have just spent several thousand dollars toward a consumer that may not have any chance of finding your product.

Suppose you're not working with DSD beverage distributors but may be selling to the natural channel directly via wholesalers. In that case, you can't exploit economies of scale to advertise in one territory as your stores are scattered all over the country. If this is you, I recommend a very targeted online advertising campaign that sells products from your eCommerce store and sends customers to your retailers. This is becoming more and more popular as large DSD beverage distributors consolidate and take fewer and fewer non-alcoholic brands in their portfolios. Not to worry, this advertising strategy works wonders, so much that I already have it as part of my procedures, and you should have it too.

Sponsorships

As a product producer, you will have no shortage of opportunities to give money away in sponsorships in return for some visibility; if well-placed, that can sell to your desired consumer groups. But like advertising, sponsorships can get very expensive very quickly, but if there is no sales or distribution, you have no means of supporting that sponsorship.

The amount of money you spend sponsoring an athlete, entertainer, motocross rider, or event will be tied to the number of eyes on it—on their exposure. An event that 10 million people will watch will cost a lot of money. You can see how a professional athlete or large event will be very expensive because there will be a large viewership and a high exposure level. Celebrity players and figures are also in the media, increasing your logo and advertising exposure every time they are photographed wearing your hat or t-shirt. Expense aside, you must have your distribution and brand recognition even to get these big names to sign with you—they all have an image, income, and a reputation to uphold, and they will not risk that by going with a no-name drink no one can find.

That speaks to large sponsorships, but you should not discount other sponsorships. Schools and community sports, and groups are a great place to start. Colleges and universities are ideal for products targeting that age group, primarily because these younger groups can provide buyers for generations. They're also more willing to try a new product. These smaller groups always need sponsors, and the cost is significantly lower than jumping into the big names. Starting a small, grass-roots campaign like this can build trust and recognition that serves as a solid foundation for upward growth and sales.

Influencers

"Use influencers as much as you can; however, make them partners, not vendors."

You'll notice I didn't include Influencers as part of the Advertising sub-chapter. That's because I don't want you to treat or pay Influencers as advertisers. It would be best to treat them as affiliates; therefore, this chapter will turn more into a profit-center instead of a cost-center.

The premise is straightforward, don't pay Influencers to take and do one post with your product. Make Influencers partners in your brand by giving them a commission of anything that sells from their promotions. This way, you can track what they do, determine what's working and not working, and compensate the Influencers that are brand ambassadors and not just in for the quick buck.

Remember, you're not Coke or Pepsi, don't try to sign long-term agreements with influencers to get them to advertise your brand. Think outside the box, think about how you can make influencers part of your brand, and they can make your product part of their brand. Find influencers that will not promote competing products as the flavor of the week but ones that are here to stay and will participate in your success.

Paying someone to take a photo or record a thirty-second video with your beverage is easy. The results could be null. On the other hand, if you have an influencer that really recommends your product and uses it daily in public, now that's a different type of relationship. That person could make hundreds of thousands of dollars on commissions.

The way to set up an affiliate program is easy. Pay your webmaster to do it for you. They'll install software and give every affiliate a unique link to promote. When someone buys the product using that link, it triggers a commission. There are also third-party affiliate networks that administer this and pay the affiliates on your behalf, so you don't have to do the work.

Sampling Events

Sampling events are different than in-store sampling or promotions, but they are still highly consumer-focused. Sampling events work well in local settings, like local community or charity events. Typically, these will be events geared to the average consumer or a group with a specific group or team in mind. You will need to gauge how appropriate that outreach is for your drink. You can have sampling events at a sporting event such as a marathon, a farmers market, a street art event, a comic convention, or other congregation.

When you do local sampling events, make sure your beverage is selling around the event in every local convenience store and supermarket. You could even use the occasion to sell the product in the stores. Don't rule out giving away tasting sizes of your product and selling full cans or bottles to the public. I also like giving away coupons, such as a buy one get one free coupon they can redeem at a local store.

You will need several things to get into and operate at a sampling event of this sort. If you open packages and serve beverages, you will probably need to apply for a local food handler's permit before the event. You will also need practical supplies, like tents, t-shirts or staff uniforms, tables, cups, and trash receptacles, and you will need product—lots of product. You have to make sure that you do it well and service consumers well, so they think highly of you when they walk away.

Sampling events sound like a lot of work and investment to give your product away. It is a lot of work. What's the return for you, then?

- ☑ Brand exposure
- ☑ Ideally, connection with your target market, or a portion of it
- ☑ Potentially extended exposure at long-lasting/day events
- ☑ Exposure to a full range of consumers across all ages (depending on the occasion, unless a very targeted, identified crowd)

These are great benefits when they are well-planned, but you need to take care in selecting the sampling events that you agree to do so you can maximize that exposure and advantage.

Nightclub Events

Another possibility for reaching your consumer is nightclub events. Nightclubs are a great place to get a product exposed, but keep in mind that they are not significant to generate many sales for your product. Here's why—if you have a nightclub and they pack it in with a thousand people, that is a thousand people with all sorts of different product choices and tastes. Not everybody is going to try your product or mix it in with their liquor of choice. A nightclub event may result in a few sales, but you should do it for the considerable exposure potential and not for on-the-spot sales. That is what most of the brands that are doing nightclub events are using them for. Because the vast majority of the sales and product used is alcohol, these will not generate sales for you as a retail choice.

Sales to consumers are the most crucial part of your business, but it is elementary. You need to get your product in front of those consumers, and you need to get them interested and committed to your drink. Basic though it may be, you can't afford to let it lapse. Selling to consumers will always be a priority for your product, and it is an area that you will need to attend to consistently and on an ongoing basis.

Develop an Emotional Connection

"There is a surefire way to ensure success in your beverage business, develop an emotional connection."

You can win a customer for life when you develop an emotional connection with your consumer. They will buy cases of your product every month, and if they can't find you in the local grocery store, they will send money via PayPal to get your product. This customer will tell all of their friends about your product. They'll even give them some products to take home and try out with their entire family. If you have this customer, you can build your beverage empire without doing anything else if you can find them and develop an emotional connection.

This book is filled with supply chain, wholesale distribution, retailing, merchandising, and many other concepts you need in the beverage industry. However, if you remember one thing from this book, it's this: the holy grail of marketing is developing an emotional connection with your customer.

How to Develop a Connection

It's not easy to develop an emotional connection with your consumer when your product is on a convenience store shelf, and you're working from your home office at eleven at night. The customer only sees your product, maybe some pricing, a sticker if you're lucky, and nothing more. So how can you, the small beverage entrepreneur, develop an emotional connection with the consumer?

Big companies like Coke, Pepsi, Bud, Miller, and Dr. Pepper, relied on advertising over time to develop their emotional connection. This connection is nostalgia for older consumers who remember the old jingles, songs, and commercials from beverage and other consumer goods companies. You and I don't have that kind of budget. We have time and personality, which I recommend using as your secret weapon against the big beverage oligopoly.

Use the internet's power to tilt the balance of power towards you and your beverage, but remember a few rules of the trade: You're not a BIG company, so don't try to act like one. Don't use commercials, branding, or advertising that the big companies use. Instead, I like entrepreneurs to be their company's voice and talk directly to consumers inviting them to try their product. Don't try to brand your logo and beverage, instead brand yourself.

Use videos, audio, and text in your social media accounts, blogs, and podcasts to discuss your entrepreneurship journey and your product. Don't use fancy recording equipment or videographers all the time. This will make it impossible to be consistent. Use your phone and record often. I aim to record one hundred long videos per year to use in vBlogs (video blogs) and podcasts, plus I use all the short videos for social media. You could have a goal of one video per week; that's fifty-two videos per year. You could then extract the video text, and you automatically have an excellent article for your blog, LinkedIn articles, or YouTube description. This is done with software, so there is no need to pay someone to type the text.

The more you record and post, the more information about you, the founder, your passion, your journey, and that of your family, employees, and your product, the better you'll do online, and the better relationship you'll establish with your perfect consumer. When your potential customer finds you and looks at your videos and content, they'll start liking you and spending time with you. The time they spend looking at your content, listening to your podcast, and reading your blogs, is the investment they're making in you. This is an emotional investment, and the result will be a long-term customer.

The beauty of the post-COVID economy, together with your ability to establish an online brand, is your secret weapon to establishing an emotional connection with your customers. Logistics, the last part of this equation, is finally cracked. The logistics part was solved when the COVID pandemic hit, and consumers started venturing out of their comfort zone and buying more things online, even beverages. Now is the very best time to start a beverage empire. All the stars have finally aligned, giving the small entrepreneur an advantage over the big soda oligopoly. The big question now is, "how will you take advantage of this opportunity?"

CONCLUSION

It's been quite a journey, but we've done it. We've gone through every aspect of the Beverage business and come out the other side. You are now well on your way to profiting in this profitable, growing business.

Journey to Success

You have journeyed with us through each part of the beverage world. You've learned about that world and the opportunities it offers you, the options that are waiting for you to capitalize on with a level of success unknown to the average drink developer.

You've gone through the entire process, from start to finish, of developing your product and positioning it for maximum sales and profits. You've learned how to produce your drink, attending to every last detail right down to the seemingly inconsequential cap on the bottle (of course, we know the reality of the importance of those finer details).

Finally, you've come to learn the most critical lessons in the business—how to plan, market, and sell your drink through every avenue and to every essential consumer. You can prepare for success and make it a reality!

I know going through a book such as this one requires commitment and dedication. Thank you for spending all this time with me. I want to hear from you. Please tell me about your projects, company, ideas, or what you think of this book. You can contact us

through the website, phone, or social media at
LiquidBrandsManagement.com

Diligence, Rewarded

I truly appreciate your diligence in staying with us through this journey and on to the end. I know this patience and dedication will mean all the difference to you and your business and future. Because of it, you are at a tremendous advantage over others who have tried and failed and continue to try and fail without the right level of knowledge and planning. That knowledge and planning are yours now, the most solid foundation we could provide for a sustainable, profitable, valuable beverage business.

Continuing Support for Success

A new venture takes a lot of time and effort, many times a whole lot of money. Ensure you use education as one of the tools to cut the amount of effort, time, and money you need for your business. If you're launching a brand or a business, read as many books as you can on marketing, branding, sales, and management. Listen to audios, attend webinars and speak to as many people in the industry as you can.

When I decided to put effort into the business world, first as an executive, then as an entrepreneur, I read hundreds of books per year on philosophy, psychology, ethics, education, and self-help. If two books per week is a bit of an overkill for you, consider that you'll have to spend thousands of hours and hundreds of thousands of dollars in your business. I recommend you get addicted to audiobooks and listen to them while you drive, exercise, walk, and whenever you're not on the phone.

Consume as much information as you can. It will not only make you better in business, but it will also improve your knowledge, communication, and relationships.

As part of continuing support for executives and entrepreneurs' success, I provide free webinars, audios, podcasts, case studies, and much more. Just visit www.LiquidBrandsManagement.com and subscribe to the newsletter to get emails on new events.

Please stay in touch, send me your beverage photos to share with other readers on my blogs and social media pages. It's free advertising for you to more than two hundred thousand followers and many retailers and distributors that can buy your products. I love to hear from readers who launched a new product, signed a new distributor, or landed a new VP job at a major soda company. Just go to my website and shoot me an email or share on social media.

As a final word, I would like to offer you my congratulations. It's no small task to complete this journey, and I congratulate you for embarking on it and for your foresight in picking a winning opportunity. I hope to see you become a raging success in the Beverage Industry—Good luck to you as you **Build Your Beverage Empire!**

GLOSSARY OF BEVERAGE TERMS

CSD: Carbonated Soft Drink (mainly soda, but now energy drinks are counted in the category).

C-store: Convenience store.

Drop shipping: a method of direct product delivery that does not rely on a distributor or retailer; the product is shipped directly from the producer's warehouse to the retailer through an outside delivery company.

DSD: Direct Store Delivery; the product is delivered directly to the retail location without passing through a distributor or warehouse. Typically, delivery is handled by an outside company specializing in delivering packages such as the postal service, UPS, FedEx, or another transport company.

Foodservice: refers to entities within the service industry, such as institutional kitchens, restaurants, bars, or companies servicing them (such as a foodservice distributor providing products and supplies to those retailers).

Mass Retail: large chain retail accounts making smaller sales directly to consumers; refers primarily to pharmacy and supermarket retail chains.

Merchandising: Refers to efforts undertaken to promote a product within the retail location—presence/use of POP/POS materials and inventory and stocking measures. It can also refer to the marketing concepts behind the actions.

New Age Beverage: a consumer drink that is not included in any traditional beverage categories; includes teas, energy drinks, new sodas, vitamin drinks, specialty waters, and others. Typically does not refer to conventional carbonated beverages and sodas or fruit juices.

New Soda: a healthier version of a carbonated soft drink developed by traditional soda producers as a foothold into the NAB market.

On-premise: accounts where a product is consumed on-site. Includes retail locations such as restaurants and bars, clubs, food service providers.

Point: percentage points of a sale.

POP: Point of Purchase. See POS, Point of Sale.

POS: Point of Sale, also called "Point of Purchase." Refers to marketing tactics and materials used in the retail location where consumers will see and buy your product. Includes advertising materials such as posters, stickers, signs, and price clings.

SKU: a unique number or identifier assigned to a product to scan for sales, ordering, and delivery (also referred to as a bar-code.

Spiff: commissions paid on a product sold organized into a program. It is meant to work as an incentive to sales teams, usually for the distributor's sales force.

Turns: volume of sales in a wholesale or retail market; for example, the number of times your product is sold and reordered by the same retailer or distributor (measured in a consistent volume, such as case, pallet, etc).

Warehouse Program: A method of selling directly to retailers without going through a distributor wherein retailers use their distribution network.

Wholesalers: Large distributors who do not specialize in beverages (or any product) but sell many different products to a variety of distributors and retailers.

3 Step System of Distribution: full-service distribution process wherein the distributor collects retail orders, fulfills them (delivers product), and stocks and merchandises the product.

Table of Figures

PART

04

INDEX

INDEX

Direct Store Delivery   240,
241, 242, 318, 323

discrepancy   131

distribute   99, 134, 221,
222, 234, 253, 256, 258, 273

distribution   4, 7, 15, 23, 54,
59, 69, 85, 87, 88, 90, 99, 101, 102,
104, 105, 115, 121, 122, 126, 142,
147, 163, 169, 172, 174, 177, 178,
179, 180, 182, 185, 192, 195, 197,
206, 216, 217, 221, 222, 223, 224,
226, 228, 231, 232, 234, 235, 237,
239, 245, 247, 248, 249,250, 251,
253, 255, 256, 257, 258, 260, 261,
262, 263, 269, 273, 274, 280, 294,
306, 308, 309, 320

distributor   13, 14, 19, 32,
34, 37, 50, 51, 52, 53, 54, 58, 72,
74, 99, 103, 114, 115, 116, 125,
126, 127, 128, 134, 147, 164, 166,
175, 178, 179, 180, 181, 186, 193,
194, 195, 210, 211, 214, 218, 222,
226, 227, 228, 229, 231, 233, 234,
235, 236, 237, 238, 239, 241, 245,
248, 250, 252, 254, 255, 257, 258,
259, 260, 261, 263, 267, 268, 269,
270, 271, 272, 273, 274, 276, 277,
278, 279, 280, 281, 282, 283, 285,
286, 287, 288, 289, 290, 291, 292,
299, 300, 301, 304, 306, 307, 316,
318, 320

Distributor Package   271, 277

distributors   14, 15, 16, 18,
19, 21, 23, 25, 32, 36, 38, 44, 49,
50, 52, 53, 54, 55, 59, 61, 68, 90,
103, 104, 106, 107, 110, 111, 114,
115, 116, 117, 119, 123, 136, 147,
148, 173, 177, 178, 179, 180, 185,
193, 194, 197, 211, 214, 215, 218,
221, 224, 225, 226, 227, 228, 232,
233, 234, 235, 236, 237, 238, 239,
240, 243, 244, 245, 249, 252, 256,
257, 258, 259, 260, 261, 263, 264,
265, 266, 267, 268, 269, 270, 271,

272, 274, 275, 276, 278, 280, 281,
283, 284, 285, 286, 288, 290, 291,
296, 297, 299, 301, 302, 303, 305,
306, 307, 316, 320

donating 18

drop-shipping   168, 250, 251,
253, 290

DSD   240, 241, 242, 243, 244,
245, 249, 250, 261, 290, 292, 295,
318, 323

E

elevator pitch   140, 141, 198

emotional connection   16, 172,
173, 174, 305

empire 15, 29, 304

Empire 13, 25, 316

energy drink   16, 31, 32, 36,
41, 42, 43, 62, 74, 77, 84, 85, 86,
90, 99, 111, 129, 132, 141, 159,
189, 198

energy drinks   17, 31, 40, 41,
42, 45, 49, 58, 59, 70, 78, 79, 83,
84, 86, 92, 129, 259, 318, 319

Energy Drinks   22, 40, 83, 86,
141

Energy Shots   22, 83

enhanced drinks 81, 82

entrepreneurs   13, 14, 18, 21,
22, 25, 29, 56, 57, 58, 59, 60, 63,
66, 85, 87, 95, 103, 174, 316

exit strategy   30, 38

expectations   13, 20, 130

experience   13, 19, 20, 61,
68, 91, 105, 119, 176, 182, 253,
264, 302

F

financial 146, 181, 213

S

sales   7, 18, 20, 23, 31, 34, 40, 42, 43, 44, 45, 47, 51, 52, 53, 54, 55, 58, 59, 63, 64, 65, 66, 68, 71, 74, 75, 83, 84, 85, 86, 87, 88, 89, 91, 92, 94, 101, 102, 105, 110, 111, 113, 114, 115, 117, 118, 124, 127, 128, 129, 133, 135, 142, 152, 169, 172, 174, 175, 177, 180, 181, 187, 192, 197, 201, 202, 206, 211, 212, 216, 217, 220, 221, 222, 223, 225, 226, 228, 229, 231, 235, 236, 237, 238, 243, 250, 252, 253, 255, 257, 262, 263, 266, 268, 269, 270, 272, 275, 276, 277, 278, 279, 280, 281, 282, 283, 284, 285, 287, 288, 290, 292, 293, 294, 296, 297, 298, 300, 301, 302, 303, 304, 305, 306, 307, 308, 309, 310, 311, 313, 315, 319, 320

Sales   10, 22, 41, 73, 89, 108, 111, 125, 127, 130, 133, 179, 285, 298, 305, 323

salespeople   25, 227, 236, 293

salesperson   19, 236, 278

Sampling events 310

save time   14

scan programs   289

Second Tier Distributors   236

secret formula   14

sell your drink   59, 200, 313

Selling 11, 61, 72, 85, 136, 172, 263, 264, 284, 286, 288, 289, 305, 312

short term   13

shortcuts   7

Shots   48, 83

Sign-up 7

size   16, 30, 39, 40, 44, 45, 64, 71, 85, 118, 119, 122, 131, 132,

133, 148, 149, 150, 154, 181, 199, 203, 232, 233, 234, 242, 268, 274

slotting 128, 129, 211, 277, 295

Snapple 93, 151, 237

SoBe   91, 92

Social Entrepreneurs   18

soda   40, 49, 70, 74, 86, 87, 150, 189, 190, 191, 198, 234, 241, 244, 316, 318, 319

spiff programs   271

sponsorships   202, 218, 277, 282, 297, 309

startups 273

statistics 40, 43, 45, 54, 65, 114

strategy 15, 38, 45, 87, 90, 107, 130, 177, 179, 182, 192, 193, 263, 280, 285

supply   14, 16, 67, 74, 76, 78, 92, 121, 132, 136, 141, 178, 185

supply chain   14, 16, 121, 136, 178

Support 271, 276, 315

sustainable business   22

T

target market   19, 50, 106, 136, 141, 145, 147, 148, 149, 150, 155, 174, 178, 183, 184, 185, 186, 187, 188, 198, 200, 215, 216, 218, 221, 232, 255, 284, 305, 310

Target market   100, 101, 136

Taste   11, 137, 156

Tea's   22

team   25, 57, 61, 63, 99, 107, 115, 117, 119, 237, 244, 252, 278, 290, 293, 310

Third Tier Distributors   238

Tops   150

trade shows   50, 111, 264, 265, 275